Freedom by Choice:
A collection of writings on America, Islam and Pakistan
By Abdul Quayyum Khan Kundi

Dedicated to my mother Hukam Jan.
Her dreams paved the path of my life.

Table of Content

Preface

Section I: Pakistan Society

Section II: Pakistan Politics

o **Building Political Institutions**

o **Tenure of President Musharaf**

o **2008 General Elections**

Abbreviations & definitions used in the book:

Abbreviations:
APL: Awami Muslim League
APML: All Pakistan Muslim League
COD: Charter of Democracy
DIG: Deputy Inspector General of Police
ECP: Election Commission of Pakistan
ES: Elah Salam, an Islamic phrase to bless Prophets
EU: European Union
FATA: Federally Administrated Tribal Areas of Pakistan
GCC: Gulf Cooperation Council
IG: Inspector General
ISAF: International Security Assistance Force
JI: Jamat e Islami
JUI: Jamiat Ulema Islam
JUI F: Jamiat Ulema Islam Fazlur Rehman
JUI S: Jamiat Ulema Islam Maulana Sami ul Haq
NAB: National Accountability Bureau
NATO: North Atlantic Treaty Organization
NRO: National Reconciliation Order
NWFP: North West Frontier Province, later renamed as Khyber Pakhtunkhwa
MMA: Mutahida Majlis-e-Ammal
MQM: Muttahida Qaumi Movement
OECD: Organization of Economic Cooperation and Development, part of EU
OIC: Organization of Islamic Cooperation
PBS: Public Broadcasting System
PBUH: Peace be upon Him.
PML F: Pakistan Muslim League Functional
PML N: Pakistan Muslim League Nawaz
PML Q: Pakistan Muslim League Quaid
PPP: Pakistan Peoples Party
PPP S: Pakistan Muslim League Sherpao
PPPP: Pakistan Peoples Party Parliamentarian

RATA: Rehmatullah Alleh, an Islamic phrase to bless sacred people
UK: United Kingdom
UN: United Nations
UNSC: United Nations Security Council
US: United States
US AID: United States Agency for International Development
USSR: Union of Soviet Socialist Republics
WMD: Weapons of Mass Destruction
WTO: World Trade Organization

Definitions of non-English terms:

9/11: This refers to September 11, 2001 terrorist attacks on USA

Awami: Peoples

Baathist: Member of a Baath party. This party is active in Syria and Iraq.

Chaudhary: a prominent agricultural landlord

Ghazwah: a term used for wars in which Prophet Mohammad (PBUH) participated

Hadith: A compilation of sayings of prophet Mohammad (PBUH)

Imam: Person that leads prayer in a mosque and usually a religious scholar

Ijma: Building consensus among religious scholars on social issues

Jalsa: political rally or town hall meeting

Jirga: Council of village wisemen

Madrassa: religious seminary or school

Majlis: a group of scholars or intellectuals

Maulana: Salutation of a religious scholar

Mohala: Neighborhood

Mohajir: Immigrant

Mohtarma: respected lady

Mufti: Grand religious scholar who has the right to issue religious edicts

NeoCon: A term used for neo-conservative group of intellectuals

Panchait: council of village elders

Quran: Religious book of Islam considered divine by Muslims

Roti, Kapra aur makan: bread, clothes and housing

Sahaba: Companions of Prophet Mohammad (PBUH)

Sardar: Chief of a Tribe

Shaheed: A martyr

Shalwar Kameez: A Pakistani national dress of a long shirt and baggy pants

Sharia: Islamic penal code

Shia/Shiite: a religious sect of Islam

Shura: A group of intellectuals that offer advice on government affairs

Sunnah: Example from life of Prophet Mohammad (PBUH)

Sunni: A religious sect of Islam

Taliban: Plural for religious student, singular is Talib

Ummah: a global community that adhere to Islamic faith

Ulema: Islamic religious scholar

Wadera: A Punjabi word for an agricultural landlord

Zakat: a charitable tax usually 2.5% of income mandated by Quran

Zamindar: a person that has large agricultural land holding

Preface

At the dawn of 21st century United States of America was the undisputed hyper power with an unmatched economic and military might. On 11th September 2001 this venerable position was challenged when 19 terrorists wreck havoc from skies. These terrorists hijacked four commercial flights; three of these planes were diverted to strike at twin towers of world trade center in New York and Pentagon in Virginia. Fourth plane crash landed near Pennsylvania when a struggle ensued between passengers and hijackers. Over 2900 people lost their lives in these attacks while economy suffered a loss estimated to be in tens of billions of dollars. Messages of support and solidarity with American people poured in from around the world. American media was quick to blame infamous terrorist group Al Qaeda for these terrorist attacks.

President Bush during his visit to ground zero in New York announced resolve of American nation to take swift actions against perpetrators of these crimes which lead to wars in Afghanistan and Iraq. Afghan war enjoyed unprecedented international support while unilateral action against Iraq resulted in heavy collateral damage. This turned public opinion against America among Muslims.

At the time of American invasion of Afghanistan, Pakistan was governed by its fourth military dictator General Pervez Musharraf. He quickly agreed to American demands of allowing ground logistics for NATO supplies, permitting intelligence assets to be based in Pakistan, and provide access to air bases to operate unmanned drone aircraft. These decisions were motivated by a desire to gain international legitimacy for his government without conducting a detailed strategic review. This deeply unpopular war produced economic loss, terror attacks claiming civilian lives and rise of extremism in Pakistan. This resulted in rising anti-American sentiment straining government's ability to continue their support for American & NATO operations.

I started writing op-ed pieces for American and Pakistani newspapers around 2004 to cover these events. Pakistani politics, society, US-Pakistan relations and regional affairs were major themes of these articles. For quite sometime many friends have suggested that I should compile these essays in a book form. I have been resisting this temptation because these articles were written for a specific event in time. I was not sure if they still retained any value for readers once that moment has passed. I started reading archived articles and began to realize that they can provide a glimpse of a past akin to looking at an old photo album. This gave me sufficient justification to compile this book.

This collection is divided in five sections to focus on a particular subject. In each section articles are grouped around a major theme. Title of some articles is re-written to relate it to the underlying content. Date of each article corresponds to the date of computer archiving and in most cases is different from date of publication in newspaper. Economic estimates and social indicators correspond to years in which the essay was written and may have changed substantially since then. Some sections provide background historical information to enable readers convenience.

This book may offer value to two set of readers. This collection could be of interest for someone curious about trends at the beginning of 21st century with special emphasis on America, Islam, and Pakistan. It can be a useful tool for a researcher focusing on events around US war on terror, US-Pakistan relations in the last decade and Muslim attitudes at large.

As a columnist I rarely get a chance to thank people who have contributed significantly towards my writings. If for this purpose alone it is worth compiling this book. I am forever grateful to my friends Mohammad Afzal Janjua and Murtaza Durrani who urged me tirelessly to start writing. Without their perseverance and prodding I would not have had the courage to embark on this journey.

Tariq Khan, Editor-in-Chief of weekly Pakistan Chronicle published from Houston, Texas provided me an avenue to convey my opinions to people. He took a chance on me when my ideas were not fully formed and needed substantial editing.

Op-ed editor of Pakistan Chronicle Mahatalat Abbasi gave me priceless insight in diction, sentence structure and continuity of thought. Her guidance enabled me to become a better communicator. Zeeshan Bhutta, former Resident Editor of The Daily Times, a daily published from Lahore, Pakistan opened door for me to become an op-ed contributor for that newspaper. Op-ed editor of The Daily Times Mehmal Sarfraz and her assistant Ishrat Saleem ensured that my articles were error free and well organized.

My dear friends Ikhlas Ahmed, Murshid Mustafa, Adeel Siddiqui, Muhammad Haroon Ilyas and Muhammad Zeeshan provided valuable feedback that helped me refine my thoughts, improve message and correct errors. My wife Dr. Zoulikha Mouffak was my best critic to keep me firmly grounded. My daughter Ayate Mankouri inspired me with her ability to survive against all odds.

I am indebted to advice and mentoring of Irfan Husain, a prominent columnist of Dawn, the newspaper founded by Quaid-e-Azam Mohammad Ali Jinnah. Over a span of three decades his writing shaped my views on society, politics and world affairs.

Any errors, omissions and misconception are my responsibility alone.

Abdul Quayyum Khan Kundi

Clovis, California

18th May 2012

Section I: Pakistan Society

Background: Pakistan became a sovereign state on 14th August 1947 at the end of British rule in Indian sub-continent. The new state had two wings, East Pakistan comprised of Bengal province while West Pakistan included Punjab, Sindh, North West Frontier Province (NWFP) and Baluchistan provinces.

Demographically East Pakistan was larger in population with an estimated 58% of total population. Geographically East Pakistan was not a contiguous part of Pakistan but separated by over 1000 miles of India territory. This created security hurdles, social separation and economic management issues between two wings of the country. In general elections of 1970 Awami League led by Sheikh Mujibur Rahman secured 160 seats out of total 300, making it the largest party in national assembly. These seats were won in East Pakistan which was an indication of an ethnic divide. On the other hand Pakistan Peoples Party (PPP) led by Zulfiqar Ali Bhutto secured 81 seats becoming the second largest party but won all its seats in West Pakistan. Both Mujib and Bhutto were ambitious and firebrand leaders with big egos. Bhutto refused to accept constitutional right of Mujib to form a government as leader of a majority party. With trepidation Marshall Law Administrator and President General Yahya called opening session of the newly elected parliament in Dhaka. Bhutto issued warning of dire consequences to his party's elected members to prevent them from attending this session.

Political deadlock between two large parties resulted in military intervention further aggravating the situation. To take advantage of the situation Bengali separatist were trained, equipped and supported by India. These militants initiated attacks on government installations, personnel and armed forces. Government tried to control a political crisis through military operations which produced widespread public discontent. Politicians on the other hand were not capable or willing to resolve their differences. On 26th March 26 1971 Sheikh Mujibur Rahman announced succession of East Pakistan to become a sovereign state of Bangladesh while West Pakistan became current day Pakistan.

Despite traumatic separation of East Pakistan, Pakistan faced many challenges in building a strong nation. First and foremost was grappling with creating a Pakistani identity from a culturally diverse society. Independence movement adopted a two nation theory defining Muslims as a culturally unique nation in a Hindu majority India. After independence leaders failed to promote one Pakistani identity derived from shared values of Islam in an ethnically diverse community. Provinces were created on ethnic bases rather than administrative efficiency that became a breeding ground for creating divisions.

Country faced social crisis that further aggravated the situation. Literacy rate has been low estimated at just fewer than 10% although the official figures estimate it at over 30% including those that can only sign their name. Women and minorities are oppressed. Political parties are controlled by families or elites that use it to further their own interest.

Judiciary has recently shown its independence but traditionally supported military dictators in the disguise of doctrine of necessity. Provision of justice is marred with delays and high expenses. There have been frequent media reports that lower court judges engage in corrupt practices.

Pakistan's GDP is estimated at $210 billion with per capita income of $1254. Inflation is officially estimated at 16% but is much higher considering steep rise in fuel and food prices. Poverty is rampant with an estimated 24% living below the threshold defined by UN. Unemployment is officially reported at 6.2%. Trade deficit is around $9 billion resulting from $30 billion of exports and $39 billion of imports. Budget deficit is estimated to be $14 billion per annum financed through aid, grants and loans from multilateral agencies. Significant portion of budget is spent on armed forces, debt servicing and state administration leaving a small portion for social services, education, law & order and health.

Doctoring the history
(March 15, 2004)

Pakistan is a young nation with a short history since gaining independence in 1947. But should this be an excuse not to make a historic record of events of national significance for the benefit of our future generations. In last few years the country has been at cross roads to define an approach that could ensure coexistence with other powers in our region. Media spot light has been on the proliferation of nuclear technology by one of the leading scientist. There are lots of theories circling that contain only a fraction of truth and are more of a fictitious nature. Dignified way is that anyone who is custodian of strategic scientific knowledge is responsible to secure it under any kind of pressure even when their life is at stake. It is even more important when the custodian is enjoying a hero like status in a nation.

Many tragic events like assassination of first Prime Minister Liaquat Ali Khan, Tashkent pact, Shimla conference between India & Pakistan, circumstances leading up to 1965 war, separation of our eastern part, acquisition of nuclear capability, imposition of marshal laws, Kargil operation etc have remained unexplained. This is just a short list to emphasize the larger point. People directly involved in these events choose not to inform the nation of facts while they don't hesitate to use that knowledge to gain material and political benefits. It is a responsibility of decision makers to inform about the motives of their decisions after a considerable time has lapsed. For instance, in America important historical documents are released for public viewing after 30 years. Anyone could have an access to this information through a freedom of information act.

Ignorance is bliss. In Pakistan facts about important events are shrouded in secrecy in the name of national security. One of the most common reasons put forward by our politicians for not disclosing facts about an important event is that it is for greater good of the people or that revelation of information could result in public unrest.

Real reason could be saving their own skin but if we take this reason at its face value it could imply that masses are not mature enough or intellectually enlightened enough to handle the truth. Let us examine this from the point of view of famous political writer Niccolo Machiavelli. He wrote a popular discourse on political theory in his book Prince and other writings. This is what he writes:

"I conclude, therefore, against the common opinion which says that the people, when they are in power, are variable, fickle, and ungrateful, and I affirm that they commit these sins in the same way that individual princes (leaders) do."

"As for prudence and stability, I say that the people are more prudent, more stable, and better judges than a prince (leader). And not without reason is the voice of the people compared to that of God, for popular opinion has been seen to predict things in such a marvelous way that it is as if some occult power enables it to foresee the evil and the good that may befall it. As for judging things, when the people listen to two speakers who argue different views with equal ability, very rarely do we see them fail to choose the better opinion and show themselves incapable of understanding the truth they hear."

"In short, to conclude this subject, I say that just as princely (dictatorship) states have lasted a very long time, so, too have republics and both needed to be regulated by the laws, for a prince who can do what he wants is mad, and a people that can do what it wants is not wise. If we are speaking, therefore, about a prince who is bound by the laws and about a people that is enchained by them, we will see more worth in the people than in the prince; if we are speaking about both of them when they are unrestrained, we will see fewer errors in the people than in the prince, and they will be less serious and better remedies."

Some people may reject this view by reasoning that western countries has higher literacy and can therefore judge things better.

But at the time of writing this concept in 15th century West had not emerged from dark ages and it would only happen centuries later. So this view of rejecting Machiavelli's doctrine does not hold ground.

It is the responsibility of a leader to speak about events, happened during his reign, with truth. He has to record history by stating facts and keeping his own personal bias and opinion separated. He has to let masses decide validity and goodness of his decisions. A person may not have the courage to do so during his life for fear of reprisal. In that case, he can record history and entrust it to someone to reveal at a later date. This was the approach adopted by Maulana Abul Kalam Azad, former president of All India Congress, requesting that his papers should be released after his death.

If we start educating the masses of our history we would not need National Accountability Bureaus (NAB) and corruption courts to punish dishonest leaders. Masses can do it better by exercising their right to vote and banishing them from echelons of power. May be precisely for that reason our leaders do not want to inform people.

At the time of making a decision a leader has many policy choices available. Effects of his decisions are evident only with the passage of time, sometimes after a considerable lapse. Mr Bhutto's decision to boycott opening session of parliament after elections of 1970 ultimately resulted in separation of East Pakistan. Mr Bhutto left no memoirs to explain reasons for his decisions. People are still speculating was it his ambition to acquire power at any cost? Or was it the realization that it is not possible to keep two parts of a country together that were 1000s mile apart? PPP zealots take one view and their opponents the opposite. On the other hand a neutral majority need historical facts to make an informed decision.

General Zia ul Haq is blamed for capital punishment of Mr. Bhutto although the court issued the verdict. So it is implied that he influenced the courts.

If it is a fact then why do we still celebrate anniversary of a person who interfered with judiciary and weakened its role? It is important that our leaders realize that recording of history of their tenure in office is important for building a strong nation. A lot has been written about our history by people who were not directly involved in it which is not a preferred method. In America all retiring Presidents create libraries where all records of their administration are kept for historians and researchers. Not all papers are released immediately but they are gradually released according to a predetermined formula.

Corruption starts with doctoring of facts. A lie is a fictitious account of an event that has never happened. When history of a nation is based on unsubstantiated facts then the whole body of people is living in a fantasy world. This weakens ideological foundation on which a stable social structure is built. This creates anxiety, frustration and disbelief in the nation. It is probably the main cause that our people do not trust politicians. Every new government informs that the departing government was corrupt and they are more responsible and patriotic. Stories are told of corruption in the past and promises are made for a better future. In a way our leaders make a mockery of the intelligence of people and assume that this game can be played over and over again.

This situation can be resolved through implementation of combination of short and long term solutions. In short term investigations of all past events including murder of Liaquat Ali Khan, oghri camp, Hamood ur Rehman commission and all other incidents should be made public. It is important that a judicial, institutional and parliamentary report is prepared and made public to highlight errors and omissions in American raid to kill Osama bin Laden to set precedence.

To learn from our past mistakes it is important that top universities conduct and publish detailed accounts of events of national significance. Speeches of all our elected leaders must be archived and made available through public and private libraries. Similarly, official records of all government affairs should be made public after lapse of certain time through promulgation of a freedom of information act.

We are still a young nation. We need to learn from our past mistakes and make a conscious effort to establish traditions that are enduring and can light the path for future. Understanding our history will go a long way in inducing a confidence that becomes a glue to build a lasting nation.

Sharing of information:
(May 15, 2011)

In Pakistan various state departments and trade associations do not share information during policy formulation or treaty negotiations. This inability to share information has many root causes. Bureaucracy feels that allowing free flow of information will erode their authority in managing state affairs. They feel that they are best suited to make decisions in state matters without any meaningful contributions and feedback from private sector associations. Ideally when a country signs a trade pact or agreement the draft agreement should be shared with stake holders for their comments. As an example, Pakistan has been negotiating a bilateral investment treaty (BIT) with America for almost 5 years but none of the Presidents of leading chambers have ever been consulted or shared draft of these negotiations. It is ironic since eventually they are the ones that have to bear consequences of this agreement or make use of it.

Similarly when Pakistan signed a transit trade agreement with Afghanistan none of the business organizations ever got a chance to review the agreement for comments. In developed countries drafts of any bill, regulation or agreement is placed in public domain for 90 days so that civic organizations and experts can provide their input. Final draft of the bill incorporates many of those comments.

It may surprise many that one of the clauses promoted by American negotiating team in a BIT is that all trade laws have to be published in public domain for comments before they come into force while Pakistani negotiators are objecting to it for lack of resources.

This shows the attitude of bureaucrats to keep public out of any decision making process through the control of information flow. This increases chances of mistakes being made and national interest concentrated in few hands.

Other cause for lack of public awareness is the absence of civic organizations or groups that employ experts to provide specialist opinion on new laws and amendments. For instance in America there are fair trade groups, anti defamation organizations, anti trust organizations, freedom of speech organizations, consumer protection bureaus, anti discrimination groups that review and create awareness about new laws before it comes into force. In Pakistan we seriously lack this kind of civic activism that can be funded by donations. Freedom of media and the success of lawyers movement has created an environment conduce to form these type of organizations to ensure that public interest is safeguarded and all voices are heard. In absence of non-political civic organizations, political parties come forward to fill this vacuum and raise their voice. These political activists can not fully divorce from their own political interest in promoting a civic cause which creates a conflict of interest. This results in political power struggle rather than protection of consumer interest.

During the British rule in India, laws were written in English language that was incomprehensible to locals who were not well versed in it. This situation was especially severe in rural areas. To understand these laws and its impact on their lives rural masses had to rely on Babu Sahib (local civil servant) in return for favors bestowed on them.

After independence this system has continued where rural majority, comprising of two third of the total population, are so engrossed in their daily survival that they do not have any interest in national policy debate. Local zamindar, civil servant and law enforcement collaborate with each other to control lives of people in villages. Even routine matters like issuance of a birth or death certificate requires help from local notables let alone seeking accountability in national matters. A strong nation can not be built until there is a strong bond of trust between various segments of society which is built on free flow of information.

Revolution or evolution?
(April 11, 2004)

Movement for creation of Pakistan was driven by an ideology to create a state where people can establish a just society practicing principles of Islam. Literary work of Allama Iqbal and leadership of Mohammad Ali Jinnah drove this movement. These efforts succeeded in gaining a landmass but the ideology could not materialize fully. One reason for that failure was sudden demise of our founding leaders Jinnah and Liaquat Ali Khan who had skills and organization to work towards that objective. This loss of leadership in quick succession resulted in a vacuum. The country struggled for establishing a form of government that could work towards actualization of its potential. Authoritarian rulers, who experimented with various approaches to lead this young nation, further deteriorated the situation. These efforts may have been sincere but they lacked fundamental ingredient of public support, moral and ethical authority. This political chaos produced a nation that does not have an orientation and is increasingly frustrated with its false starts. With the passage of time it will be even more difficult to peacefully lead this young nation with an average ager under thirty.

Ingredients of a revolution: when we look at various revolutions in human history specially three most recent ones that is French revolution of 1795, Russian revolution of 1918 and Iranian revolution of 1979. One of the three basic ingredients of a revolution is a literary movement that promotes an ideology that refuses to accept status quo and presents vision of a new future. French revolution was guided by writings of Voltaire whereas Russians took guidance from Karl Marx and later by perestroika (a Russian word meaning restructuring) promoted by Mikhail Gorbachev. These writings were published decades before the actual revolution.

Second ingredient is a group of people who deeply believe in that particular ideology who then become proponent of it and convince others to join. Third ingredient is an unjust social order in which a minority group control vast resources and deprive equitable distribution of national assets.

Once all these ingredients are present the revolution waits for a catalyst to be activated. It could be increase in taxes or assassination of an opposition leader or anything that heightens public sentiments. Once a revolution begins it results in a lot of bloodshed, complete break up of law and destruction of state institutions. Ironically people who start a revolution are almost always consumed by it. For a short period there is a leadership vacuum which is filled by people that may not totally conform to ideology of the revolution. French revolution resulted in rule of Napoleon who was not motivated by revolutionary ideology. Russian revolution culminated in leadership of Lenin and Stalin. In Pakistan, luckily or unluckily, all these three ingredients are absent to ignite a revolution. But if current callus attitude of politicians is not changed we can quickly become a breeding ground for a next revolution.

Evolution through transformation: Genesis of an evolution or a transformation is different than a revolution. Evolution is a peaceful way of bringing a sea change in mind set of people to accept reforms. Evolution starts with a band of people who understand underlying potential of a nation and how it could be released for achieving progress.

Evolution requires provision of a political, social and economic environment that encourages younger generation to utilize their potential. The leaders embark on clearing hurdles that are impediments for growth. These include introduction of merit in all parts of society, implementation of economic policies that encourage entrepreneurial activity especially in small business, introduce a social change and transforming legal system with special emphasis on imparting justice quickly and efficiently.

Japan after World War II and China in the last decade are good examples of transformation. Japanese products were infamous for their bad quality during first half of last century. After the defeat in World War II Japan was a nation defeated in a war and devastated by atom bombs. Japanese leaders instead of being demoralized from a defeat got together to conclude that they have to drastically change their direction.

A group of modern Samurai embarked on a mission to educate corporation and people in becoming the scion of quality. Now "Made in Japan" is considered assurance of quality products at affordable prices. Toyota is soon to overtake General Motors of America as the largest automobile company in the world. Japan is home to multitude of global corporation like Sony and Panasonic.

China on the other hand adopted a different approach. Their leaders realized that change should be brought at a pace that does not devastate their social and political structure. They based their philosophy on perestroika which included economic, political, and social restructuring. But they also analyzed reasons for its failure in Russia. They gradually eased government control on industrial activity and encouraged private investment in all industries. They identified their large population as an asset rather than a liability and became manufacturing center for the world. Now they are embarking on their second phase of development where they are introducing their own brands developed indigenously and marketed globally.

Pakistan became a model for countries like South Korea in early 60s but it faltered from its path of progress. Our leaders have to realize that it is their responsibility to ensure a peaceful transformation on economic, social and political front. If our professionals can be successful as immigrants in countries like USA and Saudi Arabia there is no reason they can't succeed in their own country.

Pakistan: our past and future
(August 3, 2004 & March 25, 2011)

When we celebrate our national days on March 23rd and August 14th, it is a time to reflect on our past and plan for our future. A nation is defined as a community of people who speak common language, has shared values, culture and tradition. There is a group of people who question wisdom of our founders to demand a separate state based on a theology. They argue that Muslims of India would be in a much stronger position if the country was not divided. Whether right or wrong, for a long time after independence people of India and Pakistan lived in a state of personal turmoil as their existed multitude of divided families. There were incidents during three wars with India that two brothers fought on opposite sides of the battle. Pakistan has slowly emerged as a nation with its unique set of values, tradition and culture as a new generation was born with no ties to India.

Pakistan is one of the two countries in the world that sought independence from its colonial masters to pursue an ideology and was acquired purely through constitutional struggle without a violent independence movement. A close look at countries around the world makes it quite clear that it usually takes few centuries for a strong nation to emerge with a unique cultural identity defined by its language, cuisine, clothes, festivals, work ethics and religious affiliations.

Many states went through a bloody path before they could call themselves a nation. After 100 years of independence United States of America (USA) experienced a civil war that almost divided it into two separate entities. Even today some nations are struggling with containing the forces of division. For instance French & English speaking communities in Canada; Scotland, Ireland and England struggling to maintain the federation in United Kingdom; and after last election in 2007 Belgium went without a government for six months because of the divisions between Dutch-speaking Flanders to the north and French-speaking Wallonia in south. Singapore, Malaysia and Indonesia have to manage pressures of large segments of diversified communities comprising of Chinese, Malay and Indians.

Many analysts and commentators get worried about territorial integrity of Pakistan because of small pockets of separatist movements. But they ignore the fact that Pakistanis are deeply imbibed with a sense of unity and affinity towards each other. This sense of belonging has expressed itself in 2005 earthquake, 2010 floods and fight against extremism. Anthropologist and sociologist tend to ignore slowly emerging Pakistani identity that shows its uniqueness in our daily lives. Here are some of the traits that characterize a Pakistani:

- A Pakistani has firm faith in God to be the sole benefactor of mankind and an anchor to a spiritually enriching life. For a Pakistani spirituality takes precedence over materialism.

- A Pakistani believes in family values where ambitions of an individual are always subservient to preserving a family. A Pakistani works in the framework of a family hierarchy where he has to accord due respect to both his elders and his youngsters. Success of a person is defined by the role he plays in his family as a son/daughter, father/mother, and wife/husband.

- A Pakistani is aware of rich artistic heritage acquired from his forefathers. This includes international icon of Muslim architecture Taj Mahal; famous poets Mirza Assadullah Khan Ghalib; and Amir Khusroo creator of musical instrument sitar just to name few.

- A Pakistani is bearer of the fastest growing language Urdu created from the amalgamation of international languages Persian, English, Arabic and Turkish. Despite being the youngest language, Urdu posses well defined structures of grammar and diction. In Urdu a person can be addressed in many different ways that shows his/her relation to the other person and his social status. This beauty and richness of the language has attracted many followers around the world, estimated to be around 2 billion people, to make it an international language. Indian film industry despite its best efforts to adopt Hindi/Sanskrit for movie songs has to still use Urdu as the language of choice.

- A Pakistani worker is considered ambitious, energetic and innovative in his/her approach towards their profession. This is evident from success of immigrant Pakistani community in America, UK, Canada and Saudi Arabia. In these countries Pakistanis are respected for their family values, social involvement and professional commitment.

- Pakistani cuisine is emerging with its own unique recipes and spices. Sindhi Biryani, Chicken Tikka, Nihari and Haleem have become part of international cuisine with its roots firmly planted in Pakistan.

- Shalwar and Kameez the national dress of Pakistan has become popular wardrobe of many African and Asian countries. In America, UK and Europe Muslim immigrants from Africa are seen wearing Shalwar Kameez during Eid festivals and celebrations.

Did we achieve our full potential since independence? The unfortunate answer is no. Main cause for this failure is the absence of a visionary leadership. It is important that we analyze our weaknesses to fix them.

We call ourselves Islamic Republic of Pakistan but autocratic military rulers filled almost 35 years of our history. Rest of 22 years we were ruled by weak politicians who were more interested in holding their grip on power than working for the benefit of common man. If we want to establish our sovereignty among the comity of nations then we need to create a tradition of fair elections and peaceful transfer of power. We need to provide a chance to people to cast their vote according to their wishes and elect their leaders who they deem fit to run affairs of the country. Military's role is to protect the borders of the country and leave affairs of the state to the political institutions. Police and judiciary should be made independent in their actions to apprehend and punish people fairly and justly without relenting to any kind of political pressure.

Since independence, despite promises by our leaders, we have neglected education and literacy as important nation building blocks. Our literacy rate still hovers around 8 to 10% although government classifies any person who can write his/her name as a literate, which produces the inflated 32% literacy rate. We can't fool ourselves any more, if we want to become a strong country we need to allocate more resources to education, rethink our education process, instill merit as the only criteria for success and encourage qualified people to fill teaching jobs by providing an honorable pay structure. Just to compare our priorities in the 2004-05 budget government has allocated 13 billion rupees for education and 194 billion for military, which translates into Rs. 86 per person per year for education as compared to Rs. 1293 per person per year for defense. This clearly shows that we don't think a literate population is the best defense against an enemy. Japan does not have a regular army but 99% literacy. Does this make Japan a weaker country? Education reforms are even more urgent as Madarssas are contaminating the young minds with wrong interpretations of Islamic teachings. If we do not act now then our next generation will be intolerant to other religions and cultures.

We need to change our social structure to allow women comprising 50% of our population to be productive members of society. Although our women are capable to take up any profession they choose. There are many professional choices for women available that are in conformity with our culture and traditions. For instance they can work as office or personnel assistant, accountancy, merchandising, telemarketing, healthcare, stock analysis/trading, publishing and retail sales are some of the professions conforming to our cultural norms. But even in these professions we scarcely see women given a fair chance to compete with men. We can't relegate 50% of our work force to be limited to doing house chores and raising children. Other conservative societies similar to us have successfully incorporated female in their work force like Malaysia, Turkey and Indonesia.

On economic front we cannot continue to rely on cotton and textile made ups to earn 67% of our export earnings. We need to diversify into fields where we have competitive advantage. For instance serious efforts should be made to increase our capacity in off shore software development and call center services.

We cannot progress in these fields until we make it safe for foreigners to travel to Pakistan. We need to reclaim our market share in leather made ups, carpets, surgical and sporting goods industries. We should explore the possibility of exporting light engineering products like washing machines, fans, motors etc. We have to encourage private sector to spend capital on research and development to be more competitive in international markets.

In Financial Management, we need to streamline our budget by reducing waste resulting from corruption, reduce size of government, privatize public corporations to reduce the role of government in industry, include large land owners in the tax bracket to share the burden with salaried class, encourage creation of small and medium enterprises by providing the right environment, reduce reliance on foreign loans to finance budget deficit, and regulate capital markets to provide confidence to invest in public securities.

In arts and literature, we have to encourage and introduce our artists on international platforms. Lok Virsa is playing a good role in preserving and promoting cultures of our diverse community. It should be provided more resources to introduce our folk culture internationally by organizing delegations and events. Academy Adbiyat, Iqbal Academy, Sangemeel publication and Oxford university press are providing an avenue for Pakistani writers to educate and inform citizens. We need to establish an organization that can research and publish books to record history for our future generations.

After Kargil conflict some opposition leaders demanded that a commission should be set up to investigate it. Interim Prime Minister Chaudhry Shujaat Hussain rejected this request. His argument was that this issue is part of history now and there is no point in taking the skeleton out of cupboard. This has been our attitude since independence. This deprives our future generation to learn lessons from the important events in our history. American government established 9/11 commission a year after that incident to identify mistakes and suggesst corrective action. We need to learn not only from our past mistakes but also learn from other nations who have successfully overcome impediments in their progress.

Pakistan is one of the 10 largest countries in the world in terms of its population but among the last 10 in terms of per capita income. We can maneuver statistics to show progress but real progress is shown when lives of citizen are improved.

Creating new provinces: politics of ethnicity
(August 9, 2011)

Almost all countries except few like Japan, China and South Korea, have to deal with ethnic diversity. UK is divided into Scottish, Irish and English ethnicities. Canada has French and English speaking communities. US have substantial Spanish, African American and Caucasian communities. But in all these countries they keep the nation together by equitable distribution of economic wealth as well as giving freedom of political association. American model of federation could be adopted by Pakistan as it gives considerable political and economic independence to federating units while keeping three key functions to itself i.e. defense, monetary policy and foreign affairs. To regulate various sectors of economy federal government can work with provincial governments to devise umbrella regulations as a template to develop laws for their provincial jurisdiction. Federal government can divest itself from industrial, services and export sectors through privatization or stock offerings.

Political parties are controlled by rural landed aristocracy which does not sufficiently appreciate social issues faced by communities in large cities like Karachi and Lahore. These cities are dealing with multifaceted problems including rising populations due to internal migration, deteriorating infrastructure and decreasing employment opportunities. Cost of living is higher in cities as compared to rural areas as a percentage of total income. Salaried classes from these large cities contribute close to 60% of taxes collected while wealthy landowners enjoy exemption of taxes on agricultural income, which create a sense of exploitation in the minds of city dwellers. This creates a situation where regional parties have come in and appeal to these voters as demonstrated by success of Muttahida Qaumi Movement (MQM) in urban areas of Sindh.

The need of time is to evaluate demographics of the whole country and create provinces that are economically viable and can deliver social services to their communities. It is wishful thinking to expect that new provinces can be created without major amendments to constitution. Creation of new units will require distribution of parliamentary seats, allocation of senate quotas, defining jurisdiction of provincial authority, reformulation of water accord and redistribution of National Finance Commission (NFC) award to name just few. Most pragmatic approach in this situation is to hold elections for constituent assembly that not only address question of provinces but also evaluate whether we should continue as parliamentary form of government or consider presidential form. Both forms of government have been successful in presence of large number of provinces. For instance India, comprising of 28 provinces, has adopted a parliamentary system while America, with 50 states, preferred a presidential form. Our decision should be based on our own unique cultural, social and economic realities. Next thing to consider is speed of creation of new provinces. This can be addressed by incorporating two formulae in constitution. First a phased implementation schedule should be agreed for creation of new provinces that are needed now. Second, process of creation of new provinces in future should be incorporated in the constitution by adopting a formula that defines automatic triggers to redraw units when certain benchmarks are met.

Debate on formula for creation of new provinces is revolving around two approaches that is recognition of ethnic identities verses administrative efficiency. Creation of new provinces is an opportunity to create a strong Pakistani identity which is culturally diverse but bound together by shared values of Islam as was imagined by the founding fathers. In preparing for new provinces, we have to learn from the experience of other nations that have successfully managed diversity while at the same time create a strong nation. Singapore, Switzerland, Canada, India, United Kingdom, and United States are some examples. Key to success is fair distribution of national resources, equitable application of law and acceptance of diversity.

Most provinces in Pakistan have diversity rather than one homogenous group. For instance Baluchistan has Pashtun, Baluch, Punjabi and Sindhi residents. Karachi has representation from the whole country. Creation of provinces on ethnic lines will severely affect formation of a strong nation. Redrawing of provincial boundaries does not mean that barriers will be imposed on internal migrations so demographics of a province might change over time. Politically numerical majority of an ethnic group will be reflected in the election results so this argument of rights does not hold much ground.

Other thing to consider is the economic viability of new provinces so that they can finance their expenditure without looking towards center. In many countries property taxes, motor vehicles taxes and toll charges are collected by provincial governments while value added tax, income tax and custom duties are collected by federal government. Mineral resources, airport and sea port taxes are split between province and federal at a pre-determined formula. Cities and districts collect municipal taxes from local residents to finance social services.

In most developed countries, various cities and industrial areas develop a niche for themselves. For instance, city of Detroit is famous for its concentration of auto industry, New York is known for its financial institutions and California is known for its technology industry. It is important for each administrative unit to develop its own economic development plan focusing on a particular niche instead of attracting all kind of industries at the same time. For instance, Karachi being a port city is well suited for trading and export companies, banking institutions and maritime ventures; Faisalabad has emerged as a textile center, Lahore is gaining attention from software and call center companies.

Baluchistan is rich in its natural resources and fruit production. These can be developed by not only developing mining sector as well as installation of refining and processing plants. It can attract marble industry, dry fruits packaging and export, and fresh fruit processing and export.

Gwadar deep sea port has the potential to be developed as an alternate port to not only export minerals but facilitate trade with landlocked Central Asian states. NWFP has an indigenous manufacturing of small arms which can be further developed by giving it the status of an industry and allow export to other countries for legitimate use like private security companies, game hunting and personal safety. NWFP can earn revenue from its natural resources and promotion of tourism. NWFP can become a center of transit trade to Afghanistan and Central Asian States. This industrial diversity within the country will create an interdependence on each other which can play a significant role in cohesion and unity.

To create a homogenous national character the government should stop identifying provinces on the basis of any unique separate culture and language. These cultures should be allowed to prosper at family and communal level instead of being identified at national level. Many developed countries, much smaller than Pakistan, divide their areas in administrative units to better facilitate decision making at the local level. This results in efficient delivery of social services which is important for good quality of life. A policy board should be formed to suggest provincial reforms considering geography and economics instead of a language or a culture.

Pakistan will become a strong nation when its policies promote strength in diversity and create provinces that serve the people rather than a particular ethnic group.

Background: In June 2002, Mukhtaran Mai became victim of gang rape on the orders of a Panchayat (village council) as a penalty for an alleged crime committed by her younger brother. Instead of succumbing to this oppression Mukhtaran decided to speak up and seek justice in a court of law. She was supported in her struggle by domestic and international media. On 1st September 2002 an anti-terrorism court sentenced 6 men to death for her rape. They appealed to Lahore High Court and later to Supreme Court which acquitted the accused for lack of sufficient evidence.

Ordeal of women
(June 22, 2005)

Mukhtaran Mai, a gang-rape victim, has become a symbol of women rights in Pakistan. She is attracting international media coverage but there are many more women like her that remain in the shadows and no one knows what happens in their lives. Government of Pakistan worried of getting negative media attention has prevented Ms. Mukhtaran to travel to America where she was scheduled to narrate her story to gain wider support for women rights in Pakistan. Even educated women, like Dr. Shazia, have been subjected to humiliating treatment by male dominated tribal traditions.

Pakistan is an agrarian society with almost two third of its population living in rural areas. These rural areas are indirectly ruled by landowners (zamindars). These zamindars, in some cases, have their own small armies to impose their control over farmers who toil their lands. They use their financial resources to gain political clout and coerce law enforcement to give them a free hand. They have influence over Panchayat (a group of wise men) who, more often than not, rule against farmers. Despite past promises by political parties influence of these zamindars remains unchecked. A key factor that can contain this influence is promotion of literacy in these rural areas, which is almost always opposed by zamindars who are usually Member of Parliament as well.

Other sad part is that the judiciary has been indifferent to eradicating injustices done to women of our society. According to news reports, in Mukhtaran Mai case, Court has acquitted men responsible for this heinous act because law requires that four male witnesses should be produced to convict these criminals. It is reported that the act was committed in front of a crowd of hundreds and yet there are not even four people who have moral courage to come forward as witnesses. Mukhtaran was allegedly gang raped on the orders of a rural council as punishment for a crime attributed to her brother. This shows that zamindars have totally subjugated not only the bodies but also souls of these people.

Pakistan's population is almost equally divided among male and female citizens. But literacy rate among females is estimated to be half that of male which is 60% for male and 40% for female of total literate population. Females play an important role as mothers in society especially in building character and moral values of children. They cannot perform this task until they are provided access to higher education.

This situation is even worse in rural areas where female school registration is only a fraction of total population. In rural Sindh and Baluchistan female literacy is 13% and 10% respectively. Ironically, these two provinces have a higher zamindar influence compared to NWFP and Punjab. According to a study by Oxfam International, while proportion of children not attending school in South Asia will fall by half by year 2005, Pakistan will account for an increasingly larger share of children not attending school. In fact, this study warns that by 2005, Pakistan will account for 40% of the region's children who are out of school, compared to 27% in the year 1995.

Women cannot gain higher respect in society unless they become part of the economy by participating in a gainful employment. Conservative men prevent females from pursuing a career to share economic burden of the family.

According to gender-related index (GDI) which is part of the larger Human Development Index (HDI), Pakistan ranks 120th among 140 countries and is the worst performer in South Asia.

Female workers face male exploitation in work place as well as social hurdles in the community. Pakistan cannot expect to get out of its economic quagmire until it allows its female population to fully participate in the economy. We can fix this social issue by learning from example of Indonesia, Turkey and Malaysia. In HDI report Malaysia is ranked 59th in terms of female participation in the economy while Pakistan is ranked 142nd among 177 countries rated for the purpose.

Pakistan, predominantly a Muslim country, does not even follow Islamic traditions in allowing greater social, political and economic participation of women. Mohammad (PBUH) was a business manager working for Khadijah (RATA) who was a prominent businesswoman of her tribe. No one in his sane mind can believe that she was a docile woman not fully involved in business decisions. Ayesha (RATA) was considered an authority on Sunnah, and a political activist who remain engaged in affairs of the Islamic community after passing away of Prophet Mohammad (PBUH). Even in Quran there are stories of powerful women who had a deep impact on the development of their times. Most prominent of them is Mariam (RATA) mother of Prophet Essa (ES) who was very active in her community; Sarah (RATA) wife of Prophet Ibrahim (ES) who traveled with him far and wide to spread the message of Islam, Sabah (RATA) who was queen of current day Ethiopia and who came to meet Prophet Suleiman (ES) to spread his message around African continent.

Pakistani leadership, social workers, business professionals and political leaders should appreciate the role of women for the development of a healthy and prosperous nation. We should give women equal rights and work shoulder to shoulder with them for the progress of our country. First step in that direction is focusing on the education of female child and the second is to give them security in pursuing their ambitions and talents.

Building institutions
(April 1, 2007)

For any nation to progress it has to build institutions representing ideals of the community. A nation that fails in building stable institutions is faced with chaos, confusion and ultimately breakdown of society. Founding fathers of the nation Allama Iqbal and Muhammad Ali Jinnah envisioned a society where high morals preached by Islam are exercised in all spheres of life; where appointments to government posts were based on merit; where free market economy provided level playing field to all; and where no discrimination was allowed based on religion, caste, color or sex. Allama Iqbal promoted the vision through his poetry while Jinnah led a constitutional struggle to make it a reality. Ironically this dream turned sour as soon as independence was achieved when the nation soon lost its visionary leader and opportunists gained control.

In sovereign state armed forces, especially a voluntary force plays an important role of shielding nation from external aggression. Nation provides their hard earned income to finance such a force while mothers lend their sons/daughters to shed their life to protect the nation. In Islam it is considered a highest honor to serve in the army to protect ideals of the faith. For a professional soldier charged with zeal of faith it is disgraceful to be inspired by material possessions and social status. In Pakistan first institution that was destroyed by politically ambitious Generals was army itself. This lack of focus is not only destroying the morale of a large number of professional soldiers but creating a gulf between the nation and their protectors. Army has become an elite class of ambitious individuals who have no regard for constitution or masses. For the first time in history of Pakistan militant groups have taken up weapons against their own soldiers. This is evident from heavy loss of soldiers in Baluchistan and NWFP. Tribal leaders that were strong allies of military generals are now considered traitors. If we do not radically change this situation, so that professional soldiers are not used for political purposes, it will further undermine this institution.

Police is an institution that imposes writ of law according to the constitution as well as implements decisions of judiciary. Without a highly trained and resourceful police force it is a fantasy to believe that law and order can be maintained in mega cities like Karachi and Lahore. During British rule police was used as an official instrument of extortion and keeping populations in control through extra judicial means. Same practice has carried on as government officials use police to punish political opponents. If we want to strengthen our society we have to reform police department on modern lines and give them resources to implement law without prejudice or political pressure.

Judiciary does not have the right to write laws but once a law is passed by a legislature it is their right to interpret that law fairly for all citizens of the state. A free and independent judiciary is one of the basic requirements to create a civic society. Throughout our history governments have tried to subjugate this august institution for their own political advantage. Appointments of judges were inspired by political affiliations to ensure they will interpret law in favor of government.

Pakistan is struggling for its survival. It is pressured from both inside and outside to maintain unity which is getting weaker by the day. Reason for this erosion is directly related to our inability to build strong institutions. We still have time to get hold of our affairs and embark on a journey of creating a civil society governed by institutions created on solid foundations. If we fail we can not blame it on any external force.

Individuals Vs Institutions
(June 2, 2011)

Leo Tolstoy dedicated last part of his classic novel "War and Peace" to the discussion whether a leader is made by the hand of destiny or a person makes his own destiny through sheer hard work and ability. There is no definitive answer to this riddle and the debate continues to this day. But it is certain that a nation is as strong as its institutions that are immune from individual failure of its leaders. Pakistan today faces crisis of institutional failure that can easily be traced to failure of handful of individuals. The questions that need to be answered is how able leaders can be allowed to rise to the top of institutions based on their capability and merit? And how an institution can be indemnified from failure of individuals?

Catastrophic failures result from accumulation of small errors that goes unnoticed. A strong institution is defined as one which is not dependent on an individual or a small group of people for its continuing success. This requires that a deep bench of leaders is available that are ready to take up reins at a short notice. In Pakistan it seems that all institutions are weak as whenever time comes for replacement at the top a debate starts whether to give an extension for a year or another full term as if the institution is dependent on that one individual for its survival. In some instances a leader occupies top spot for many terms further contributing to damaging morale of others that are waiting for their turn to serve the nation. In political parties the situation is quite severe as there is no concept of retirement and the top position becomes inheritance of a single family. Political leaders in Pakistan have been pushed to oblivion by the circumstances. No leader has ever announced their retirement and assumes the role of a mentor to guide younger generation. Leaders that have already served in top positions for many years are still trying to get another chance. They are willing to go as far as to amend the constitution to be eligible without giving due consideration to long term consequences of this action.

Other effect of extension of leader's term is that to maintain their grip on power they start appointing people in their team that do not exhibit a challenge to them which usually means sacrificing talent for loyalty. Since most top positions involve some kind of political maneuvering that means that various institutional heads have to cut deals with each other for mutual survival. This result in damaging healthy relations between institutions that should be based on national interest rather than short term interests of few individuals. Agreements like National Reconciliation Ordinance (NRO) are the result of this desire for coexistence that have damaged credibility and moral authority of state and political institutions.

A strong institution is one that has the ability to continuously evaluate their performance to make changes in operating processes to stay abreast with dynamic technology and social environment. These adjustments can only happen when fresh leadership is allowed to rise up at regular intervals that bring with itself fresh ideas and new thinking. When this cycle is broken status quo starts to seep in that stiffens the organization affecting their adaptability to change.

In any society, institutions can not perform as closed systems without taking input or feedback from other institutions. In a healthy environment institutions have to perform as open systems where they evolve together as new technologies, management practices and social changes occur. When one institution becomes too strong to start dominating others then the delicate balance gets distorted which ultimately result in deterioration of the whole social structure.

Long term survival of the institutions requires regular addition of new recruits. Rigorous implementation of merit and fairness in hiring process without political, racial or sectarian bias, in public institutions is very important to gain respect of the community. Unfortunately there has been political interference and corrupt practices in selection and hiring of teachers, policemen, district officers and social sector workers.

This is an in injustice to qualified people. It creates bases for corruptions of these officials as they want to recoup the bribe paid or repay the favor incurred to get their job. On the other hand this damages reputation of public sector organizations becomes disincentive for capable people to seek opportunities there. Instead they prefer to work in private sector with better compensation as well as merit based promotions. Similarly there has to be fairness in reward and punishment of performance of leaders to ensure that they do not abuse their powers or slack in their performance.

There are many solutions to correct institutional deterioration in Pakistan. First and foremost is abandonment of extension in term of service. Second is hiring on merit with full public disclosure of hiring process and criteria. Third is implementation of a compensation system that provides a decent living standard for public servants. Fourth is strict adherence to performance measurement standards and punishment for negligence. Fifth is adequate training for new hires especially teachers and policemen.

A nation belongs to every member of community. It is important that all of us take ownership of our affairs and get involved through various forums and civic organizations. If nothing else we can form mohala (neighborhood) committees to monitor state functionaries.

Foreign Intervention in domestic affairs
(September 3, 2011)

Press conference of a senior leader of PPP Zulfiqar Mirza in Karachi showed lighter side of politics which is full of action, comedy, and drama. One of the revelations was a letter written by MQM to former British Prime Minister Tony Blair. This letter was an open invitation to a foreign power to intervene in domestic affairs of a sovereign state which has become a norm of our politics rather than an anomaly. In last decade Nawaz Sharif's exile agreement, National Reconciliation Ordinance (NRO), reinstatement of judiciary, are all resolved through intervention of foreigners bearing pressure on our political parties. In this environment who would blame MQM, a junior partner in PPP led coalition government, to seek foreign patronage for political expediency. Real questions to ask are why political parties resort to get help from foreign patrons? How to contain this practice?

Principal reason for this behavior can be traced to failure of local institutions to resolve political disputes. Institutions that play significant constitutional role to resolve political disputes are judiciary, election commission and law enforcement. Judiciary throughout Pakistan's history has been a biased party in judging political matters. For instance they have legitimized rule of military dictators citing doctrine of necessity; awarded death penalty to an elected Prime Minister under pressure from a military dictator; and were unable to punish military dictators for abrogating constitution. Not withstanding recent activism, this track record resulted in loss of credibility of the court to be a fair arbiter of political disputes and constitutional matters.

Election commission of Pakistan (ECP) has the vital function of ensuring that citizens have a chance of awarding their mandate, without coercion, to the political party of their choice. It is expected that ECP will ensure no member of its staff or supporting departments engage in voting fraud or that any external factor affect the results.

Historical and empirical data suggest that it has failed miserably in discharging this important national responsibility. This failure may not affect larger parties substantially but it affects smaller parties who do not have resources or wherewithal to fight for their rights. This creates discontent that not only produces militancy but encourages parties to seek foreign patrons to bear pressure on stakeholders. Failure of local institutions to hold free and fair elections has invited foreign observes to monitor our elections which is a mild form of foreign intervention. It is unwise to think that a foreigner is more sincere to help our country than ourselves. No respectable society will allow a foreigner to tell them they have been dishonest to each other.

Peaceful transfer of power is essential to reduce political tensions and animosities arising from hotly contested elections. It is ironic that when politicians are in power, no law enforcement agency is able to prosecute their crimes which give an impression that survival depends on clinging to power. Crime committed by any citizen whether elected, uniformed or bureaucratic, which is termed as white collar crime, must be persecuted by law enforcement.

Institution of National Accountability Bureau (NAB) is a stigma on the face of the nation. It has become an instrument of political exploitation and wasteful use of national resources. NAB should be abolished, even if constitutional amendment is required, and white collar crime cell of Federal Investigation Agency (FIA) should be given powers and resources to investigate and prosecute these crimes. Most democracies have a parliamentary ethics committee that penalize parliamentarian that have breached law or abused powers separately from law enforcement that prosecute for the crime. Foreign powers offer protection against corruption charges as we have seen in NRO deal brokered between Musharraf and Benazir by Saudi, British and American.

America, United Kingdom and Canada have immigrants from countries around the world, but Pakistani community is the only one which has international chapters of their political parties.

These chapters not only show cleavages of our society to the whole world but also make our Pakistani identity subservient to ethnicities or narrow political ideologies. These party offices operate like embassies engaging in lobbying with policy makers, securing funds, organizing political rallies and making appointments for their leaders during their foreign visits. This situation has gotten so out of hand that even mediation between political parties is organized by these offices usually under foreign patronage. This practice becomes an avenue for foreign interests to create their sympathizers in political parties which in most cases create conflict of interest. Political parties should be required to make full disclosure of their foreign offices, its activities, office bearers and their financial accounts.

An office bearer of a registered political party is a custodian of sovereign interests. He/she is required to preserve and maintain interest of the State. It has become routine practice that Pakistani politicians meet with foreign delegations and policy makers outside the country without presence of a note taker. Rules must be amended to ensure that all meetings of party office bearers with foreign delegations are recorded, reported and archived with Ministry of Foreign Affairs and ECP as they have a direct impact on the relationships between nations and strategic interests.

Individualistic and dynastic politics of Pakistan has given rise to another form of foreign intervention where other nations dictate who they prefer to be in power to provide aid, economic incentives or provide market access for our products. This situation will be fixed when political parties are organized on democratic principles and state institutions are staffed with people of merit.

Our sovereignty is only as strong as our desire for the self-respect and dignity. If we don't respect ourselves no one will.

Building national character
(*May 25, 2004* & September 9, 2011)

The soap opera that started on 27th Ramadan, when Zulfiqar Mirza of PPP held a press conference to lay allegations against MQM, has been a positive development as the nation is able to see true faces of its politicians and get an appreciation of their capabilities. This is very important as it is the guiding hand of these leaders that will ultimately decide future of this nation. There are two trends clearly visible in all this drama. First, whenever a party is blamed for their involvement in crime against society, then instead of denouncing it, they start narrating a history of similar crimes committed by other parties. Second, when corruption of a minister is highlighted, then instead of taking responsibility for it, they start mentioning a long list of departments that should have prevented the corruption. This is an indication that the menace of corruption is deep rooted in our society and all of us are involved in it one way or the other. Confucius, famous Chinese philosopher, wrote a complete chapter on how incorrectly writing official's names can become basis for corruption of a community. We are engaging in far bigger acts of corruption while, at the same time, hoping that we will become a civilized society as if both are mutually exclusive. It is very important to analyze the root cause of corruption and how it can be fixed.

There is no short cut to fixing the issue of corruption as we have to develop a new generation based on a strong moral character. This will require a commitment of least 30 years if we start today. While this new generation is growing up we can take short term measures to develop an environment of merit, fair play and justice.

Fundamental civil right of a child is getting good education, both academic and social, to become a productive and effective member of community.

Dismal state of affairs at public schools has prompted parents to enroll their children in private schools. These schools have made it upon themselves to develop a curriculum and dictate course material for their students. In theory though these schools do get licenses and monitored by government education boards. Private school curriculum may provide a good knowledge of sciences but is devoid of providing necessary social skills that conform to our culture and traditions. Education has become big business in the hands of industrialist whose prime mover is making money. It is dangerous to play with minds of children to create a class base social structure. There will be those who graduate from public schools but do not have necessary skills to compete with those who have been trained in sciences and languages at a resourceful private school.

Experts of human behavior have identified that first few years in a child's life are most critical in formation of character and personality. Values learned, voices heard and events experienced during these years of infancy stays with us throughout our life and play a significant role in our decisions. During these formative years two groups of people play an important role i.e. parents and teachers. They have to work together to ensure that ethical, moral and spiritual values are ingrained in the child's character to develop good citizens. One way of collaboration is creation of parent teacher counsels in elementary schools that can meet on weekly or monthly basis to discuss progress as well as assign responsibilities.

In most developed countries a large majority of elementary school teachers are women. This is very important because in early years a compassionate and motherly guide is needed by an insecure and fragile child. In cities female teachers are taking an increasingly larger role especially in private schools although they do need training and mentoring in child psychology. But in villages where levels of female education is low usually male teachers are hired which is not a preferred solution. At the same time most of these primary teachers are not hired on merit rather through political influence which further dampens the hope of producing desired results.

Responsibility of civic education lies with parents to shape the character of a child in etiquettes, social responsibilities and cultural traditions. In Pakistan, parents are not mindful of their behavior in presence of small children thinking that infants are not observing. For instance in their child's presence some use profanities while other breaks traffic rules or tell a blatant lie. All these events are observed by children and become part of their memory. So right from beginning we corrupt the soul of a child by distorting the benchmark needed to separate right from wrong. The child observing these events naturally adopts these bad habits. It is inculcated in his personality that getting around these social responsibilities is an intelligent or smart thing to do. On the other hand when the child goes to school he is exposed to another unbridgeable paradox in the form of values promoted in syllabus and the ones practiced by a teacher. For instance cleanliness, we tell our children that according to Islam cleanliness constitutes half the faith but at the same time our classrooms are dirty, our school bathroom stink and our streets are littered with garbage.

Once a youth acquire adulthood they need avenues to express their talents and creativity. These creative energies come out in the form of drama circles in colleges, forming a music band with peers, becoming member of sports teams, and organizing painting exhibitions or any other form that suite their talent. But most of these avenues are not available to youth, which result in suppression of their creative instincts.

Our colleges lack funding and support from the faculty to form drama societies. In a city like Karachi, with an estimated population of over 10 million, there are only 12 art galleries and three art schools. These galleries cannot be successful until people buy these works produced by young artists. Our ill formed tradition imposes restriction on certain form of expression. We look down upon artist who wants to become dancers or choreographers. This dearth of expression creates a frustrated youth who feel suffocated and wants to retaliate against society. They become prey to political exploiters who come in many shape and form. Religious and ethnic groups recruit these disoriented youth to forward their own agendas.

Historically we were part of a community whose system revolved around caste system. This caste system was derived based on the nature of job. Kasturya were good warriors, Brahmans were good administrators, maulana become an expert in religion etc. That system still prevails in our country even after independence. If a person does not become a doctor, engineer or an MBA he feels opportunities are limited for him. Any one graduating in social sciences like economics, arts, and mass communications has either very limited opportunity or if there is one it does not offer sufficient compensation or growth opportunity to be attractive. A student in these fields considers himself/herself as a second rate citizen and is already under pressure to prove that he adds value to society. This lack of professional diversity in our community is reflection of superficiality of our social structure.

In developed societies, like Europe, America and Japan, students are encouraged to go through apprenticeship in various fields during their summer vacations. It helps them understand requirements of a practical life even before they enter it. Students are encouraged to do part time jobs to gain maturity and assume financial responsibility. These students even do blue collar jobs like working in a grocery store or a petrol pump to appreciate dignity of work.

In Pakistan we seek high sounding titles instead of dignifying work. Majority of our youth that pursue higher education abroad, get part time blue collar work with pleasure and confidence because they know no one will look down upon them. Some international consumer retail chains like McDonalds and KFC has started hiring part time workers in Pakistan to provide an income source for students. It is a good trend which should be adopted by local retail chains to establish dignity of labor in the minds of our youth.

At the end of academic life the young adult knows the theory of what is right but is devoid of finding living example of it.

When they join workforce they get another doze of corruption practiced in our offices and factories where dignity of work demands that a person discharge their function truthfully and to the best of their capability. Instead fresh recruit observe people coming late to work, wasting company resources, accepting or giving bribes, evading taxes and looking for shortcuts to make money or get promotions.

One of the most important social building blocks is conscientious use of authority and power. Our system has gotten so weak that it is not able to punish abuse of power and social status. A military or government officer consider him or herself above law and mistreat police when they are apprehended for even a small breach of law. Our industrialists breach tax code and do not feel any burden on their conscience. These characteristics are ultimately transmitted to our youth who feel it is their right to grab what is not due to them without giving thought to damage done to the society at large. In just a matter of few years the person who got out of college with bright eyes to change the world has now fully accepted the reality and instead decides to swim along. With every passing year his desire to listen to conscience gets weaker and weaker so much so that this corrupt way of life actually becomes the accepted norm.

Towards the end of life an honest person, who has maintained dignity of his soul and pursued an honorable life, is hoping to become a guide to the next generation. National awards are created to honor those few that have given more than their fair share to the nation by achieving new heights in sports, arts, philosophy, science, administration, defense and other spheres of society. Awardees are expected to inspire next generations by keeping the flame of honesty and value of hard work alive. Final nail in the coffin of a just society is installed when national awards are bestowed on friends and loyalist.

If you agree with what you just read, then next time before telling a lie or breaking a traffic rule remember that your child idolizes you as a parent. Honesty of your actions will decide future character of your children and destiny of this nation.

Changing the mind set
(November 28, 2011)

Change has become the buzz word in Pakistani politics. All parties are aspiring to introduce one or the other form of change in the country. There are some who are rebranding their promise of *roti kapra aur makan* (bread, clothing and home) through an ATM card in the form of Benazir Income Support Program while others are promising newer models of yellow cabs. An emerging party of the youth, Pakistan Tehreeke Insaaf, is promising to eradicate corruption and force politicians to declare their assets. But these words have no meaning in itself unless they are backed by a policy and an instrument to achieve the desired change. Most important change we need is the change in our mind set and a fresh start.

To start this journey of change most important riddle for us to solve is the unity of purpose. After 65 years of our independence we are still confused whether our founding fathers were seeking to establish a secular state for a Muslim nation or an Islamic state. It is important that we resolve our differences on this important question and come to an agreement.

Independence movement of Pakistan was based on the two nation theory which defined a nation based on Islamic faith. To convert this concept into a political movement, Allama Iqbal became instrumental in bringing back Mohammad Ali Jinnah, from self-imposed exile in England, to assume its leadership. Allama became political mentor to him. Jinnah understood a paradox faced by secularism whereby religious motivations of individuals can not be extricated from their political decisions. Without this understanding it would be impossible to imagine that he will assume leadership of a liberation movement based on religious definition of a nation. After independence religion has become the unifier of a diverse group of people with long histories of separate languages and cultural traditions. In the absence of this string to connect there will be no Pakistani nation. We should accept this reality and focus more on understanding true Islamic concept of a social state.

For above theory to be valid it is important to resolve disagreements between various schools of religious thought. These differences can be eliminated by adopting Quran as basis of our social contract as all sects have an agreement on its text and centrality to Muslim lives. It is important to note that Quran is a forward looking book. This requires that each generation should engage with it to interpret its message according to contemporary thought. Western scholars are conducting an extensive research on Quran based on prevalent knowledge of science and technology while Muslims are still looking backwards to establish an archaic society. To create a progressive society, we have to liberate Quran from shackles of traditionalist Maulvis to embark on the path of understanding and enlightenment. We should emphasis on reading Quran in native languages to enable masses to understand its message while maintaining Arabic recitation for spiritual meditation and prayers.

To eradicate corruption we have to first realize that this parasite has infiltrated deeply into the roots of our nation. Every member of society is engaged in one or the other form of corruption limited only by reach of their authority and influence. All of us have to be conscious that corruption is like a bad karma, every corrupt action comes back to haunt us in one form or the other. It benefits no one and affects everyone. Honesty and integrity as a social policy are the best approach to survive and progress as a society. In communities corruption produces inflation, dilapidated infrastructure, produce loss of dignity, moral decline and ultimately loss of sovereignty.

In individuals corruption produces anxiety, stress, paranoia, heart illness and diabetes. So it is better to act with honesty and lead a contented life. It is important that we realize that corruption in a society starts from small things like breaking a line at the passport office or not respecting traffic rules in the middle of the night. Famous Chinese philosopher Confucius has written a full chapter on how a society is corrupted by misspelling the name of a state official. We are committing far graver acts and expecting the society to somehow remain healthy.

At the government level it is important that salaries of state officials are raised to a level where they can lead decent lives but at the same time impose a strict code of ethics. Those officials committing corruption should be severely punished. It was the recipe adopted by Singapore to develop into a rich and prosperous nation.

Corruption has prevented us from engaging in high precision manufacturing or produce premium priced products. For instance, consider a machine that has 10 parts each manufactured by a different vendor. Just 1 % corruption by each vendor will produce a machine that has 10% defects. Pakistan is one of the top producers of cotton but has not been able to produce high quality spindles locally. And the main reason for this failure is the prevalent corruption in the society.

It is a fact that our politicians refuse to learn from mistakes of the past. Biggest impediment in their lack of intellectual development is their big egos which are easily malleable and their chronic impatience to gain access to the seat of power by hook or crook. Corruption is not limited to public representatives but it is expected that they will somehow control their dishonesty while other segments of the society can engage in it without apprehension or fear. Majority of current cadre of politicians were groomed under military dictatorships which genetically tie them to wishes of establishment no matter how much they try to extricate themselves from it. On the other hand mean spirited verbal fights on national media create a perception that there is something larger at stake than serving people selflessly. These animosities in the end spill over to streets between die hard supporters of these politicians affecting everyone that has no particular interest in their fight.

In political arena we have to progress from politics of inheritance to politics of merit. We have to move from politics of power to politics of people. The will of the people is not only important to elect public representatives but it should be an ingredient of political parties as well. A 25 year old should not become chairman of majority party just because he was conceived by the chairman of that party.

Similarly, party nominations should not be awarded based on back door deals rather local voters and party workers should be asked to recommend qualified candidates from among their midst.

In long run democracy is certainly a better form of government but in short term it produces nepotism, conflicts between state institutions and distorted foreign relations. The source of these ills is lack of trust and rapport between elected representatives and bureaucracy who are real managers of the country. In a stable democracy role of legislature is to formulate policy which is then implemented by bureaucracy under their watchful eye. Legislators should have no say and influence on day to day decisions but they do get engaged in it, producing tensions and corruption. To have influence on decisions they try to get their favorite bureaucrats transferred at choice appointments and award promotions without merit which further deteriorates relations. On the other hand during military rule bureaucrats are able to function more independently and are able to get things done with little interference from a morally tarnished dictator. This provides bureaucracy a vested interest in failure of democracy and reemergence of military dictator. They achieve this objective by going slow, during civilian rule, in delivery of social services creating social unrest and intentional waste producing larger budget deficits.

Soldiering is one of the most honorable professions in the world. Our Generals must realize that keeping one eye on the seat of power and the other on borders is creating a security risk for the country.

Abbottabad incident, terrorist attack on GHQ, attack on Mehran Naval Base and November killing of 24 soldiers, to name just few, should give our corps commanders a pause that they are not able to perform their duty of protecting the state which in a way is professional dishonesty. Their focus should be to make sure that our soldiers are adequately trained, equipped and managed to fight enemies that are circling us from all sides. They should leave politics to civilians. Protection of ideology is responsibility of all citizens and no army can protect its erosion so that should not be their reason to intervene in domestic affairs.

There should not even be a question of army's involvement whether President Zardari stays or leaves or whether elections should be held on time or early. Investigation of federal crimes, including treason, should be the responsibility of Federal Investigation Agency (FIA) that should then prosecute the culprits and seek judgments from the Supreme Court for these crimes.

It is not impossible to break the vicious circle of a dictator followed by a weak democracy and then a repeat. Recipe is quite simple but difficult to implement because it requires cooperation and mutual respect from all institutions. First step is for managers of three legs of democracy i.e. legislature, judiciary and executive to realize their constitutional roles and not overstep it. This will only happen when capable and honest leaders are allowed to prevail in all three functions. Capable judiciary will rise up when merit is instituted in selection of judges. Executive will get stronger if bureaucracy is allowed to function without political interference and establishment of merit in its selection.

Pakistan needs change in mind set to build a dignified nation rather than pursue political slogans that does not mean anything by itself. Let us all agree to change ourselves first before we ask the other person to change. That's the first step. Building a nation requires hard work and engagement from every citizen. We mistakenly assume that honesty of one segment will be enough to produce a chain affect that will change destiny of the nation. Change agents are usually a small number of people but they have to be from all segments of society linked through a common ideology. Until then we will have more of the same.

Constitution & tradition
(January 21, 2012)

A stable state rests on three legs of legislative, executive and judiciary. Balance of power between these three is derived from constitution and a political tradition. Political culture builds its legality from constitution while traditions provide a moral fabric dictating behavior of the stakeholders. In Pakistan unfortunately this political culture has not developed because of repeated usurpation of power by military establishment. PPP administration can be rightfully blamed for their lack of governance and delivery of social services but they have, so far, successfully sustained pressures to maintain continuity of democracy.

As we develop our political culture we must remember that in an Islamic republic Quran provides the constitution while life of Prophet Muhammad (PBUH) is a living tradition and manifestation of it. We can also learn from Western democracies which has nurtured their political traditions in last three centuries. For instance in England there is no written constitution but a deep sense of adhering to traditions. It was the pressure of these customs that forced Vice President Al Gore, during 2000 American presidential elections, to abandon his constitutional right to seek recount of votes in the State of Florida. He could have done that by submitting a petition to the US Supreme Court. In the hind sight he would have been elected president if he had chosen that path but by doing so he would have weakened not only the legitimacy of his own presidency but also that of President Bush if the vote count turned out not to be in his favor.

Supreme Court of Pakistan is the right forum to interpret constitutional articles in their letter and spirit. But while it exercises this right it should consider the impact of their decisions on development of democratic traditions.

For instance, Supreme Court's adoption of doctrine of necessity has legitimized unlawful rule of military dictators. Similarly, taking oath under a Provisional Constitutional Order (PCO) has raised questions about impartiality of judges.

Seeking written guarantee to ensure continuity of service of government officials is another example of a tradition that could damage the balance of powers between constitutional pillars.

In Prime Minister Gilani's contempt of court case some prominent lawyers have rightfully come forward to defend elected government while another group of lawyers have criticized this action. Ironically some of these criticizing lawyers have considered it their moral obligation to defend actions of an American citizen responsible for a mysterious memo sent to Admiral Mike Mullen resulting in a political crisis. These contradictory actions from prominent members of legal fraternity strike at the heart of developing a political culture based on principles and ethics.

Media plays a critical role in developing tradition of politics by allowing politicians of all stripes to debate their respective ideologies and educate people to make an informed choice. Unfortunately one of the compulsions of commercial media is to attract larger audiences, and hence more advertising dollars, by dramatizing important political debates and turning it into personality feuds. It is the similar compulsion of being first to break a news story that pressures editors to make public announcements without carefully collecting and analyzing the facts. A cordial meeting between high stake players presented wrongly can create disagreements and promote wrong perceptions without any chances of repair. Media has to come up with a code of conduct that helps in building an environment of trust, fairness and mutual respect among political stake holders.

Politicians have an implicit responsibility in building political culture that is a guiding light for future generations. In their personal conduct they have to set highest standards of adherence to law, constitution and social values. If their car is towed for wrong parking then instead of cursing the policeman they should apologize and pay necessary penalties.

In their debates on policy matters they have to remember that it is not a personality clash but two sides of a coin. They have to remember that their constituents understand that they have to balance competing interests of their constituency, political party and national interest. It is not expected from them that they will always be right but that they will try their best to fully understand the issue and come up with best solution. Personal attacks and name calling hinders the chances of a compromise that is usually the outcome in politics.

As voters, we should give benefit of doubt to politicians and assume that they have honorable intentions in presenting their policy position. If we are sure of mal-intention of a politician then we should not vote for that person or party in elections as by doing so we become partner in crime.

We are a four years old infant democracy so it is not unusual for us to make childish mistakes. But as a nation we should try to nurture this child to grow and become an adult rather than kill it in the infancy.

Who is next?
(February 8, 2012)

A UN petition to authorize military intervention in Syria, lead by America and supported by 13 out of 15 members of Security Council, was vetoed down by two permanent members China and Russia. This could be a starting point of drawing of demarcation lines on world map between West and Russo-China alliance. Premise of the resolution was humanitarian crisis ensuing in Syria. As soon as the petition was rejected Western Media embarked on propaganda drive to blame Russia and China as enemies of humanity. Ironically West did not saw humanity at risk in Yemen, Somalia and Bahrain. Killing of innocent citizens in Iraq in indiscriminate bombardment and drone strikes in Pakistan are conveniently labeled collateral damage without impinging on human right sensitivities of UN members. Israel has repeatedly engaged in human rights violation but no economic sanction was ever imposed on it by UN. This selective interpretation of human rights violations is striking at the legitimacy of UN as a neutral entity to arbiter conflicts and prevents wars. If this trend continues the world will fall back to the pre World War II condition that was dominated by regional blocks engaged in violent struggle to safeguard their strategic interests.

There is a pattern emerging from Arab spring. A disgruntled population, unwilling to accept continuation of an unjust and autocratic ruler, is covertly supported by foreign elements to rise up against the state. In the process of uprising, community is divided along ethnic and sectarian lines so that cleavages are created. These divisions are then used to maintain control of government as long as it serves a strategic purpose. If not then a country is carved out into smaller pieces. This scenario has played in past after First & Second World Wars and is now playing again as the world moves towards a multi-polar arrangement. The question to ask is who is next in line after Syria? Which country has the strategic interest for the powers?

Pakistan, luckily or unluckily, lies at a strategically important geopolitical location.

It is the historical gateway for landlocked Central Asian States and their mineral wealth to be exported via warm water ports of Indian Ocean. It is on the eastern side of Strait of Hormuz through which 20% of oil is shipped out to the world. Strait of Hormuz was the location of military tension between Iran and United States. This geostrategic position can be a blessing if the nation state is strong or a worst nightmare when there are internal divisions and weaknesses. To fully exploit its geopolitical asset Pakistan require a cadre of leaders that has good grasp of history of our region; a deep understanding of founding values of our state; and appreciation of diversity of our cultural heritage. In absence of these skills short sighted and narrow minded approaches would weaken the state from inside and make it vulnerable to exploitation by foreign powers.

Unfortunately it is later scenario that has played out in Pakistan in last 63 years of its existence. Today ethnic divisions are wide, sectarianism is rampant, corruption is widespread and injustices happens everyday. To add to the risk is proliferation of sectarian militancy which is controlled by a narrow minded intolerant leadership.

These sectarian organizations are armed by illegal weapons that infiltrate from war torn Afghanistan or probably shipped in thousands of Afghan transit containers that disappeared within Pakistan in last few years. Add to the mix presence of foreign intelligence officers whose presence was reported by international media. It is now a known fact that intelligence officers from Belgium, Germany, America and Israel are operating in Pakistan. It will hardly be a surprise if agents from other countries are also present. What these foreign elements are doing is any body's guess but they are certainly not dreaming about a united Pakistan as their top priority.

In this environment we may be fooling ourselves to think that territorial integrity of Pakistan is in our hands. Fact is that it is more contingent on strategic interest of outside forces. It is fortunate that masses of Pakistan understand these dangers and share a desire to live together.

They will be helpless in front of violent forces that could be unleashed. In these dire times, it is responsibility of politicians and security establishment to understand dangers lurking around us and work together to put our house in order.

It is in our national interest to contain our ethnic identities and work progressively towards building a community where merit, justice and equal rights are granted to all citizens. We have to share more with down trodden and bring them to par with others in terms of economic opportunities, social services and quality of life. It defies all logic that our planners ignored citizens of Sui to have natural gas at subsidized prices when it was made available to far off places in other provinces. It would be a natural consequence that fertilizer plants that use natural gas as feed would be built in Sui. So that jobs could be created for locals as well as others. But in reality fertilizer plants were built where gas was piped not found.

Sui is not a lone example there are many examples around Pakistan where natural resources were not shared with local communities. It is these kinds of policy and planning mistakes that has weakened our nation. We have many assets that could generate billions of dollars revenue for the country. Lahore and Peshawar can attract millions of foreign tourists as they are no less significant, than Greek and Egyptian cities, for their historical importance. But instead of preserving our cultural assets we are throwing garbage around it. Karachi can be a financial and trading hub for South Asian region but instead it is a venue of targeted killings everyday and land mafias operating without any apprehension of law. Fertile lands of Punjab and Sindh can feed half the world but are devoid of capital infusion. Large deposits of key mineral in Baluchistan and Sindh are untapped because of local grievances. These are just some examples of our treasures, not to forget our human capital that expresses its talent around the world as immigrants.

Nation building requires hard work. It is always easy to divide than uniting people. Brotherhood is developed when people are willing to share the bounty and ready to die for each other.

Politics of Flags
(March 7, 2012)

As humanity emerged from caves to engage in agriculture there emerged a need for protection of their surplus wealth from robbers and looters. This became a prime mover for creation of a tribal culture. It had some prominent features including unique symbols hoisted on flags. As long as a person pledged allegiance to a tribe he was considered part of community enjoying its protection but at the same time conforming to its cultural and religious beliefs. Each tribe had its own code of conduct and system of justice that was adhered to by all. This penal code was applied through a council of elders called panchait or jirga in our part of the world. The system worked fairly well to ensure peace within community but produced violent clashes with neighboring tribes in times of stress like famine or epidemic or when the population of a tribe grew forcing them to acquire more land to accommodate them.

Advent of industrial revolution, in the mid 18th century, started migration of rural masses to cities to provide manpower to run those factories. Pace of urban migration increased in sync with improvements in quality of life as a direct result of growing economy. Later introduction of railways, airlines, telephone and internet enabled intercity commerce which ultimately lead to creation of nation states managed through secular democratic institutions, capital markets and equitable system of justice. This development directly struck at viability and existence of tribes. In 21st century tribes are almost non-existent in highly industrialized countries of Europe and America. But on the other hand in lowly developed countries of Asia, Latin America and Africa there are still existence of tribes which compete for dominance that has produced some violent clashes in Africa. War in Afghanistan is largely a tribal war where Pashtun tribes, under the umbrella of Taliban, are not willing to accept presence of foreign forces in their lands.

Pakistan is a lowly industrialized agricultural country with broken system of justice, elite control of resources, business controlled by oligarch and patriarchal system of incentives.

In this environment Pakistan is experiencing a unique situation. It is home to reemergence of new kind of tribes in its cities and villages defined in sectarian and ethnic terms. Each tribe promotes its own unique ideology and symbolism to differentiate from others. Some wear green turban, others have checkered ones, some has a unique cap or a uniform. Since most political parties are controlled by families they are also run like tribal interest groups. Some are promoting narrowly focused cause for Saraikis, Sindhis, Baloch, Pashtoon, Hazara etc. etc. It seems with each passing day more and more of these tribes are adding to the list.

All these tribes have their own flags which are then hoisted on a particular territory to claim it as their own. If you travel around the country, you will experience that various regions are demarked by these interest groups. In these marked territories competitors are slowly pushed out either through conversion to become their members or pressured to move out.

These tribes have short sighted agendas that they promote for benefit of their members. Initially they start with peaceful promotion of their interests. Once they have sufficient strength in members and resources they are willing to go to any length to protect their domain without regard for justice or law. Members are so indoctrinated in their ideologies that they become intolerant to presence of other ideologies among themselves. Allegiance of these tribe members are not with the nation but with their own vested interests. In many instances these tribal members refuse to accept validity of national flag or anthem. These groups are amenable to foreign interference and influences which further complicates the situation. This is a dangerous development and directly hits at national unity and integrity.

The question arises as to how we can reverse this trend? There is no short term solution to this problem rather a long term approach is needed to arrest this trend.

First, there should be introduction of a unified curriculum for education implemented across board in private, public and madrassa schools.

Second is implementation of a fair, expedient and creditable judicial system that can deliver speedy justice regardless of cast, creed or other associations. Third creation of political parties that appreciates democratic practices to promote its next cadre of leaders picked from the grass roots and enjoys public support. Fourth ban on hoisting political party flags on public property regardless of their position in government. Fifth all civic organizations that engage in mass appeal, movement and politics should be regulated to submit their accounts, charters and membership details. Sixth national flag should be promoted in all public rallies rather than party flags as our allegiance should primarily be with the state rather than narrow interest of a party or association.

A nation is as strong as its weakest member. Dividing allegiances along sectarian and ethnic lines weakens all of us. If we want to survive as a strong State in a volatile South Asian region then we have to give up our narrow interests and join hands to become one nation. A Pakistani nation gathered in the shadow of a green flag decorated by the crescent and star.

Section II: Pakistan Politics

Background: Pakistan has struggled with building stable political institutions throughout its existence. Within a year of independence Pakistan lost its founding father Mohammad Ali Jinnah who was one of the foremost constitutional minds of 20th century. Mr. Jinnah was not able to help in preparation of constitution because of his struggle with deadly decease tuberculosis (TB). First Prime Minister of Pakistan Liaquat Ali Khan, a key lieutenant of Jinnah during independence movement, struggled with juggling priorities between settling vast number of Muslim immigrants pouring in from India; arranging financial resources to kick-start a non-existent economy; manage first war with India for control of Kashmir and drafting of first constitution. Liaquat Ali Khan was credited with formulation of the Objectives Resolution (Qarardad-eMaqasid) that became a corner stone of all future constitutions of Pakistan. After assassination of Liaquat Ali Khan in 1951 drafting of the constitution was further delayed by infighting between various political factions and civil bureaucracy.

At last in 1956, after 9 years of independence, first constitution of Pakistan was adopted. Within two years of its promulgation, in 1958, that constitution was abrogated by first military dictator Field Marshal Ayub Khan to install himself as President. To legitimize his rule Ayub Khan held a referendum in 1960 in which 80,000 union councilmen voted yes or no to the question "Have you confidence in the President, Field Marshal Ayub Khan?" In 1962, Ayub Khan promulgated a new constitution which promoted parity between East & West Pakistan; sanctioned a unicameral National Assembly comprising of 156 members with equal representation from both provinces; and provided executive authority to President elected through indirect elections by an electoral college comprising of basic democrats. Presidential elections were held in 1965 in which Ayub Khan was challenged by Fatima Jinnah, who was sister of the founding father Mohammad Ali Jinnah. At the end of a bitter contest Ayub Khan claimed victory but lost credibility as widespread election fraud was reported by observers and media.

Ayub never fully recovered his moral authority to hold public office and resigned on 25th March 1969 by handing over power to his hand picked Chief of Army Staff General Yahya Khan.

Yahya announced first general elections of Pakistan to be held on 7th December 1970. Election campaign was dominated by two charismatic leaders Zulfiqar Ali Bhutto of Pakistan Peoples Party (PPP) and Sheikh Mujibur Rahman of Awami League. Although 1970 elections are considered one of the most fair and clean elections in the history of Pakistan but results showed an ethnic divide of the country. In East Pakistan, a Bengali majority province, Awami League emerged as the majority party with 160 seats while in West Pakistan PPP emerged as the leading party by winning 81 seats. Bhutto refused to accept Awami League's majority and created hurdles in announcement of an opening session of the parliament to allow formation of government. Political deadlock could not be resolved resulting in succession of East Pakistan to become Bangladesh while West Pakistan province became current day Pakistan.

In 1973 Zulfiqar Ali Bhutto was able to form a consensus among all political leaders to promulgate a new constitution. This constitution is still enforced in Pakistan with 20 amendments to date. The new constitution changed structure of legislature from a unicameral to bicameral comprising of 100-member Senate (after 20th amendment it is increased to 104 by adding 4 minority members) and a 216-members (after amendments, increase in population and inclusion of women & minority it has increased to 342 seats) National Assembly. President is the head of state and Commander-in-Chief of the Armed Forces. President is elected by an Electoral College comprising of National and Provincial Assembly members. Executive branch is run by a Prime Minister who is usually leader of the largest party in National Assembly. If the largest party does not have a clear majority it has to form a coalition with other parties to enable the Prime Minister to clear constitutional hurdle of seeking a vote of confidence from the parliament. Zulfiqar Ali Bhutto formed government as Prime Minister as mandated by the new constitution.

In 977 elections were held by Bhutto government to seek fresh mandate from people. PPP secured 155 seats in 216 seats National Assembly. Alliance of opposition parties, Pakistan National Alliance (PNA), refused to accept these results blaming their dismal performance to an election fraud. Bhutto government sought military's help to suppress street protests organized by opposition.

Negotiations failed in resolving differences forcing opposition to demand fresh elections. On 5th July 1977 Chief of Army Staff General Zia ul Haq took advantage of this political stalemate to impose second marshal law of Pakistan suspending the constitution yet again.

General Zia promised to hold elections in ninety days but that promise was never fulfilled. Instead he installed himself as 6th President of Pakistan in September 1978 while retaining the position of Chief of Army Staff (COAS). Deposed Prime Minister Zulfiqar Ali Bhutto, still commanding mass popularity, was charged with murder of a political rival Ahmed Raza Kasuri to crush any chances of his return to power. Supreme Court found him guilty as charged and awarded a death sentence.

Soon after taking over, President Zia disbanded parliament and appointed a 284 member Majlis-e-Shoora (council of advisors) which mostly comprised of right leaning politicians and intellectuals. To legitimize his rule a referendum was held on 19th December 1984 in which a controversial question was asked to appoint or reject General Zia as President. According to official results 95% of voters answered in favor of General Zia to elect him as President.

In February 1985 general elections were held on non-party basis. Most political parties boycotted these elections which seriously undermined political authority of the parliament. President Zia nominated Mohammad Khan Junejo as Prime Minister from among members of the newly elected parliament. To ensure his control of reins of power, parliament was coalesced to pass 8th Amendment by inserting article 58(2)(b) in the constitution. This article granted extraordinary powers to President to dissolve national assembly. Prime Minister Junejo was an honest and respectable man. His exercise of executive powers soon created a gulf between him and the President. On 29th May 1988 President Zia invoking article 58(2)(b) of the amended constitution dissolved Senate and National Assembly thereby removing Prime Minister Junejo. Constitution stipulated that elections to be held within 90 days of dissolution. While politicians were busy in their election campaigns President Zia died in a mysterious plane crash on 17th August 1988.

An experienced civil servant and Chairman Senate Ghulam Ishaq Khan assumed office as 7th President of Pakistan after death of Zia. Fresh elections were held on 16th November 1988 for 336-member National Assembly and 100-member Senate to reinstate 1973 Constitution. Leading contenders were PPP lead by Benazir Bhutto, daughter of Zulfiqar Ali Bhutto, and Islami Jamshoori Ittehad (IJI) lead by Nawaz Sharif, who was considered a prodigy of General Zia. Elections were held peacefully and elevated PPP to become a majority party by winning 94 seats while IJI secured 56 seats. As per constitution President Ishaq invited Benazir Bhutto to form government. On 4th December 1988, Benazir Bhutto became first women Prime Minister in any Muslim country.

President Ghulam Ishaq Khan was a conservative at extreme right while Prime Minister Benazir Bhutto was a liberal at extreme left. It was a mismatch that was doomed to fail from the beginning. Strains were evident soon after she took oath of office. President frequently exercised his constitutional right to veto proposed laws and regulations creating hurdles for executive to function effectively.

Prime Minister Benazir Bhutto enjoyed support of people but her term in office was tarnished by frequent reports of her husband and Senator Asif Ali Zardari's involvement in corruption. In August 1990, President Ishaq levied charges of corruption, nepotism and despotism to depose Prime Minister and dissolved national assembly exercising the power vested in him by 8th amendment. Dissolution of a democratically elected government with a mandate for five years term was a serious set back to development of political institutions in the country.

General elections were held in November 1990 in which Islami Jamhoori Ittehad (IJI) lead by Nawaz Sharif won 106 seats while Peoples Democratic Alliance (PDA) lead by Benazir Bhutto was reduced to a minority party with 44 seats. Nawaz Sharif, leader of right wing conservative alliance, was invited to form government as a leader of the largest party. It was expected that since both head of state and executive were conservative they will be able to run government with better understanding. But this proved to be too much to ask from people with big egos.

Soon differences developed between these two severely affecting functioning of government. To break this political deadlock a deal was brokered by Chief of Army Staff Abdul Wahid Kakar which required both President and Prime Minister to resign to pave the way for fresh elections. This was second time in five years that a democratically elected government was not allowed to complete its constitutionally mandated five years term.

General elections were held on 6th October 1993 results confirmed that Pakistan has progressed considerably towards a two party rule. Benazir Bhutto leading PPP campaign secured 89 seats while Pakistan Muslim League Nawaz (PML-N) secured 73 seats. None of these parties had absolute majority but as a leader of the largest party in parliament Benazir Bhutto was invited to form a government. To ensure that her second term is not disrupted, PPP was able to elect one of its members Sardar Farooq Ahmad Khan Leghari as 8th President of Pakistan.

It was expected that in her second term Prime Minister Benazir Bhutto would demonstrate better performance in governance, contain corruption and putting economy back on growth track. President Leghari, although a member of PPP, did not hesitate from dissolving parliament and deposing Benazir in November 1996 once again blaming her government to engage in widespread corruption. This was third time a duly elected parliament was dissolved by a President exercising powers vested in him by now infamous 8th amendment. Action of the President in dissolving parliament could be legally justified by constitution but this seriously hampered development of a political tradition which is important for emergence of a political culture for peaceful transfer of power through popular mandate.

General elections of 1997 once again moved pendulum in favor of Pakistan Muslim League Nawaz (PML-N) which secured 137 seats providing it enough parliamentary majorities to form a government while PPP was reduced to just 18 seats curtailing its ability to offer a viable opposition. Nawaz Sharif became Prime Minister for second time in a decade.

Nawaz Sharif government was tested with a serious crisis when India became a nuclear power by conducting test explosions on 18th May 1998. Despite international pressure especially from President Bill Clinton, orders were issued to carry nuclear tests. On 28th May 1998 Pakistan became a nuclear powered state and member of the elite seven nation club with declared nuclear arsenal. These tests produced extreme economic hardship for the nation as economic and military sanctions were imposed by the largest trading partner and ally United States.

General Pervez Musharraf was appointed as 13th Chief of the Army Staff by Prime Minister Nawaz Sharif. Army as an institution has exercised considerable political influence throughout history of Pakistan whether it was in the form of a marshal law or brokering political deals to break deadlock. Military Generals were reluctant to allow civilian leaders to control military operations and planning. This inability of civilians to control military proved fatal for Nawaz Sharif as he was not taken into confidence when a covert military action was initiated in Kargil sector to reclaim territory in the Indian occupied Kashmir. When incursion was discovered by Indians they used their diplomatic influence to damage international standing of Pakistan as a responsible nuclear state. Dangers of a conflict between two nuclear powers did not sit well with capitals around the world.

President Clinton pressured Prime Minister Nawaz Sharif to pull forces behind internationally recognized borders. Pakistan complied but produced a growing rift between powerful Chief of Army Staff and a civilian Prime Minister. This institutional struggle terminated when on 12th October 1999 Prime Minister exercised his constitutional powers to replace General Musharraf as Chief of Army Staff. General Musharraf was on a foreign trip in Sri Lanka when this announcement was made. He immediately got on a PIA, national carrier of Pakistan, commercial flight to return to Pakistan. In panic executive branch tried to delay his arrival by preventing the plane to land in Karachi. These efforts failed and a marshal law was imposed in Pakistan for the fourth time. General Musharraf government ruled the country as a Chief Executive for almost three years.

In 2002 general elections Pakistan Muslim League Quaid (PML-Q), also called kings party as it was formed by military establishment, won 126 seats in parliament becoming the largest party. Benazir Bhutto was in a self-imposed exile to avoid prosecution in corruption charges. While Nawaz Sharif was exiled after a deal was brokered by Saudi government. President Musharraf refused to allow these leaders to participate in political process which severely damaged credibility of these elections. In Benazir Bhutto's absence PPP participated in elections as PPP Parliamentarians headed by Makhdoom Amin Faheem. PML N was lead by Makhdoom Javed Hashmi. In the absence of key leaders PPPP and PML N secured 81 and 19 seats respectively. PML Q formed a coalition government which was first lead by Mir Zafarullah Jamali and later by Shaukat Aziz, a pro-American former top executive of CitiBank with no political roots in Pakistan.

For the first time in Pakistan's history a government completed its constitutional term of five years and held elections in 2008 to seek fresh mandate. During this time General Musharraf reached out to Benazir Bhutto to negotiate a political deal which was later termed as National Reconciliation Ordinance (NRO) (full text of this ordinance in Appendix IV). Media reported that a deal was brokered by British, American and Saudis seriously eroding public support for both Musharraf and Benazir. At the same time Benazir Bhutto reached out to her political rival Nawaz Sharif to sign a Charter of Democracy (COD) (full text of COD in Appendix II) to collaborate for establishment of strong political institutions.

In retaliation for its support for American war in Afghanistan, Pakistan was subjected to frequent terrorist attacks. Despite incurring heaving economic and human sacrifice, American's were asking Pakistan to do more to curtail infiltration of insurgents from Pakistani FATA region. American drone attacks were producing increasing numbers of civilian deaths raising anti-American sentiments in the country.

American involvement in brokering a deal between Musharraf and Benazir produced strong reaction from people. While Pakistan was experiencing deteriorating international relations, President Musharraf sought reelection by this handpicked assembly. He feared annulment of his election by activist Supreme Court Chief Justice Iftikhar Mohammad Chaudhry. Musharraf decided to depose the Chief Justice by issuing a judicial reference against him on 9th March 2007.

Justice Chaudhry instead of complying with wishes of military dictator decided to pose an opposition. This initiated a tug of war between lawyer community and government which ultimately resulted in an imposition of an emergency rule on 3rd November 2007 just 2 months before elections scheduled for January 2008. This action was later termed as a soft coup.

In this backdrop Benazir Bhutto returned to the country in October 2007 despite warnings from her American and Pakistani friends that there is a serious threat to her life. These fears proved real when a bomb blew off in the procession gathered to receive her at Karachi airport. She avoided any injury but the incident claimed 134 dead and 450 injured. Undeterred by an attempt on her life, Benazir filed her election nomination papers on 24th November 2007. Ignoring security alerts she embarked on a series of political rallies to campaign for her party candidates. On 27th December 2007 she spoke at a large rally at Liaquat National Bagh, Rawalpindi in a run up to the elections. While returning from this rally, she stood out in her sports utility vehicle to wave to the cheering crowd. Bullets were fired at her together with twin suicide bomb explosions. She was critically injured and rushed to the hospital but could not survive the wounds. Death of Benazir was substantial loss for the nation in building democratic institutions. Her 19 years old son Bilawal Bhutto Zardari was elevated to become Chairman of PPP while her husband Asif Ali Zardari became the co-chair. These appointments were made based on a handwritten will of Benazir which raised questions as no expert was allowed to examine it.

Death of a national leader raised fears that elections could be postponed but majority of parties decided to participate in elections with a slight delay of 30 days. In 2008 general elections PPP and PML N participated with full vigor. Death of Benazir produced a large turnout of sympathy votes for PPP candidates but was not enough to give absolute majority to the party in parliament although it became the largest party with 124 seats.

PML N secured 91 seats while PML Q lost significantly to be reduced to 54 seats from its previous total of 126. PPP formed a coalition government with MQM, ANP and JUI F which was later joined by PML Q. Yousuf Raza Gilani became 16th Prime Minister of Pakistan on 25th March 2008. At publishing of this book PPP government was on course to complete its term of five years.

President Musharraf faced threats of an impeachment because of his judicial reference against the Chief Justice and imposition of an emergency few months before elections. He succumbed to the pressure and resigned from Presidency on 7th August 2008. In the subsequent presidential elections held on 8th September 2008 co-Chairman of PPP Asif Ali Zardari became 11th President of Pakistan.

Elections in Pakistan are managed by Election Commission of Pakistan (ECP). ECP is an independent and autonomous constitutional body headed by a retired judge. The commission is comprised of a Chief Election Commissioner and four members each drawn from the sitting judges of the High Courts of the four provinces. Day to day affairs are run by a Secretary, Provincial Election Commissioners and a secretariat staff. According to ECP there were 80 million registered voters in Pakistan as of February 2012. On ECP web site there is a list of 193 registered political parties which in a way is reflection of deep divisions in the country which produce divided legislature and force formation of coalition government. In last elections ten parties won seats enabling them to manipulate policy agenda of the government. There is rising influence of regional parties like MQM, Awami National Party (ANP) and fractionalization of larger parties into splinter groups like PML dividing in to PML Q, PML F, PML N or PPP dividing into PPP S. Recent surveys and polls indicate that forthcoming elections in 2013 will produce a divided parliament resulting in another coalition government.

Building Political Institutions: Politics of self
(June 6, 2004)

If you ask a politician why is he in politics? The most likely answer you will get is to serve people. It sounds good but then if you continue with the argument and ask them why don't they do charity work? Their first reaction is of surprise and then you would get as many reasons as there are members in the assemblies. Politically motivated people would find this argument distasteful but reality is that we have a small group of people who have an iron grip on political institutions. It is musical chairs where players remain same but we get different winner at the end of each game. Sons inherit party leaderships from their parents.

Difference between politics and charity is quite simple but substantial. In charity a person affect life of people who are in need of some basic human necessity like food, shelter, education, medical attention etc. so it tries to address a deficiency in a society. Politics on the other hand a person decides direction of the nation by formulating laws that affect every segment population. It has much wider and deeper effect on society as compared to charity. It is extremely important for the survival of a nation to elect capable people from its ranks to manage government according to the aspirations of the community. Opportunity to serve should be open to any person who aspires to assume that responsibility. But in our society a large number of people are excluded from election process.

Today's social structure of Pakistan is a continuation of how the society looked like during British Raj. There is civilian and military bureaucracy, which compete for power with landlords created by British when they were granted revenue collection rights in return for their support of colonial rule. Another class of people was added to this spectrum when a renowned industrialist Mr Nawaz Sharif got elected to become Prime minister of Pakistan.

This power struggle between upper classes frustrated a large number of people who were then manipulated by religiously motivated leaders.

These political clerics aspired to gain political clout in the name of Islam. Motivation of these classes is to retain control of resources of the country to advance their own personal gain. They blind side people by presenting their self-interest as interest of the nation. If an opposition is offered to them they consider it an assault on the national interest. These groups bargain with each other to get maximum advantage from a political situation. There is a long list of actions of our leaders that were taken in the name of national interest and proved to be for self-interest only.

Pakistan's population is fast approaching 150 million. Out of these 150 million total numbers of people belonging to five ruling classes is not more than 8 million. You can do the math. Strength of military 750,000, strength of bureaucracy around 625,000, substantial land owner families are not more than 325,000, consider 200,000 top tax payers as leading industrialists, according to one estimate there are 30000 madrassas in Pakistan consider imams of all these as religio-political leader. This total comes out to 7,600,000 people including their siblings. It is amazing that a nation of 150 million is ruled by a class structure constituting not more than 5% of total population. Answer lies in the fact that these classes realize importance of their dependence on each other and negotiate compromises to retain status quo.

Another question is how long will it take for people to realize power of their vote and what they can achieve by exercising this right. Our leaders, both military and civilian, understand that best way to rule is to divide people. That is probably one reason we talk more about being a Baluch, Pathan, Punjabi, Sindhi, Saraiki or Mohajir instead of being a Pakistani first. Then to further bifurcate we bring religious differences into picture. These divisions have served politicians well but have increasingly frustrated the people and produced increased chaos.

Another reason people do not get courage to exert their influence is by keeping them illiterate. We spend almost 40% of our budget spending on debt servicing and military expenditure. Education on the other hand gets just 2%. This neglect of education is in direct interest of ruling classes. Knowledge gives a person power to differentiate between good and bad leaders. It gives them dignity to stop following blindly and question actions of politicians. Mr Musharraf has been tolerant of criticism of the press but then how many people are actually reading those news stories. In 1997 circulation of Dawn was 500,000, Jang and News International combined was around 875,000 multiply this with the pass through rate of 3 and you arrive at a figure of about 4 or 5 million people which also include those from the ruling classes. This is less than 3% penetration of information. Advent of satellite TV has changed the landscape but it is still not more than 15 to 20% of population.

Ruling classes have a stronghold on political parties. It is evident from the fact that 2 of the 4 largest political parties carry names of their leaders. In this situation it is very difficult for a person, for instance a salaried professor, with knowledge and integrity to consider running for a representative position. In past decade an ethnic party successfully tried to prove that a middle class person can be elected to provincial and national assemblies. They collected small donations from their constituents to finance election campaign of their candidates. There are a lot of questions marks about method of collecting these donations but they did prove that if efforts are made it is possible to get a middle class person elected to the assembly. Main factor in their success was presence in urban areas where education and awareness is higher. The party was able to unite people under one banner to politically ask for their right. But like many other good things in our nation that party became prey to greed and thirst for power. They soon forgot the fundamentals of their struggle and joined elites of the society.

We can not build strong political institutions until we refine the political process to include all people rather than exclude.

To close the argument here are some recommendations to reform electoral process. Election commission should be given more powers not only to execute election process but also to monitor constitutions and democratic values of political parties. Any party engaged in an activity deemed undemocratic should be asked to amend its constitution or lose their registration.

For instance appointment of a party Chairman for life is anathema to democratic values. A party should be required to prove membership throughout the country before they can be qualified to participate in national elections. Staff of election commission should be increased to reduce reliance on temporary staff from judicial bodies. Campaign finance reforms should be promulgated. Serving people is one of the basic rights of a citizen. As implemented in democracies like Europe and America, government should allocate fund to distribute among political parties who achieve a certain number of votes in national elections. For instance any party achieving 15% or more votes in national elections are eligible to get federal funds for their election campaigns.

In the current parliamentary set-up there are 60 seats allocated for women which are filled proportionately by parties according to their seats in assembly. This is a non-democratic system. All seats should be filled through direct elections including Senate.

A fatal flaw in 'First past the post' system of elections is that in case of large number of candidates the winner could only get mandate from a small fraction of voters. This should be replaced by system of majority votes. Winning candidate should be required to secure absolute majority of 50% plus 1 vote to be elected. If no candidate secures that many votes a run-up election should be held within a set period of time between the top two vote getters of the first round.

These are just few suggestions to improve political process in Pakistan. We cannot expect democratic institutions to gain roots until we liberate our electoral system from clutches of ruling classes.

Building Political Institutions: Why do we accept military rulers?
(October 19, 2004)

For a large part of Pakistan's 57-year history military Generals have ruled the nation. Most of them have derived popular support from people in initial period of their marshal law. Our current military ruler, General Musharraf, is citing this wide support to hang on to a morally wrong precept of keeping both political and military office at the same time. The question is: why do we accept a military ruler?

Answer lies in our history, culture and society. Numerically, we have had more civilian rulers than military Generals. We have had only four (including Yahya despite his short tenure) military rulers whereas we have tried over a dozen civilian governments. In last decade, before the Musharraf took over the reins, civilian presidents dissolved three democratically elected governments. Ironically, these dismissals came from presidents who were from the same political party that was controlling majority in Parliament. President Ghulam Ishaq Khan, a sympathizer of Pakistan Muslim League dismissed Nawaz Sharif who was a parliamentary leader from the same party. Benazir Bhutto, chairperson of Pakistan Peoples Party, met same fate. Farooq Leghari, who was appointed to presidency by PPP dismissed her. This shows egocentric and personality orientation of political parties in Pakistan. People see and understand party dissents and get a feeling that these civilian rulers are more interested in their personal agendas rather than working for benefit of the nation at large. Military, on the other hand, works as a disciplined organ where personal preferences are succumbed to greater good of the institution. Regardless ethnicity background of the chief, corps commanders and soldiers offer their complete loyalty and pledge their allegiance to him. This creates an impression of credibility and respect in the eyes of people.

Psychological make up of human beings is such that they prefer to maintain a status quo and resist change. Quick changes create anxiety, confusion and frustration among people.

65

Civilian governments are mired by in-house struggles for authority and non-stop conspiracies while there is relative calm during military rule. This gives an impression of progress and prosperity but reality surfaces once the dictator is no longer in power. We have heard praise for Field Marshal Ayub Khan and General Zia while they were in power. But soon after their demise realities that came to light were much different than the rosy picture painted during their tenure. Both, General Zia and General Musharraf, were helped by a geopolitical crisis to uplift economic situation of the country. General Zia used Russian invasion of Afghanistan as a pretext to gain economic aid from West especially USA. General Musharraf used 9/11 and war against terror to seek economic benefits and support for his military rule. Since we do no have any tradition of writing and investigating history as it happens, we will have to wait, for a time when he is no longer in power to find out effects of his decisions.

Socially we are a conformist community. We are educated and trained to accept decisions of our elders and teachers without questioning their wisdom. We do not encourage debate and acceptance of divergent views. Political system does not provide equal opportunity for an aspiring social worker to rise to the political high office. Political parties nominate people with certain amount of financial standing and land assets to contest for national and provincial seats. Party volunteers in lower ranks are limited to earn gain from success of party leadership, which becomes an impetus for their loyalty to personalities controlling it rather than the institution itself.

Religiously we have relegated understanding of our religion to maulvis who are educated in orthodox madrassas and do not appreciate and welcome questioning while giving *khutbas* (sermon) from the polemic. Any deviations or dissention with the views of maulvis is considered a blasphemous act.

At the family front, head of family does not consider it necessary to explain his/her decisions to other members. In all we are a society where submission to authority without questioning is the way of life. This kind of social make up plays a role in our acceptance of the rule of a military dictator.

Culturally we are an agricultural society where two third of our population lives in villages. Livelihood of these people depends on land owned by a small number of landlords in all four provinces. These landlords consider it a threat to their dominance to impart education, give equal rights and civil liberties to these peasants. Wealth created from sweat and blood of farmers is used to gain political office and control policy for their own benefit. Democratically strong political institutions run counter to the interest of this landlord class. A military ruler looking for legitimacy relies on alliance of this landed aristocracy to maintain his control on power. Continuation of a political process for a long term could mean retaliation against these political elite. One example of influence of land holdings on political landscape is evident in our neighboring country India. Impact of Nehru's land reforms in early days played a vital role in establishing enduring Indian political institution.

In this environment General Musharraf has no real political threat from any quarter. In reality he is competing with his own image of a person who has moral authority and mandate of the people to implement a vision of economic prosperity, social justice and political stability. His insistence on keeping offices of both a General and President shows conflict between these two personalities. His political actions to amend a constitution to retain political power shows his lack of respect for it as well as a desire to ensure his control at any cost. This is in direct conflict with an image of a leader who has integrity, moral strength and farsighted wisdom.

In order for us to become a sovereign nation we need to respect rights and liberties of each individual, give equal opportunity to all without considering his or her ethnic background, religious affiliation, and gender.

Background: There were two great leaders engaged in struggle for Indian independence from British Empire i.e. Gandhi representing Indian Congress and Mohammad Ali Jinnah representing All India Muslim League. Difference between Gandhi and Jinnah was that Jinnah believed in a constitutional struggle without resorting to violence. On the other hand Gandhi promoted social disobedience by advising people to refuse showing up for work or pay taxes. Jinnah refused to cooperate with Gandhi because he felt that non-cooperation movement can get out of hand and turned violent. Jinnah was proven right as riots broke out in many parts of India resulting in arrest of Gandhi as well as imposition of a ban on his entry in Punjab province.

Building Political Institutions: Jinnah- a constitutional leader

(June 16, 2005)

Difference between a politician and a leader is that a leader has a vision for the nation where as a politician has a desire for power to achiever short term objectives. A leader does not compromise for his personal benefit while a politician manipulates to ensure his continued advancement in power circles. An average leader has a short-term vision while a great leader leaves his mark on history and inspires future generations. Average leaders are dime a dozen while a great leader is born once in centuries and stands taller in stature with each passing decade. Founder of Pakistan, Quaide-e-Azam Mohammad Ali Jinnah, is one of those great leaders who believed in democratic values and stood his ground against all odds to seek an independent state for Muslims who were the largest minority in united India. Debate ignited by L K Advani's comment that Jinnah was a secular leader deserves some merit to be viewed and analyzed in historical context.

Core of the controversy is Jinnah and other Muslim leaders' faith based definition of a nation, which culminated in adoption of the Two Nation Theory by All India Muslim League.Henry Kissinger, former American Secretary of State, validated that in nineteenth century concept of a nation was a linguistic and cultural unit.

Based on this definition, Indian people following Islamic faith were different from their Hindu neighbors. Muslims predominantly spoke Urdu, a language derived from Arabic, Persian, and Turkish, while Hindu majority preferred communicating in Sanskrit and Hindi. Culturally Muslims were almost a counter creed to Hindus. Muslims cuisine included meat dishes, wore different style of clothes, and had unique architecture significantly different from Hindus.

Societal attitudes of Muslim and Hindu communities were also different. Muslims believed in equality of all humans regardless of their ethnic and racial origins. Hindus, on the other hand, divided community on religiously sanctioned caste system with Brahmans enjoying highest social stature while other lower casts were subservient to them. Lowest order of the caste was considered untouchables or social outcast. Members of a caste were barred to rise in social stature in their life times regardless of their talents and achievements. Although they lived together for many centuries these divergent social attitudes demonstrated that Muslims and Hindus were two unique communities. Adherence to a common faith became an anchor for Muslims throughout India to unite, despite diverse ethnic backgrounds, to form a political movement for their rights.

Historians of India project Gandhi as a unifying force while Jinnah is, wrongfully presented as a divider of India. Historical evidence negates this myth. According to John Keay in his book "India: a History" all foreign born citizens, including Arabs, Turks and Persian were called Mleccha defined as "foreigners who could not talk properly, outcasts with no place in Indian society, and above all inferiors with no respect for dharma".

Further more, John Keay writes that Hindus considered Muslims essentially marginal, negative and destructive. Congress leaders repeatedly exhibited adherence to this philosophy during their struggle for independence.

Although on surface Congress claimed to represent all segments of Indian society, their reaction to key historical events made it clear that Hindu majority Congress could not tolerate Muslim majority in any part of India. First evidence of this attitude was exhibited when, for purely administrative reasons, Viceroy Lord Curzon, in 1904, divided largest Indian province of Bengal into Hindu majority West Bengal and Muslim majority East Bengal & Assam. This administrative arrangement created first Muslim majority province. This political loss by Hindus in an important province ignited a countrywide protest lead by Indian National Congress ultimately resulting in loss of life and property forcing government to reverse that decision in 1911. After 1935 elections, a report of "Muslim Sufferings under Congress Rule" was published in 1939. In this report over 100 incidents were reported from Bihar, the United Provinces, and Central Provinces where Muslims were violently attacked, killed or looted between July 1937 and August 1939. In all these cases local officials were charged with aiding Hindus while ignoring cries and complaints of Muslims. Besides these two major events there were other numerous instances when it was evident that majority Hindus would subject Muslims to genocide after removal of a British protective umbrella.

Jinnah, on the other hand, believed in Hindu-Muslim unity for their common cause of attaining independence from colonial rule. He started his career as a member of the Indian National Congress in 1904 and remained a member until 1920s. Although he participated in annual sessions of Muslim League, he did not formally join it until 1913. On many occasions Jinnah championed the cause of Hindu-Muslim unity.

Speaking to Bombay Provincial Conference in October 1916, Jinnah said in his address:

"I believe all thinking men are thoroughly convinced that the keynote of our real progress lies in goodwill, concord, harmony and cooperation between two great sister communities. The true focus of progress is centered in their union."

In his statement to Associated Press in 1934 he wrote: "nothing will give me greater happiness then to bring about complete co-operation and friendship between Hindus and Muslims"

Muslim League, under leadership of Jinnah, struggled for independence of India, presenting formula of a confederacy of two or three states forming a union at the center. This was central principle of Muslim League's political strategy until 1938 when reports of atrocities against Muslims surfaced under Congress run administrations around the country.

This view was further strengthened by intransient negotiating tactics employed by leaders of Indian National Congress especially Jawaharlal Nehru, who later became Prime Minister of India after independence.

Historical fact is that Indian Sub-continent was divided into two separate nation states, India and Pakistan, and both nations should accept this fact. A student of anthropology can see that there is an emotional pull between these two nations to live peacefully and harmoniously that is based upon 5000 years of common heritage. Indian leaders have to respect sovereignty of Pakistan instead of exhibiting an attitude of Akhand Bharat. Mr. Advani's recent statement about Jinnah is a positive step in that direction. Pakistani leaders should give due respect to India and accept that it is one of the dominant players in South Asian region. Pakistan's foreign policy should look more towards India for cultural and trade association.

History always travels in a continuum, instead of broken threads; our common historical heritage should compel leaders from India, Pakistan and Bangladesh to form a South Asian Union with free markets and common currency to compete with other unions being formed around the world.

Building Political Institutions: Developing Democracy
(April 19, 2006)

Last year, during Houston city council elections, I went to a town hall meeting with our candidate Khalid Khan. After that meeting, we met with citizens and one person made a very interesting comment that participation of good candidates in an election is a sign of a strong democracy. Those nations where best and the brightest decide not to participate in an election can learn from this simple statement. By abstaining from political process educated elite are in a way responsible for lack of development of democratic institutions. Unfortunately, Pakistan has been plagued by this malice since its inception when members of influential groups like bureaucrats, military and *zamindar* took control of democratic institutions and political parties.

Democracy has always struggled in Pakistan because of absence of certain basic ingredients for institutional development. First ingredient is an informed and empowered electorate. Empowerment of people can only be achieved through education, economic independence and awareness. Proliferation of electronic media is doing a good job of creating awareness among people about actions of political leaders and parties. Influenced by the media even Benazir's own party, Pakistan Peoples Party (PPP), is showing their concern about public backlash in case of a probable deal with a military dictator. But awareness can not be effective unless people have self-respect and understand power of their vote. This can be achieved through higher literacy rates. Considering low levels of literacy there is a slight chance that an enlightened, moderate, and loyal political leadership will emerge anytime soon. But even worst form of democratic rule is better than a military general. If democracy is allowed to prevail, people will start understanding power of their vote and exercise it better.

Second ingredient for durable democracy is creation of political parties that practice basic tenets of democracy itself before expecting it from the electorate.

In Pakistan, almost all political parties are undemocratic with an individual or a family at the helm requiring unquestioned loyalty to them instead to an ideology they represent. These families draft charter and constitutions of parties to legitimize their control. In many countries a person receiving a party nomination has to give up their party position so that there is no conflict of interest. Keeping both offices gives rise to cronyism and corruption in appointments, award of contracts and allocation of funds. This runs anathema to traditions of democracy where votes of people should decide who can represent them not only at the party level but also as elected representative. Some parties that started with support from educated middle class like MQM or ANP have fallen prey to personal domination and interests. During Imran Khan's visit to Houston few years ago, he was asked when he would leave chairmanship of the party. He gave no satisfactory answer. A similar question was asked from a PPP elected representative about lifetime chairmanship of PPP of Benazir Bhutto. Again, there was no satisfactory answer. This situation prevents development of future leaders rising through party ranks to assume responsibility later on. Since military rule has dominated a large part of our independent history, it is in the interest of the ruling Generals that their cronies, who are always ready to make a compromise at the expense of people, control political parties. This makes it easier to manipulate this small group of people to ensure the continuity of their military rule.

Third ingredient for durable democracy is equal economic opportunity for all citizens. Almost two third of Pakistanis living in villages are employed by jagirdars and waderas as peasants on their lands. These people are paid subsistence level income and deprived of education to keep them subservient through generations. Peasants are forced to cast their vote to the wadera or face their wrath.

Jagirdars do not pay any taxes on their agricultural incomes running into millions. Large majority of these are absentee landlords.

As their peasants toil they enjoy good life in urban centers like Lahore, Karachi and Islamabad. With a lot of time at their hand they seek political power to protect their interest. Members of the same family join different political parties to hedge their risk. On the other hand, to generate revenue for the treasury salaried people of the cities and private business owners are subjected to heavy taxes without an equal voice in legislation.

Fourth ingredient of durable democracy is fair justice for all. Reinstatement of Justice Chaudhry as Chief Justice through a popular movement has given people renewed hope in imposition of rule of law. But this is only a pipe dream. For any judicial system to succeed it needs an impartial, just and qualified police department that can impose the will of law. Politicians, during their stint at power, instead of strengthening this vital state function has meddled in its affairs by recruiting people of their choice, favoritism in placement of officers in their constituencies and granting promoting out of merit. It acts more as a state arm of extortion than an institution to enforce justice. Similarly military rulers neglected the training, organization and empowerment of this civilian institution. It is in the interest of the army to keep Police as a weak institution to prevent them from resisting imposition of martial law. Unless we empower the judiciary and police we can not expect the rule of law to improve and allow people to exercise their rights without fear.

Fifth important ingredient of durable democracy is people's desire to control their destiny and refuse to allow exploitation. It seems preposterous to think that 160 million people are exploited by less than 7 million elites comprising of military and civil bureaucracy, jagirdars and their families. People should wake up to refuse to be silent about injustices and inequalities. This can only be achieved if they are guided by an ideology like Allama Iqbal presented the concept of Khudi to Muslims of India.

Musharraf's enlightened moderation is devoid of passion because of his own unethical ways to acquire and retain power. Religious leaders have tried to present Islam as an ideology for the people.

But this is not a religious struggle as the exploiters and exploited are both Muslims. This is a struggle for attaining national dignity and improving the lives of the people.

For a candidate or political party to succeed, financial resources are needed to manage election campaigns of candidates and running of regional offices of the political party. Most educated middle people do not have these financial resources available to compete with well-financed larger parties funded by landlords or industrialists.

Ironically, these landlords and industrialists have accumulated their wealth by enjoying no-farm tax benefit or write-offs of large loans by government owned banks. This is another reason vested interest do not want to lose political control. In last decade, some religious and ethnic parties have tried to collect campaign funds from people through small contributions in mosques or neighborhoods. But after gaining political power they conveniently forgot the sacrifices of their constituents and follow in the footsteps of other political parties.

In established democracies like India, America and England, people with middle class backgrounds who have knowledge, experience, intellect and a desire to serve get an opportunity through their political system to represent their people. This is achieved by separating party positions from elected representative positions. Once a person gets party nomination to compete in an election for a representative body he/she has to give up their party positions so that other people can get an opportunity. Secondly, serving both on party and representative body creates a conflict of interest because an elected official has to serve all people without giving preference to their party patrons.

In established democracies, candidates raise funds for their campaigns instead of spending their personal money. A person who has spent his/her own funds for an election is tempted to recover it once elected which creates a conflict of interest and results in corruption.

People who support a political party or a candidate should not only honor it with their vote but help them financially as well to get elected.

In Pakistan, if we are interested in establishing strong democratic institutions, we have to reform the regulations governing political parties, campaign finance and qualification of the candidates. It should be made mandatory for all political parties to hold elections for their party positions where individual members cast their votes to elect their party leaders. It should be made mandatory that a person elected to a public office should vacate the party position for other people. We need to clearly establish the academic and intellectual qualification of a person to run for a public office. Recently imposed condition of a Bachelors degree is a step in the right direction, although many candidates have made a mockery of this condition. We need to overhaul the campaign finance rules so that a person is compelled to raise funds for his campaign instead of spending their own money.

Pakistan is located in a highly volatile region where the country has to be strong internally to maintain its independence and territorial integrity. This cannot be achieved unless we create an environment where qualified people are given an opportunity to reach legislature.

Building Political Institutions: Politics of emotions
(February 20, 2011)

Politics is an art of manipulating emotions of a community to inspire them to pursue a vision. In established democracies election campaigns are run on emotions while government is run on rational derived from tradition, laws and constitution. That is probably the reason that elected leaders, who won in landslide victories, lose popular support within first few years of their term because governance requires making hard choices. Emotional quotient forms a substantial part of Pakistani decision making process in all walks of life. Pakistani politicians understand this dynamic very well. They run election campaigns on feudal loyalties & alliances while govern through manipulation of public sentiments instead of focusing on tangible results.

In recent years this situation seems to be getting out of hand. Murderer of Governor of Punjab Salman Taseer, by appealing to religious emotions, is showered with rose petals and valentine gifts in the process mocking rule of law on which a society maintains its moral authority. Even economic decisions are subjected to emotional arguments rather than factual analysis. Decision of Kalabagh dam should be solely based on engineering data that could be debated by experts holding diverging points of view. Instead local politicians make it an emotional issue without any appreciation or criticism of project's engineering data. Same tactics of emotions are being used when a foreigner killed two Pakistanis on busy streets of Lahore. Instead of allowing law to take its course to decide fate of the accused, it has become an emotional drama on which all sides are seeking political benefit for their future election campaigns. This issue will be resolved one way or the other but any damage done to national interest will take some time to recover. Pakistan is in a volatile region where it needs skillful diplomacy to ensure it has more friends around the world especially among its neighbors and strategic allies.

We have to explore reasons for prevalence of high emotions in our society.

It might be interplay of three factors that are hierarchical structure of our society, low level of literacy and our outdated educational system.

From our childhood we are taught to comply with decisions of our elders without ever raising a question or seeking logical explanation. A father or an elder brother, as a patriarch of the family, might as well be insane in his decision making but younger lot has to obey no questions asked. In our villages many families have been damaged by the wrong decisions of elders. Critical decisions of our lives like choosing discipline for higher education, marriage and jobs have to be approved by elders. This undermines a young person's ability to have confidence in their independent decisions which is an important step in gaining experience and maturity. In some cases, consequences of a bad decision made by others are borne by a person who was not even consulted. We express same command and follow behavior in our professional lives where obedience to a superior's orders is an important consideration for raises and promotions. This hierarchical structure has greatly undermined our ability to agree to disagree which is an important ingredient for a democratic society where constant debate is held on national issues. Debating or reasoning are not equivalent to disrespect and should be encouraged.

Our school syllabus, for primary and secondary levels, is filled with distortions of our history to provide us a false sense of pride. Language used is laden with words that are extreme in their expression rather than using diction that convey a neutral view. In our schools and colleges the emphasis is on memorizing the content rather than have a discourse in the class rooms where concepts are fully explained and understood. Our examination system encourages reproduction of memorized content rather than promote expressions of creativity, innovation and imagination. That might be the reason for our uncanny ability to copy or improvise ideas rather than create new ones.

Politicians and political parties are derived from within our society so they exhibit same behavior.

Political speeches are loaded with emotionally charged words without shedding light on solutions to the issues or inspiring people on a vision for future. A look at sampling of speeches from all parties seems similar in content, language and ideology. Press briefings in response to terrorist attacks, accidents or natural calamities are an exhibition of competent authority's play on emotions of the people. They make promises to accord severe punishment will be given to culprits or irresponsible officials without providing a road map to prevent disasters to happen.

A dynamic and progressive nation honors those who contribute to advancement and well being of community. Shaheed (martyr) and Ghazi (victor) are the highest and most esteemed titles in a Muslim society. But even in bestowing these titles we are emotional and careless. A murderer who did not perform his duty of protection is entitled with Ghazi severely undermining the value of this sacred title. Similarly, sudden death of a person in an accident or terrorist crime is termed as Shaheed putting him in the same league with a soldier who knowingly faced death to protect his nation. We exhibit same behavior in showering flattering titles on our political leaders whose abilities are at best average when compared with ultimate outcome of their past decisions. This erodes inspirational value of rewards to become an incentive for younger generation to contribute to the nation with pride.

Emotions are an integral part of a person's character and can not be ignored. But in a civilized society it is important to keep emotions under check or they start tearing the social fabric apart. Open debate on Pakistani media is a positive step in allowing all voices to be heard to cool down emotions. But we need to reevaluate our social and educational structure to develop a nation that appreciates emotions but allows prudence to prevail in making critical decisions.

Tenure of President Musharraf: A disappointing Charter of Democracy
(June 6, 2006)

As the date for 2007 elections in Pakistan approaches, there is increased activity in political circles inside and outside the country. Latest development is the meeting in London between Chairman of PPP, Benazir Bhutto (PPP) and Chairman of PML N Mian Nawaz Sharif (PML), leaders of two largest parties. Outcome of that meeting was declaration of a "Charter of Democracy" signed by them. President of Pakistan, General Musharraf responded, in a manner suited to his military habits, denounced the charter as empty words of shallow politicians. Pro-government parties have rejected the charter as was expected while opposition parties of all shades and colors were quick to approve it. The Charter has opened floodgates for journalists and political pundits to create as many scenarios about future political landscape of Pakistan as there are voices.

For quite sometimes there has been speculation that President General Musharraf has struck a deal with former Prime Minister Benazir to end her self-imposed exile and participate in next general elections. As a savvy politician she grabbed this opportunity to gain wider public support by approaching her opponent thrown in exile by the dictator. With this, she killed three birds with one arrow. First, she established herself as a national leader by gaining sympathy of all political activists. Second, she made an alliance with second largest party in the country to ensure they don't act to impede her plans. Finally, she exerted greater political pressure on the General to ascertain that he does not go back on his words as he has done in the past.

Nawaz Sharif on the other hand had no other option left but to support his old political nemesis to secure his return to the country. It is clear from one of the articles of the charter and subsequent statements of leaders that Benazir has agreed to nullify the agreement he signed with Musharraf government once she comes into power.

It is speculated that US has played a role in pressuring Musharraf to abandon his uniform and allow prominent political leader to participate in elections. General Musharraf's recent meetings with pro-government PML-Q and his directive to reorganize the party for 2007 elections prove that point. Rumors are circulating that General Musharraf is now looking for a graceful exit from political scene and wants to avoid the closure faced by his predecessor General Zia.

Charter of democracy declares military intervention as an enemy of democracy. It proposes a joint platform to pressure military Generals from grabbing power by using similar tactics used by them to coax politicians. It outlines formation of an accountability commission to question military brass about their financial gains. One positive proposal is establishment of parliamentary committees consisting of both treasury and opposition members to conduct public hearing for the appointment of judges and accountability commissioner.

Abolition of National Security Council is probably another step taken to undermine power of the military establishment. In many countries National Security Councils are formed consisting of both civil and military members. It would be unwise for politicians to ignore military in matters of national security. Other article to note is allowing a Prime Minister to seek a third term in office. This, in plain words, is in self-interest of both these leaders as they have served two terms already and wants another chance at the helm.

Another agreement is formation of a caretaker government three months prior to election date. Removal of graduation requirement to run for a public office is a setback to the democracy, as it will bring all those old zamindars into parliament.

Reading "Charter of Democracy" reminds one of old times when a political party would announce a platform to take revenge on the other party during elections. This time the foe they are united against is military establishment.

Although these leaders are targeting military in their own self-interest it is a fact that for democracy to prevail political parties has to unite to erect an insurmountable hurdle for the establishment. To undermine military's political meddling, it is important to have a transparent defense budget, audit of financial assets of military generals, and closure of political wings of intelligence agencies.

In its essence, this Charter of democracy is a political platform announced by two large parties for 2007 elections. Surprisingly, the charter does not introduce any reforms in the structure of political parties to make them more democratic. Charter does not address how it would handle sectarian and ethnic terrorism that has plagued Pakistan for two decades. It is silent about how it would create harmony between center and its provincial units. There is no mention on how it would handle economy of the country. It does not address issues like reorganizing police and enforcing speedy judgments to improve law and order situation.

Nation needs selfless leaders who understand the fine line between personal and national interest. Country should not be treated as an inheritance that can be divided among political elite. It has its own soul and body. It is important that people elect leaders who can steer the nation according to its potential and ambitions.

Full Text of charter of democracy is provided in Appendix II

Aftermath of COD:
(February 4, 2007)

It was obvious from language of the charter that it was a political ploy by Benazir Bhutto. The charter was a smart political move as it was an all win for her. If General Musharaf did not come forward to form a deal she could continue with applying the charter. This would improve her chances to gain leadership in parliament as it would have been too tall an order for military machine to beat coalition of two large parties. As she anticipated Musharraf came forward with a deal which among other things include her return to the country as well as dropping cases against her and her husband Asif Zardari.

As rumors of the deal surfaced, Nawaz Sharif tried to keep her on his side by announcing an all parties conference in London. It was an ill timed and ill conceived effort by him to stay politically relevant in the upcoming elections. Choosing between them is a no brainer for Ms. Benazir. She will not hesitate even for a moment to side with General Musharraf as she needs military support to rule in Pakistan. She understands that a uniformed dictator does not have necessary skills to get a political base among people. She appreciates that it was still not time for her to part ways with Nawaz Sharif so she convinced him to postpone the all parties conference for a month. This way she can keep pressure on Musharraf to get most from their deal while keeping the charter alive as a political card.

General Musharraf showed his political acumen to handle this situation by diverting the debate whether he can be elected by present assemblies or not. The kings party, controlled by Chaudhry's, are struggling for their political life by appeasing.

For their political benefits they don't care if they abrogate the constitution one more time as long as they keep military on their side. From statements made by Benazir Bhutto it seems she is not against reelection of General Musharaf for another term but she would not accept him in uniform.

Benzazir knows too well that in absence of a political base Musharraf derives his power from his uniform. If she can get him to give up his uniform as a political compromise for his reelection then she can get rid of him later through political maneuvering. Musharraf on the other hand understands this risk and is resisting giving up his power base. This is probably for this reason that the deal has not been formally announced so far.

There is no doubt that Pakistan needs a moderate leader that can arrest rising tide of fundamentalism, sectarianism and ethnicity. Ms. Bhutto can fill that void but she needs to develop a second tier leadership which can execute her plans at grass roots level. She is surrounded by political opportunist who does not have the courage or intellectual depth to give her frank advice on matters of national interest. Speaking to her party officials makes a person feel that loyalty to Ms. Bhutto is prime qualification to rise in her party's hierarchy. This not only breeds cronyism but also shield honest patriots from gaining a voice in the party. In her last two terms at government she relied more on her party's strength in Sindh and Punjab to form federal government. Defection of Aftab Sherpao to form his own faction of PPP has substantially weakened her party position in NWFP province. Even if he decides to come back to the fold it will be an uphill task to make a dent on MMA's strong grip on NWFP politics.

During the tenure of General Musharraf unity of the country was seriously damaged by military action in two provinces namely NWFP and Baluchistan. This not only resulted in loss of lives on both sides but severely damaged image of the military as a national institution.

A poor country does not pay a huge defense bill so that its soldiers can open fire on their own people. Never before in the history of Pakistan were soldiers made target by terrorists and suicide bombers. Political differences are defused through negotiations rather than pulling a trigger. It is true that tribal chiefs, in rural areas, have mostly been driven by greed and self-interest. But the power of a tribal leader cannot be undermined unless education is introduced in these areas.

With an education budget of Rs. 89 per capita it is not possible to eradiate illiteracy to introduce a rule of law in tribal areas.

In international arena Musharraf realizes that his honeymoon with America is over since democrats took control of congress and senate. This is indicated by a bill pending in Congress to limit military assistance to Pakistan (it was the Kerry-Lugar-Bergman bill). From op-ed articles it seems likely to pass without much resistance. Another development which did not get much media attention was invitation of Benazir Bhutto and Asif Zardari to attend presidential breakfast in White House in January. It is likely that next American president will be a Democrat with a political mandate to correct past wrongs done in Afghanistan and Iraq.

Pakistan played a key role as a frontline state in American war against terror lead by General Musharraf,. Despite risking its federation and heavy cost to social structure, Pakistani diplomats did not succeed in convincing American nation that we are an all weather friend with a long history to back it up. If America change course in Afghan war there is a probability that Democratic president will not be willing to lend support to Musharraf as was accorded by Republican President George Bush. He realizes this shift in winds which is obvious from his desire to form an international forum of Muslim states to maintain his relevance on the international scene.

***Background**: On 9th Mar 2007, at the advice of Prime Minister, President General Pervez Musharraf filed a judicial reference against Chief Justice of Pakistan, Iftikhar Muhammad Chaudhry, effectively suspending him from the office. Picture of this meeting published in newspapers showed five military generals in uniform meeting with the Chief Justice. This initiated a public outcry and a lawyers Movement to reinstate him. In this political struggle on one side were government allied parties including PML Q, MQM, JUI F while in opposition were pro-democracy PML N, PPP, JI, and Pakistan Tehreek-e-Insaf. Justice Chaudhry took an active role in this movement by addressing bar associations around the country. On 12th May 2007 he was scheduled to arrive in Karachi, capital of Sindh province, to address bar association there. MQM, an allied party of government, advised him to refrain from visiting as it could jeopardize the law and order situation. Violent clashes, on that day, between political activist left many dead. Lawyer's movement was applauded around the world and is considered an inspiration for reform movements in Middle East called Arab Spring. This movement resulted in the forced departure of General Musharraf and installment of a democratically elected parliament that reinstated Justice Chaudhry as Chief Justice in March 2009. In a March 2012 Time magazine survey Justice Chaudhry was one of the 100 most influential figures in the world.*

Tenure of President Musharraf: May 12th incident- Rally for what?
(May 14, 2007)

12th May 2007 has become another dark day in the history of Pakistan. Political ambitions of handful of individuals claimed 35 lives and hundreds injured. Key players of this dark day are familiar to all of us. On one side was king's party including Muttahida Qaumi Movement (MQM) and Pakistan Muslim League Quaid (PML-Q) while opposition parties included Pakistan Peoples Party (PPP), Jamat-e-Islami (JI), Awami National Party (ANP), Pakistan Muslim League Nawaz (PML-N) and Pakistan Tehreeke Insaf (PTI). Indirect participants in this drama were military establishment and legal fraternity represented by Chief Justice Iftikhar Ahmed Chaudhry. Worst part is that all these players are driven by their own ambitions while interests of the nation are taking a back seat.

It is an open secret that MQM was founded by military government of Zia ul Haq to undermine the influence of PPP in Sindh province. In hind sight it is clear that this strategy failed. Since its inception MQM has been a political instrument as and when needed by military establishment. It may not surprise anyone that MQM rally, to prevent entry of CJ in Karachi, might have been planned and executed by the blessing of military establishment.

While Karachi was experiencing mayhem on its streets, PML (Q) rally in Islamabad was in full swing with bhangra dances and spirited speeches. Leadership of PML (Q) knows that their best bet is to keep control of Punjab provincial government while maintaining marginal presence in other provinces. It was sad that while Karachi was burning their rally organizer's allowed playing of music and performance of dance. President Musharraf for the first time spoke from behind bullet proof glass which is an indication he was concerned for his life among his own supporters.

As MQM emerged Jamat-e-Islami (JI), a strong supporter of military governments in the past, lost its control of major urban centers including Karachi, Hyderabad and Sukkur. Apparently it is in the process of changing their political affiliations for the upcoming elections. Recent announcement by JI's Ameer Qazi Hussain Ahmed that he wants to relinquish chairmanship of MMA could be an indication that they want to get out of their alliance to be free to pave way for negotiations with other major political parties. Failure of Muttahida Majlis e Amal (MMA) government in North West Frontier Province (NWFP) has made it clear to Jamat leaders that politics has its own dynamics separate from religious affiliations. Under Qazi Hussain Ahmed Jamat has tried to emerge as a modern religio-political organization capable of adjusting to changing times. JI is the largest party in MMA but has not been able to exercise its influence in key political decisions. Jamat has used protests for reinstatement of CJ to come closer to other opposition parties.

Reading few pages of General Musharraf's autobiography makes it quite clear that he is driven by blinding ambition. He narrates in his book that during political crisis of 1998 between President Leghari and Prime Minister Nawaz sharif it was decided twice in corps commander meeting to send a message to Supreme Court to behave and remain impartial. Apparently hisloyalist in army decided to use similar tactics to ensure his reelection by current assemblies before upcoming elections. Presence of five senior military officers to pressure CJ gives credence to this view.

Army is an institution where loyalty to institution supersedes personal ambition. In last one year General Musharraf has tarnished the image of military to further his own political ambition. Losses incurred by military in Baluchistan and NWFP operations are substantial not only in personnel but also damaging to its image as a national institution. Further more in his book General Musharraf has criticized his senior officers which is against norm of military tradition. Thirdly GHQ (military headquarters) recently announced plans to change structure of military command by adding another layer to the chain of command. This plan suggests formation of three regions each commanded by a three star general. This would undermine powers of thirteen corps commanders who have traditionally been most influential in military decision making. This has further created division among military high command. These developments suggest that as an institution military is starting to consider General Musharraf a liability rather than an asset. This is probably the only thing worrying him more than any political unrest in the country.

Chief Justice Iftikhar Mohammad Chaudhry has attained a legendary status in the history of Pakistan by refusing to resign under pressure from military. But he is currently used as a pawn by political forces to further their own cause. One of his lawyers Barrister Aitzaz Ahsan is a key political figure in PPP and held many senior positions in the party.

As this political crisis deepens to other segments of society CJ will outlive his utility for political parties and will be dropped as a spent force. To maintain dignity of his office CJ should rely more on professional lawyer forums with little or no political connections instead of allowing politically motivated lawyers to use him.

It is apparent that a bloody struggle has started among various power brokers. Ambitions of these individuals will claim many more lives before the situation stabilize. Loser once again will be poor who will suffer the most. Current leadership does not have the vision, ideology or selflessness to solve daunting issues faced by the nation. We need reincarnation of Allama Iqbal and Mohammad Ali Jinnah to unify the nation with a sense of direction. Until these kinds of leaders emerge we will be sacrificed as sheep at the altar of political opportunist.

2008 Elections: pre-election analysis I
(December 1, 2007)

Storm that started brewing on March 9th after General Musharraf filed a reference against the then chief Justice Iftikhar Mohammad Chaudhary has at last claimed his uniform. But clouds are still casting a shadow over the horizon and seek further sacrifice from the now retired General Musharraf. His rise to power was on the back of his military credentials which means as soon as he gave up his uniform he lost support of that very institution that brought him to power. A retired general does not enjoy same unquestioned obedience as a serving general. Institution is now behind its new chief General Ashfaq Parvez Kayani whose political views, ambitions and contacts will slowly reveal itself with each passing day. Only support left standing behind Musharraf is America and its western allies. But American public opinion is slowly turning away from supporting a dictator to restoration of democracy in the country. This does not bode well for the retired General who just sworn himself in as President for second five year term.

Political leaders from Pakistan Peoples Party (PPP) and Pakistan Muslim League Nawaz (PML N), have refused to accept Musharraf as President and are demanding restoration of judiciary and constitution to its pre November 3rd position. Political parties, although talking of boycott, are submitting nomination papers to contest in upcoming elections. It is obvious that both Nawaz Sharif and Benazir Bhutto need the door of election to regain access to political power. They are threatening to boycott January 8th elections because they want to buy time to reorganize their parties whose local leadership has withered during their eight years exile from the country.

Major political parties would prefer that a limbo is created by questioning legitimacy of General Musharraf's reelection. They would prefer that he is forced to resign thereby elevating chairman Senate to replace him which incidentally is interim Prime Minister Mohammad Mian Soomro.

We have precedence of this when Ghulam Ishaq Khan took over power after death of General Zia ul Haq. This will produce a new interim government and delay of election up to spring 2008. It will provide ample time to PPP and PML N to create an election organization to ensure their rise to majority positions in provincial and national assemblies.

Chaudhries of PML Q on the other hand will prefer elections to be held on January 8th as they had all the time to prepare themselves for it. They know that it will be difficult for them to form a government in Islamabad but they will strive to maintain hold on Punjab with help from military establishment. Despite dissolution of previous assemblies they still enjoy considerable power over the provincial establishment to use it to their advantage. This is their single point agenda to lend support to Musharraf who used their allegiance to legitimize his rule for eight years. But they face a formidable competition in the form of PML N. It is quite likely that PML N emerge as a leading party in the province.

In North West Frontier Province (NWFP), socialist Awami National Party (ANP) has a natural tendency to align with Pakistan Peoples Party (PPP) and hope to achieve slight majority in the province. PML N has long history of political alliance with Jamat-e-Islami (JI) which is falling out from MMA after their disagreements with Jamiat Ulema Islam Fazal (JUI-F) leader Maulana Fazl ur Rehman were made public. Muttahida Majlis e Amal (MMA) has substantially damaged political standing of JI which is a religious moderate as compared to extremist views of JUI F.

Although JI leadership is insisting they will boycott elections but they fully understand that staying out of elections could be politically damaging. JUI-F and PPP Sherpao both benefited from supporting the military regime. They can once again form an alliance to not only soften the image of JUI-F in the province but also improve their chances of forming a government. It is likely that they would need more allies to have any majority in the province.

In Sindh, Muttahida Qaumi Movement (MQM) understands that they are at best a regional party which means they have to align with whoever has the best chance of forming a government. They have already started sending feelers to PPP to ensure their participation in future Sindh government. MQM needs to still recover from political damage inflicted upon them by the Chaudhries of PML Q during judicial crisis of May 12th when PML Q was celebrating in Islamabad as Karachi shed blood of its citizens. PPP/MQM alliance should not have any problem in forming a majority provincial government.

Baluchistan once again will produce a patch work of religious, socialist and ethnic parties. This does not bode well for the province. Baluchistan voters should decide which national level party serves their interest best and align themselves with it to get some resources for the province.

In final analysis it seems that Musharraf will be forced out from Presidency and elections will be delayed until spring 2008. But then again politics in Pakistan does not follow any pattern and winds of change could produce a totally unforeseen scenario.

2008 Elections: pre-election analysis II
(January 6, 2008)

Pakistan is slowly albeit grudgingly moving towards general elections on 18th February 2008. All major parties have agreed to participate in elections while maintaining a pressure on government by demanding fair and free elections. Statements made by Pakistan Peoples Party (PPP), Pakistan Muslim League Nawaz (PML-N) and Pakistan Muslim League Quaid (PML-Q) leadership suggest that elections will not achieve end which is a stable political environment in which people can feel safe and advance their lives. PPP co-chairman Asif Ali Zardari has gone so far as claim that next government will be formed by PPP by winning the elections. PML-N Chairman Main Nawaz Sharif has repeatedly demonstrated that they will not accept leadership of President Pervez Musharraf. PML-Q leadership is targeting their opposition with negative campaign slogans which are reciprocated by Asif Ali Zardari. In this environment the nation is nervously watching next phase of their volatile political life while prices of basic commodities are sky rocketing beyond the reach of common man. The question no one is willing to answer is how do they define fair and free elections?

In a nation where there is no balance of power between institutions it is quite natural that various parts of government will strive to gain maximum advantage from any future setup. Military leadership abusing their powers uses Inter Services Intelligence Agency (ISI) to maintain a dossier on civilian political leaders which is not part of its mandate. These secret files are used for political arm twisting whenever a General grabs power. Since military leadership abuse this institution it is unnatural to assume that officers in field will not try to have their own view included in the equation. It is beyond doubt that new generation of army officers are more inclined to be religious and conservative in their lifestyles. To conduct fair and free elections it is important that political wing of ISI should be rolled back. It is also important that Chief of Army Staff ensure that it will focus more on fight against terrorism and prevention of external threats rather than keep one eye on seat of power.

Blame for desperate state of affairs in Pakistan lies with the whole nation itself rather pointing fingers at one or two segments. How is it possible that without consent of masses people with questionable reputation comes to power either in bureaucracy, politics, military, or judiciary? No rule or law can ensure fair elections until people engaged in managing elections feel the responsibility for it. Election duties are performed by lowly paid education department employees and district officers. These subsistence level functionaries are already stressed for mere survival. It is hard to believe that they will jeopardize their jobs if a higher officer in civilian and military establishment demands certain unfair actions from them while conducting elections. Unless election staff is fused with certain nationalist ideology it can not be expected that they will risk their livelihood as well as their life for an election result that do not matter much to them. Elections are organized by over one million officials and supported by an even larger number of soldiers and policemen. If not a single person among these have courage to stand up to the rigging of elections then the nation can not blame internal or external forces for a bad government. It is responsibility of law enforcement and citizens to protect election whistle blowers from vengeance.

In a world driven by social network technologies, like twitter, blogger and facebook, have provided an avenue to each member of society to express their views on policy matters. On the other hand political analysts have access to tools like surveys and polls to gauge public sentiments during the term of a mandate. Pakistan civic society is fast becoming a vibrant participant in the cyber space which has started showing its influence on views of public. All major political parties and politicians have web sites, facebook profiles and blogs to communicate with their voters. In coming years these mediums can be used effectively to monitor election process to prevent rigging and ensure that winning party has moral authority to rule for a full term. Geo-political location of Pakistan attracts intervention from world powers to affect the election outcome. Pakistan should rely on its own indigenous election monitors instead of allowing international monitors that may have vested interest in the outcome of an election.

Elections are not an end in itself. It is a means to elect politicians that can provide law & order, institute a viable economic policy and protect sovereignty of the nation. No political party is presenting an ideology that will solve social, economic and political crisis faced by the nation. Most of them are looking outward by seeking help from other countries to gain political clout. It is believed that return of Nawaz Sharif was orchestrated by Saudi government which wants to maintain an influence in any future political set-up of Pakistan. It is not a secret any more that Benazir Bhutto signed a deal with Musharraf brokered by US and UK. In this environment of mistrust when leaders are not in synch with the nation, fair and free elections can not be expected.

Foreign powers operating in Pakistan are well aware that fair and free elections might produce results that are not in their interest. They have already experienced this scenario in Algeria, Palestine, Lebanon, and Turkey where Islamic political parties gained widespread support in elections. For these powers it is better to maintain their grip on government through a distorted democracy resulting from election rigging rather than face prospect of dealing with a conservative force which has people's mandate. In a poverty stricken country it is not difficult for them to spend small amounts of money to buy people who are willing to interfere with election results. These foreign powers have enough networks in the country comprised of locals that executing this strategy is not too difficult.

Independent media plays a pivotal role in maintaining transparency of electoral process. Media plays a significant role in disseminating the message of different political parties. In last 6 years media has strengthened its role as a bridge between government and people. Open debates between differing political factions have contributed in education of people about views held by their representative. During his struggle for re-election President Musharraf has struck a serious blow at the independence of media by forcing cable operators to pull plug on many channels.

In order to continue their operations media outlets have to agree to an amended Pakistan Electronic Media Regulatory Authority (PEMRA) ordinance which imposed strict broadcasting conditions on television channels. In this hostile environment it can not be expected that media will be able to point finger at irregularities during the elections.

Tradition in Pakistan is such that winning party assumes that they will stay in power for ever and engage in revengeful actions against losers. We have seen this play out during two terms of Nawaz Sharif and Benazir Bhutto when both of them went after throat of the other. When both these leaders decided to work together there was a feeling that at last there will be some decency after elections. Election campaign slogans suggest that old tradition of revenge will be repeated. This feeling of survival of the fittest creates an environment where losing an election is sort of a death warrant. Unless this kind of hostility is defused we can not expect to create stable institutions. Our politicians have to learn to live with an election loss and wait until next elections to convince electorate for a mandate.

We have to agree that the country belongs to all of us and we have to work together to build it. A stable government is one of the necessary components for a nation's prosperity and progress. All of us whether a policeman, a teacher, a leader and a solider have to understand that any unfair actions under their watch is going to damage the nation. After that if the leaders do not accept results we can all stand up to make it clear to them that enough is enough. Either they work together or the nation will get rid of them to make room for others that can work together.

2008 Elections: post election analysis
(March 2, 2008)

A glimpse at February 18ᵗʰ election results makes it clear that collective intelligence of people of Pakistan is much deeper than any political leader on the horizon. People of Pakistan have listened to the statements of their leaders and realized that if they gave overwhelming majority to any one party their lives will be worst off as that party will break all bridges of reconciliation. Nation has forced politicians to work with each other if they want to form a government. Electorate has ensured that their local interest is safeguarded at provincial level while nationalist coalition is encouraged at the federal level.

In national assembly Pakistan Peoples Party (PPP) despite being the largest party did not won enough seats to form a government. This could be an outcome of Asif Ali Zardari's appointment as party co-chairman ahead of many senior leaders like Raza Rabbani, Makhdoom Amin Fahim, and Shah Mehmood Qureshi. People have not forgotten corruption stories associated with Asif Zardari regardless whether a court has convicted him of those crimes or not. His presence as co-chairman of party did make a dent in its ability to gain clear majority in the assembly. His subsequent role as a power broker with other parties is a sign he is preparing himself for the Prime Minister position in a very near future. It is very difficult for a person to change his basic instinct regardless of the circumstances surrounding him. Asif Zardari likes to exercise power and it will be difficult to contain this instinct for very long. His actions suggest that he is buying time through a conciliatory tone to prevent break-up of the party before his loyalist are installed in key party positions.

Pakistan Muslim League (PML N) has realized from the results that they made a mistake by not nominating their candidates on all national assembly seats. Their statements to take revenge on PML Q leaders in Punjab are not an encouraging signs for future stability.

Mian brothers should understand sentiments of people and adopt a more conciliatory tone. If they refuse to listen to the voice of people then they will once again encourage fragmentation of PML in more factions. In national assembly PML N should not erect hurdles for majority party to form a government and in return can expect to get some cabinet positions. They should seek support of PPP in Punjab to form a government.

ANP, MQM and independents have a narrow agenda to pursue which is to gain more resources for their ethnic groups or make personal gains in case of independents. It has become quite apparent that MQM prefers to be in power regardless which party forms government. They have realized that their voter base will always be urban centers of Sindh especially Karachi and Hyderabad.

Withdrawal of military from politics resulted in emergence of ANP as leading party in NWFP. They have a liberal agenda for the province but they have to realize that they can not look toward Afghanistan as an extension of their ethnicity. They have to understand that historically Afghans have exploited people of NWFP to their advantage. ANP has an opportunity to improve lives of their constituents by investing in education, job creation and tourism. ANP traditionally has had good relations with PPP so they should not have a difficulty forming a coalition government in province with itself being a senior partner.

Baluchis have to understand that they can not gain resources from center unless they provide mandate to candidates from large national parties. At provincial level PML Qs majority should be respected and allowed to form a government with support from smaller and independent parties.

PPP should not have a problem forming a government in Sindh but MQM should play the role of an opposition instead of trying to become part of the government as a junior partner.

Nation has provided an opportunity to politicians to reconcile their differences and coexist with each other in a more dignified manner. Sitting in opposition is not a stigma but rather an important role to check policies of party in power. PML Q members should respect these results and form an opposition rather than offering themselves for trading. Media is playing a positive role by exposing back door deals of these parties before any deal is struck. This media spotlight should make politicians realize that all their actions are watched and will have consequences on their political future.

2008 Elections: why PML-N should sit on opposition benches?
(May 14, 2008)

It seems honeymoon is over between the two largest political parties in Pakistan. On 12th May 2008, PML-N parliamentary members resigned from their cabinet positions because of failure of PPP to reinstate the deposed judges. Despite this exodus they have announced to cooperate with the ruling party to ensure continuation of current assemblies. We know that politics forces odd couples to share bed but even then no one willingly agrees to lose their identity in the process. This means that if both parties maintain their ideological position then they can not agree on all policy matters. They can agree to disagree which will ensure continuation of the fragile democracy in Pakistan.

Pakistan Peoples Party (PPP) at its core is a socialist secular party. In recent years they have tried to change their position to become capitalist. Their political manifesto of *roti, kapra aur makan* (bread, clothes and shelter) time and again forces them to adopt socialist views. When promising these basic necessities which should be norm rather than the exception they do not seem to find cooperation from other segments of society especially large land owners, civil bureaucracy and industrial oligarchs. Another alternative available to them is to nationalize assets. When that fails they recruit people without regard for financial health of the corporation that hires them. This may solve the problem in short term but in long term it sucks the nation dry as government has to write checks to cover for their corporate losses. PIA, WAPDA and Pakistan Railways are some of these examples. It is always better to teach a beggar how to earn a living rather than just buying one day ration for them. Pakistan's labor is not looking for charity but a dignified way to earn decent livelihood.

Politics is about making compromises without a fixed position on a policy issue.

But that does not mean that there are no rules of the game or ethics to follow while negotiating with opposition parties. Founder of PPP Zulfiqar Ali Bhutto preferred to compromise integrity of the country by refusing to give up control to a rival party, Awami League of Sheikh Mujibur Rehman that had majority after elections of 1970. Some might argue that succession of East Pakistan was inevitable but Mr. Bhutto contributed significantly to accelerate that break up. It was an ugly divorce with loss of life and goodwill between the two nations.

Before her assassination, Mohtarma Benazir Bhutto emphasized that she was negotiating with a dictator to return the country to democratic rule but retirement of a General does not signify return to democracy. As long as elements of autocratic rulers remain in the system they will ensure democratic foundations never gain strength. She negotiated with military dictators who hanged her father and imprisoned her husband. It might be argued that she did it for the nation. Only history can justify if she was right or wrong but so far those actions did not help the country rather only provided short term benefit by brining her party to power. Struggle for stable Pakistan with social justice, equal opportunity for all and solid democratic foundation require a longer struggle.

Pakistan Muslim League Nawaz (PML-N) is a party that derives its ideology from Islamic teachings. It does not believe in socialism but an open market approach which is similar to capitalism with a minor difference of acceptance of interest as part of an economy. The party believes that Pakistan should be an Islamic country with close ties to the Muslim world. During their two terms in office PML-N has gained considerable economic support from United Arab Emirates (UAE) and Saudi Arabia. Party believes that diversity combined with the binding force of a common religion can keep cultural differences at minimum to ensure unity of the nation. They may be right to a certain extent but ignoring rights of provinces for autonomy in local decision making can severely undermine this unity.

PML-N, a variant of PML, was creation of military ruler Zia ul Haq which means that they can not go against the very institution that created them. In current political environment PML-N is not opposing influence of army as an institution rather their opposition is against acceptance of President Musharraf. On the other hand PPP is bound to maintain status quo as part of their secret deal with President Musharraf which was sponsored by Bush administration. Failure to reinstate deposed judges will not damage political standing of PML-N but it will provide them a reason to get out of government rather than accept blame for economic breakdown eminent on horizon.

PML-N is trying hard to remake itself as a political force independent of any military influence. They can achieve this objective by filling the void of an effective opposition that is driven by ideological differences rather than personal vendetta. Opposition can ensure a balance in policy making without breaking the institution. Pakistan needs an example of a dignified opposition to create a democratic tradition. Current position of the PML-N to be an undefined force in parliament will damage their position in long term.

Democracy is full of contradictions and disagreements. Media is playing a vital role of bringing views of all shades in the broad day light. But media should not play role of a defacto opposition without real power to influence policies. It is a role suitable for elected representatives. PML-N is ideally suited for this role as they have clear ideological differences with PPP and have enough parliamentary clout to be effective.

2008 Elections: Zardari as President- what it means for Pakistan
(August 26, 2008)

Year 2008 has already proved to be an eventful year for Pakistan. In February the nation elected a new parliament through an election that are largely considered free and fair. These elections forced President Musharraf to resign and cleared way for a new president. PPP decided to nominate Mr. Zardari as their candidate for the office of President of Pakistan. Is it a surprise pick or was it on the horizon throughout this political turmoil? The answer lies in history of Mr. Zardari and organizational structure of PPP.

Before Benazir Bhutto decided to return to Pakistan, The Wall Street Journal ran a full-page story on Asif Ali Zardari when he arrived in America immediately after release from prison. That story outlined that Mr. Zardari feels it is birth right of Bhutto family to rule Pakistan and no other option is acceptable to him. During his two years stay in America, Mr. Zardari held frequent meetings with policy makers and politicians facilitated by current ambassador to America Mr. Haqqani. Their objective was to create a lobby favorable to him. Concern showed in the article was the tarnished reputation of Mr. Zardari and its effect on American image if they supported his accession. But rapid turn of events in Pakistan after assassination of Benazir; Mr. Zardari's success in imposing his authority on PPP leadership and dwindling popularity of Musharraf forced it to look for a new partner. It is no secret to any of his associates that he savors power and likes to accumulate it at any expense. Influential individuals rather than an elaborate democratic process are prevalent in all political parties in Pakistan, including PPP. It was in the interest of these opportunist politicians to accept Zardari as heir to Benazir Bhutto instead of holding intra party election to give a chance to other senior leaders to compete for chairmanship.

Symbolism used in PPP press conferences gives insight into the thinking of party leadership.

When Senator Raza Rabbani announced candidature of Mr. Zardari the backdrop was pictures of Bilawal Zardari in the middle while Mohtarma Benazir and Zulfiqar Ali Bhutto on each side of it. This means that anyone sitting in front of these pictures is accepting patronage of Bhutto family to announce a key decision without much regard to the country and its ideals. It is only a matter of time when formalities are completed and Mr. Zardari becomes the next President of Pakistan.

It will be a challenge for Mr. Zardari is to strike a balance between competing interest of America, military establishment, China and Saudi Arabia. It will be unlikely that he will stop cooperating in war on terror in foreseeable future. All he can hope for is that Democratic Presidential nominee Barack Obama wins elections and changes his war policy to include dialogue. Saudi Arabia historically supports Muslim League, JUI-F and military dictators in Pakistan. This means that they could play a positive role by forcing PPP to have a working relationship with PML (N) to complete their term of this assembly. PML (N) cannot afford to jeopardize their relationship with Saudi Arabia by assuming an extreme opposition to government. Pakistan's military establishment on the other hand may not welcome this appointment and undermine the rule of PPP.

What would be the effect of President Zardari on Pakistani nation? Supreme Court judges will be restored after oath of president's office. It will ensure that Chief Justice Iftikhar Mohammad Chaudhry will be saved the embarrassment of installing an National Reconciliation Ordinance (NRO) tainted president. Mr. Zardari will have presidential immunity during his presidential term while repeal of NRO can be used to twist arms of his opponents.

Separatist movements in Baluchistan and NWFP will continue to gain strength as PPP does not have moral authority to solve these issues since Zulfiqar Ali Bhutto was the first political leader to authorize military operation in Baluchistan. PPP has never been popular as a business friendly party. Their socialist views are quite apparent from the budget presented by them. Economy of Pakistan will continue to rely on oil subsidies from Saudi Arabia and economic aid from USA.

Considering Mr. Zardari's desire to have absolute powers repeal of 58 (2) (b) will not happen under his watch as it will take away an important source of his presidential powers. Zardari is guardian of a party founded by Chairman Zulfiqar Ali Bhutto who was a creation of a military ruler General Ayub Khan. Ayub appointed Bhutto as a foreign minister in the first marshal law government of Pakistan. Mr. Zardari fully understands political cycles in Pakistan that oscillates between civil and military rulers. It is the civilian cycle and if he does not gain control of presidency it will be difficult to create foundation for next generation of Bhutto family, Bilawal Bhutto Zardari. We can hope that he will remember that without Pakistan there cannot be a parliament or a prime minister.

To resolve its problems, Pakistan needs a leader of Mohammad Ali Jinnah's stature. Unfortunately, current cadre of leaders of all major political parties comes with a baggage which cracks their resolve to stand up to contain vested interest in the country. People of Pakistan have demonstrated time and again that they want to live as one nation but decisions of their leaders have worked against these feelings of unity. We need fresh ideas and a new start. Unless we are ready to change, this situation will not improve and we will not gain dignity in the comity of nations.

Tenure of President Zardari: Midterm Elections- is it the answer?
(December 18, 2010)

It seems democracy is feeling heat from citizens around the world. Italian Prime Minister Berlusconi barely survived a vote of confidence. French President Sarkozi is still recovering from bribery allegations from sale of submarines to Pakistan. British Prime Minister Cameron faced violent student protests when announcement was made to raise tuition fees. Democratic party President Barak Obama lost congressional majority to Republican Party creating a serious hurdle to his legislative priorities. Irish government is facing loss of mandate because of the economic crisis.

Democracy as a form of government is chaotic by nature. It becomes a pressure cooker when there are a large number of political parties, a coalition government, an opinionated media and no mutually agreed ethics of behavior. In successful democracies all players understand their roles, responsibilities and boundaries. They understand that overstepping a line may offer a short term benefit but in the long run it will affect their interests as well. This behavior of stakeholders is conditioned by their long political tradition as well as fair application of law. In Pakistan all instruments of state carry a stigma of overplaying their hands whether it is politicians undermining each other or judiciary legitimizing dictators using doctrine of necessity or military establishment abrogating the constitution.

For established democracies in West, change in public opinion is not a new thing. Over course of two centuries they have developed checks and balances between various state institutions that may get rocked in turbulent times but survive and continue in the end. President George W Bush saw his popularity go down to 39% near the end of his first term but still got re-elected for a second four year term.

President Obama inspired the whole nation with his message of change but within two years his popularity has gone down significantly resulting in losing majorities in US House of

Representative even after approval of the historical health care bill. Prime Minister of United Kingdom (UK) David Cameron has lost his popularity even faster than his American counterparts. It should not come as a surprise to people in Pakistan that PPP government has seen its popularity gone down because of their handling of economy, flood relief and abatement of terrorism. But this unpopularity should not be used as a pretext to overthrow them before completion of their five years term. If electorates are dissatisfied then it should be expressed in their voting patterns in next elections.

Since formation of Pakistan Peoples Party (PPP) government, after 2008 elections, there have been many occasions when it seemed that they will not be able to survive but they did. In latest crisis, Jamiat Ulema Islam Fazal (JUI-F) has announced to break away from the coalition government and sit on opposition benches. As soon as this was announced multitude of rumormongers and conspiracy theorists started spreading all kinds of scenarios to emerge from this development. The most talked about are two i.e. an interim government of technocrats that would economically stabilize the country before next elections in 2013 or that mid term elections should be held to seek a fresh mandate.

Some politicians and analysts argue that the nation can not sustain bad economics for another two years, so a change in government should be pursued through constitutional means. This may be a viable solution for countries with long history of democratic tradition. In Pakistan, with a feeble democratic foundation, an attempt to remove a sitting government through constitutional means will unleash a torrent of undemocratic forces that could then hijack the government. More suitable approach would be to maintain pressure from the opposition, judiciary and media to reverse bad decisions. In last year we have seen effective collaboration between these institutions to force government to change their decisions. This is a positive trend and should be allowed to play its role.

Politicians will pursue a path that suits their interests but the nation has to ponder over this and decide if mid term elections will be helpful in formation of a better government. Early elections will just be a musical chair between existing cadres of politicians but will cost the nation a lot of scarce treasure. There are only two years left in the term of current government which is not a long time to wait. During this time local bodies elections should be held so that an institution for developing future leaders is reinstated. These elections will be a litmus test of the nation's choice for next government in provinces and center. It will allow emerging parties like Pakistan Tehreek-e-Insaf (PTI) to demonstrate their ability to appeal to the electorate to give them a chance to rule and show their governance capability.

Real issue is the structure of our government and how various institutions should behave to create a stable environment for the nation to thrive. A Minister is supposed to provide a policy direction to bureaucrats based on ruling party's manifesto promises. It is never a good idea that a Minister gets involved in actual operational decision making which become breeding grounds for corruption and cronyism. It undermines authority of professional bureaucrats and damages merit by appointment of choice candidates on key positions to facilitate corrupt transactions.

Military establishment has controlled strings of government directly or indirectly throughout history of Pakistan. A soldier or policeman without a moral authority provided by the law is not different from a criminal. When a General captures power from civilians he is undercutting his moral authority thereby damaging an institution that is held in high esteem by the nation. People realize that military rulers have done more damage than the combined damage of all politicians.

There is no denying the fact that army is a leadership development institution. In many countries military Generals become part of political parties after retirement and even become Presidents like Charles De Gaulle in France or Eisenhower in USA.

There is a widespread rumor in America that General David Patraeus will be the Republican Party candidate in 2012 presidential elections. Pakistani Generals should consider that route for their political ambitions which is more appropriate and will provide them moral authority to make tough decisions. General Kayani has been referred to as an intellectual person and will be a good politician after his retirement. It might be a good idea for him to consider giving up his term extension as Chief of Army Staff and join a political party by requesting exemption from the two year no politics rule after retirement.

Patience as a virtue is not part of our national psyche. Traffic congestion on our roads, cutting lines to get served, our approach towards business and our expectations from politicians are evidence of our deep rooted impatience. There are always multiple options available to tackle a national issue. Best approach is one that offer safeguards against long term negative implications. We have to ensure development of political institutions which can not happen until we let them continue. In short term there will be disappointments but in long run capable people will rise to the top. If the nation can stay united after a major earthquake, a historic flood and daily rampage of terrorists then fears of survival from a political storm are unfounded.

Tenure of President Zardari: next elections-tsunami of change
(October 16, 2011)

A visit to villages in Punjab and Khyber Paktunkhwa (KPK) shows that season of election is getting ready to start. There are street banners and billboards from probable candidates of various parties, political rallies, corner meetings and local deal makings are in full swing. But there is a deeper current flowing that suggests that the country is preparing for a revolutionary change in its political structure. There are various factors in play for this sea change.

Youth activism in politics can be credited to celebrity appeal of Pakistan Tehreeke Insaf (PTI) Chairman Imran Khan. It started as a fan appeal but as these youth got indoctrinated in the ideology of change they have become a potent political force that is eager to demonstrate its ability to affect future of Pakistan. Challenge for PTI will be to mentor and guide this youthful energy with experience and mentorship of seasoned politicians. They may be political novices but they are savvy in using social media, mobile sms and communication technologies to connect and mobilize at a very short notice. Effectiveness of these abilities was in full exhibit during political rallies organized by PTI. This phenomenon was initially discarded by old guard politicians but success of rallies in Faisalabad, Multan and Gujranwala has forced them to rethink their approach.

Other factor is emergence of regional media in small towns across the country. It is showing an ability to educate local masses. They are beginning to influence their decisions by highlighting poor performance and broken election promises of incumbent politicians. As national media focus on larger issues regional publications has carved its role by dictating political agenda filled with local issues that can not be ignored by candidates and must become part of their election manifesto. Most of these media outlets are using social media and internet to spread their message to registered voters that have migrated to other parts of the country.

Regional media is showing their desire to have an independent voice despite lack of financial resources to challenge establishment and local landlord. If used effectively they can become a key factor in monitoring election fraud.

Third factor is the ever widening gap between rich and poor. As an illustration, Faisalabad is the second largest city in Punjab and an industrial center of Pakistan. Just few miles off GT road, in vicinity of Faisalabad, are located poorest villages of Pakistan. In these villages streets are unpaved, children are unclothed, sewerage is flowing in uncovered channels becoming breeding grounds for viruses, streets are littered with garbage and houses are made of dirt walls. In midst of this abject poverty rich landlords are driving in shinning new Prado's or Land Cruisers comforted by cool breeze of an air condition while masses are struggling below poverty line burdened by worry for their next meal. Rich are totally oblivious of the misery happening around them. They spend large part of the year in cities which are stocked with best merchandize produced locally or imported. Even when they spend few months in villages their villas are built at a distance from the village featuring latest amenities construction technology can offer.

While villages of central Punjab are poor ironically Mosques are modern and adorned with best marble inside and out. One wonders how people could afford to build such beautiful edifices when their own lives are below subsistence level. This paradox is solved when a person is informed that funds for mosque and attached Madrassa's are provided by international benefactors. This is a recipe for disaster as orthodox Imams of these mosques are impregnating mind of people with hatred for rich in the name of religion. This phenomenon has made Pakistan a breeding ground for extremism. Religious establishment has become so powerful that no one has the strength or courage to challenge them. Anyone who dares to hint at bringing these institutions under state control is threatened with dire consequences. But it can not be totally ignored and will play a role in the elections.

In next elections all these factors will come into play and will impact the outcome. Larger struggle will be between rich and poor. Youth, media and religious establishment will all join hands to defeat influential status quo. PTI can become the vehicle for this dynamic if party plays its card right. Realizing its potential to break out as a majority party, it has suddenly become darling of old political elite that had lost its luster or lost last elections. Debate within the party is how to handle this challenge and balance interest of loyalist against electable. If too many old faces get nomination then it will lose the prized status of a party of change while ignoring it might not produce much desired parliamentary majority. It is a test of party's ability to gauge political current and use it to their advantage without losing their core constituencies of youth and undecided voters. PTI rallies and jalsas are drawing increasing crowds but the party strategists have to ascertain whether these are voters or fans of cricket hero Imran Khan.

Against this backdrop PML N looks tired and out of ideas. PML N President, Nawaz Sharif seems awakening from a long slumber and behaving more like a reactionary than a visionary. PML N is fighting an existential threat as its core vote bank is attacked by PTI, MQM, and JI. PPP seems to be confident that status quo in parliament will hold up with minor losses in its current numbers. PML Q looks like a party that will be most affected, many of their dissident leaders have joined ranks with PML N while some others might be unseated in next elections. ANP, JUI F and MQM are expected to maintain their numbers except that ANP might lose its provincial majority in KPK. They are eager and open to make alliance with next emerging power center.

Revolutions are bloody while transformations are comparatively peaceful. Pakistan is at the cusp where it can tilt either way. One must hope that the nation will choose path of transformation and emerge as a beacon of light for larger Muslim world.

Section III:
American Society, Muslims & Pakistan

2008 American Presidential Elections

Background: 43ʳᵈ President of United States Mr. George W Bush took oath of office on 20ᵗʰ January 2001. America faced terror attacks of 9/11 within nine months of his Presidency which claimed around 2996 lives as well as billions of dollars of damage to economy. In retaliation military operations were conducted against Taliban government in Afghanistan and dictatorship of Saddam Hussain in Iraq. Iraq war was based on questionable evidence linking Saddam government to Al Qaeda and development of weapons of mass destruction (WMD). Once American forces deposed Saddam and took control of Iraq it became clear that evidence provided to justify war could not be validated by facts on ground. During Presidential elections of 2004 when Mr. Bush sought re-election, Iraq became top item of election campaign debates. Democratic Party nominee Senator John Kerry questioned wisdom behind Iraq war and its impact on American economy.

US Presidential Election 2004: Democrats vs Republicans
(March 7, 2004)

After a protracted electoral fight John Kerry secured Democratic Party nomination for presidential election. So far Mr. Kerry has focused all his energies on securing this nomination. He has not clearly outlined his election strategy to win against incumbent Republican Party President George W. Bush.

When differentiating between Democrats and Republicans we hear about left and right ideologies. One wonders about emergence of this right/left philosophy. This term was first used after when at the end of French revolution, in 1795, a republic was formed. People who favored status quo were seated to right while those vying for change were seated to left. In American politics left and right are defined as liberal and conservative philosophies respectively. Republicans are considered conservative and so is a right leaning party. Differences between these two parties on some key policy issues have been blurring. Most election fights are between the two leading men and their campaign teams rather than party ideologies. Political pundits agree that a majority who are still in middle or center of these two extremes decides election outcome. It is important to understand each party's positions and their performance on notable policies.

Foreign Policy: US emerged, as world power soon after World War II when leading European powers like England, France, Germany and Russia were considerably weaker in terms of military and economic strength. It provided an opportunity for America to take a leading role in ensuing world affairs and exert its influence on development of an international framework. America was a leading contributor to cease fire agreements signed with Germany, Japan and Italy. This superpower status reached its zenith with break-up of former USSR into thirteen independent states in 1991. Since then American hegemony is unrivaled with some potential challengers emerging in European Union and China.

Superpower status imposes responsibility on her to act in a more responsible manner. Performance of Bush administration has been murky in this regard. American diplomatic efforts to gain support from NATO allies Germany and France for Iraq war failed which created a gulf between these Atlantic partners. American inability to secure a UN resolution to overthrow Saddam Hussain through a multilateral military operation undermined their moral authority. Ensuing discussion on missing Iraqi WMD and legitimacy of war will become a major point of contention in the presidential race. Traditionally Republicans have been in favor of expanding American international influence.

Democrats on the other hand are more inward looking and are more concerned with domestic policies. Mr. Kerry is professing to make America a safer place by abandoning isolationist strategy. He has expressed to engage NATO member countries and UN in Iraqi nation building. His agenda for war against terrorism envisage uprooting terrorist organizations by collaborating with other governments. Democratic candidate is also suggesting making changes in Patriot Act to make it more in tune with American principles of treating all people fairly and justly. This is especially important for immigrant community.

Economy and Jobs: American economy is showing signs of emerging from the longest recession in its history. Economic theory suggests that a recession typically lasts for 18 months as compared to current decline that lasted for almost 39 months. Theoretically government spending is increased in recessionary times to stimulate growth. Recent uptick is credited to American war spending. But this spending is financed by a deficit of 500 billion dollars that is crowding out capital from private sector, a more reliable growth engine. This lack of capital for private enterprises could have a long-term adverse effect on the economy. When Mr. Bush took office there was a budget surplus of 300 billion dollars. So net effect of last three and a half years is a deficit of almost 800 billion dollars and this figure is expected to grow in coming years.

Prominent Republican leaders have downplayed impact of this deficit. It will be a major debate point between the two candidates. By cutting down interest rates central bank has tried to encourage private sector to make investment thereby creating more jobs. America has one of the lowest savings rate in the world which is an untenable position in long term. Most of the capital is provided by foreign economies China, Japan and Europe. These countries are substantial investors in US government securities. Bush administration is claiming to create 2.4 million jobs during 2004 but estimates released on 24th March 2004 indicate that the target could be missed by almost 50%. With low job creation numbers Mr. Bush could lose support among his voter base during his reelection bid for White House.

Senator John Kerry has yet to define his economic policy. From his speeches it is indicated that he is in favor of reducing budget deficit and stop tax cut for wealthy. To create and retain jobs, his campaign is considering imposing some form of tax on companies that are exporting jobs out of America. America has its longest economic boom in history during the tenure of democratic president Mr. Bill Clinton. If economy does not perform well in next 6 months Mr. Bush would have a tough time convincing his electorate to reelect him.

Immigration Policy: America has been an immigration friendly country since its independence. It is considered a land of opportunity for talented people because of its openness to accept diversity and providing a level playing field to express talent. American constitution guarantees equal opportunity for all legal residents. But it also attracts a multitude of illegal immigrants especially from neighboring Mexico. The illegal immigrants provide steady flow of cheap manpower for labor-intensive industries although it poses a security threat. During his 2000 campaign Mr. Bush promised reforms to provide relief for undocumented (an American euphemism for illegal) immigrants who have stayed in America for a certain length of time. After incidents of 9/11 these plans were put on back burner.

Instead a Patriot Act was enacted which gave more powers to law enforcement authorities. They now have powers to detain illegal immigrant for a period of 7 days without presenting them in court. This is considered a violation of human rights and anathema to principles laid down by founding fathers in the bill of rights. Structural changes have been made and a new department of Homeland Security is created which is entrusted with handling immigration.

Immediately after its creation the department initiated a special registration program that focused on Muslims with sole exception of North Korea. Officials announced that other countries will be added later. But as soon as registration of immigrants from 25 Muslim countries was completed the program was abandoned for lack of fund and utility. Historically Republicans are considered pro immigration control whereas democrats have favored liberal immigration policies.

Besides these major issues there are some minor policy differences like abortion, gay rights and medicaid. Speculation is ripe in political circles that Mr. Bush is considering to replace Mr. Dick Cheney, as Vice President, with Rudy Giuliani former mayor of New York. Mr. Giuliani claimed prominence during his leadership role in the 9/11 crisis. Mr Kerry has yet to name a running mate. Some analysts are predicting that John Edwards is his top choice for the position. Muslim voter turnout in American elections has been dismal. It is important to change this and encourage voter registration as well improve turnout on Election Day.

US Presidential Election 2004: Republican Party convention
(September 7, 2004)

From 28th August to 3rd September 2004 Republican Party held its convention at Madison Square Garden in New York. This marked formal acceptance of Mr. Bush to seek reelection as well as start of his campaign. Venue was carefully chosen to focus this election campaign on war against terrorism and homeland security. It was an effort to create nationalistic sentiment, which is required to galvanize support for any war time leader. Mr Bush may not be savvy in international affairs but it is evident from selection of venue and speakers that Mr. Bush has deep understanding of local politics and voter psychology.

One outcomes of the Republican convention was show of exceptional unity within party lines which was noticed by majority of political analysts. To create dissent within Democratic Party convention scheduled a speech by Democratic Senator Zen Miller who spoke passionately about inability of his Party's nominee Mr. Kerry to be an effective commander in chief in a war like situation. This speech was meant to put Kerry camp on defense but it failed to achieve that objective.

Republican convention planners allocated prime time slots to center-left speakers like former mayor of New York Mr. Rudy Giuliani and California Governor Arnold Schwarzenegger. Mr. Giuliani is credited with managing the chaos created by incident of 9/11 and keeping morale of people high during that time of tragedy. His speech was filled with references to 9/11 that gave him personal glory and used it as a justification to reelect Mr Bush. He ignored reports that indicated President Bush failed to act when he was briefed by intelligence on creditable terrorist threat on American soil soon after his inauguration. Mayor Giuliani made repeated reference to terrorism against Israel although that is unrelated to election of American President. He made a passing reference to wisdom of Winston Churchill in checking expansionist agenda of Adolf Hitler but he did not mention former's political defeat as soon as the war was over.

Mayor Giuliani endorsed Bush Doctrine of preemptive action against nations considered potential threat to American security with or without support of international alliances. This could be a hint of adopting a much stronger diplomatic stance towards Iran and Syria. Mr. Giuliani is considered a strong contender for the position of Secretary of State if Mr. Bush is reelected. Secretary of State Colin Powell has decided to step down when media reported his disagreements with Vice President Dick Cheney. Governor Schwarzenegger on the other hand was given prime time to convince undecided voter among minorities, gay and abortion rights activists to support Mr. Bush.

Senator John McCain was given an opportunity to address Republican convention to show unity among party leadership as his name was mentioned as a probable running mate for Democratic Party candidate John Kerry. He tried to make case for the necessity of Iraq war and its conduct which is a focal point of this campaign.

To smooth edges of an otherwise war convention Ms. Laura Bush spoke about goodness of her husband and elaborated on his softer side. As they say in our native language *Wojode Zan se ha tasweer-e-qainat ma rung* (women bring colorfulness to life), she tried to add color to a white and black convention. She is an eloquent speaker and her speech targeted women and conservative to vote for her husband.

Vice President Dick Cheney gave his acceptance speech in which he initiated attacks on election manifesto of Mr. Kerry. He questioned Democratic candidate's judgment in making tough decisions that will be required during American military engagements in Iraq and Afghanistan.

In his acceptance speech on Thursday September 2, 2004, Mr. Bush spoke about his plans for next four years in a speech that lasted over an hour.

Key elements of his plans are permanent cuts in taxes; introduction of a privately managed social security program; retooling of laid off workers; proposal to form special opportunity zones; reforms in healthcare to make it affordable for small business owners; reduce cost of liability insurance for healthcare providers; and public school reform program to improve standards of education. He was the only speaker to avoid direct attacks on his opponent's credentials. His speech was considered reenactment of his state of the union address in January. Political commentators gave average rating to the speech for its delivery and content.

In this Republican Convention most of the time was spent talking about September 11 terrorist event, war on terrorism, credibility of Mr. Bush to be an effective commander-in-chief and unsuitability of Mr. Kerry to lead this nation in a state of war. No one elaborated or tried to clarify allegations that Bush administration lied about presence of WMD in Iraq, about cooperation between Iraq and Al-Qaeda and failure of Pentagon to plan for political reconciliation in the aftermath of Iraqi occupation. No one talked about enormous loss of life and treasure in Iraq. No one expressed concern about reducing unemployment or rising trade deficit. Creating new jobs was not given any attention. There was no discussion about minority rights and immigration policies. This convention will always be remembered as a war convention as peace and economy had no place in it.

Bush's campaign team is trying to create a perception that Kerry has no plan for ending Iraq war, improve economy or reduce trade deficit. If Bush wants to win both popular and electoral votes he has to talk about domestic issues. Mr. Kerry has to make efforts to explain his manifesto to the people and highlight its difference's with Bush's program. It is a close fight so far but Kerry could lose ground if he does not emerge as a stronger personality who can lead the nation in tough time.

US Presidential Election 2004: Congratulations Mr. Bush
(November 9, 2004)

At last a hard fought campaign for White House has ended. President George W. Bush has become 12th President in American history to serve for two terms. Although Senator Kerry, Democratic Party candidate, ran a high spirited effort focusing on domestic issues to unseat Republican Party contender but in the end war on Iraq proved to be an insurmountable hurdle for him. Bush campaign was vulnerable because of his failure in creating new jobs, harnessing budget deficit and losing major allies in Europe. They faced questions about legitimacy of Iraq war once it was clear that there was no creditable evidence about Iraqi WMD and their link with Osama Bin Laden's Al-Qaeda terrorist network. Surprise appearance of a Bin Laden video just days before voting began on 2nd November 2004 raised questions about American intelligence's knowledge of his whereabouts. In the end Bush campaign team understood preference of voters better than Kerry. They focused their campaign on questioning credibility of Senator Kerry as a war president which proved to be a right political strategy.

Mr. Bush emerged as a strong leader based on his popular vote count as well as securing 286 electoral votes although he only needed 270 to cross that threshold. He is the first President since 1988 who secured more than 50% popular votes. Emerging political map of America is getting redder in support of conservative ideology represented by Republicans. Liberals are removed to Eastern and Western Border States, which is not enough to claim an Electoral College victory at national level.

On 9/11 destiny provided President Bush an opportunity to leave his footprint on history. Once initial euphoria settled, strategy Mr. Bush pursued has isolated America internationally. A unilateral war was waged rather than forging international alliance to fight expansion of terrorism.

Collateral damage from war has since flared the increase in terror networks. Success in preventing any terrorist act on American soil is cited as proof of effectiveness for this strategy. Objectives of terrorists are to create confusion and chaos in the minds of people by inflicting economic and human loss. They have succeeded in achieving that objective. American forces in Iraq provide 138,000 walking targets for these terrorist coupled with an economic loss to the tune of $200 billion dollars and counting. War in Iraq has created a community of over 200,000 people who has lost one or other relative and is angry enough to become recruits for Al-Qaeda.

In his second term, Mr. Bush can realize that war never solves any problem. Conversely it increases hatred and widens gulf between people. He should extend his hand towards countries in Middle East and Europe to form a broader alliance to address current situation in Iraq. Europe and America can provide necessary technology, financial aid and political know how to build Iraq while Muslim countries can contribute forces not only to maintain law and order as well as to train local security forces. Instead of making Iraq an American responsibility it is important to make it a global opportunity and let all stakeholders share this burden of nation building. It will help to contain this chaos spreading to other countries in the region.

American presence in Iraq is creating an anxiety in neighboring countries Iran and Syria. Current Iranian push for uranium enrichment, a precursor to an atomic bomb, could be a result of American occupation of Iraq. Greater involvement of Muslim countries in Iraq could contribute to improving relations with Iran. America needs to use EU as a bridge to strengthen its diplomatic/trade ties with Iran and Syria. If America did not reduce its reliance on military might, to solve global issues, chances are that war in Iraq could get out of hand and become a regional conflict bringing Iran and Syria to the battle front.

It is usually said that during their first term American presidents consolidate their grip on politics while in their second term they try to create a lasting legacy.

In his second term, destiny has provided President Bush an opportunity to go down in history as a peace maker by resolving Israel Palestine issue. Mr. Yasser Arafat, President of Palestinian National Authority, long considered an impediment in resolving the conflict will be replaced for health reasons. Mr. Arafat during his tenure was not able to muster support for the peace plan. During last four years America has given a free hand to Aerial Sharon's government to take an aggressive posture towards Palestinians which is igniting anti-American sentiments in Muslims. It is now time for America to moderate the peace process by forming a council of Palestinian leaders to negotiate with Israel. Any lost opportunity will provide an impetus for militant organizations like Hamas to increase their political influence among young Palestinians. Israel should realize that military might does not produce peace until negotiations are conducted in a balanced and compassionate manner.

Mr. Bush should strengthen its ties with Pakistan not only as an ally in war on terrorism but also improve trade and cultural ties. This can only happen when American aid is spent to improve law and order situation in Pakistan. This will enable increased tourist traffic between these two countries. America should increase numbers of educational visas and grants to Pakistani scholars.

Patriotic Act coincides with foundation of American constitution. It has created an anxiety among Pakistani and other immigrant communities in USA. Even Democratic Party Congressmen have expressed concerns about it. With increased political influence, in both the House of Representatives and Senate, Mr. Bush should review and amend Patriotic Act to bring it more in line with civil liberties act as well as bring equality among all legal permanent residents.

In next four years Mr. Bush has a critical choice to make, more of the same or a radically different approach to bring peace and harmony; to make this world an environmentally better place to live by adopting the Kyoto protocol; to welcome economic immigrants who want to pursue the American dream; to create more jobs and reduce the budget deficit.

Second Term of President Bush

Background: America was engaged in two active wars in Afghanistan and Iraq after terror incidents of 11th September 2001. To create a favorable public opinion for these wars, American media actively engaged in presenting Islamic fundamentalism as a risk to their way of life. This raised emotion in among Muslim producing steep decline in American goodwill on the street there.

Bush 2nd Term: US war against terrorism- who is winning the war?
(June 26, 2004)

On 18th June 2004 international news media were flashing pictures of a masked terrorist claiming to strike against American interest using Islam as an ideology to legitimize those actions. That same terrorist was later accused of beheading an American citizen working in Saudi Arabia for Lockheed Martin Corporation. Saudi Authorities claimed they killed four terrorists, including the masked man, involved in this heinous crime against humanity. But will this be an end to targeting of American interests by terrorists? There is a growing debate among American intellectuals to find reasons behind escalating hatred against their country in many parts of the world. This hatred, most often, is projected to be emanating from the Muslim world. If it was true, a girl wearing a t-shirt with American flag printed on it would not be asked by her German school teachers to refrain from wearing it again as it raises negative emotions among other students.

There is no doubt that American political, military and economic power is unmatched. This position of superiority imposes a responsibility on it to act in a compassionate manner giving due consideration to how its actions will be perceived especially among its close European allies. Muslim world dose not pose any threat to American long term interests. Probable challenger to its dominance will emerge from European Union (EU) or China. Recent political developments in EU increasingly point in this direction.

Just last week EU summit approved its constitution, established a foreign ministers office and a military agency to develop defense technology. This is precursor to the emergence of a United States of Europe. Even in its current form it is the largest economic body encompassing over 350 million people. Two largest members Germany and France have been increasingly vocal criticizing American foreign policy and its strategy of unilateral tackling of Iraqi problem. During G8 summit, at Sea Island in Georgia, French President Jacques Chirac refused to lend support to the proposal of sending NATO forces to Iraq despite President Bush's formal request.

China is dependent on Middle Eastern Oil for smooth functioning of its growing economy. It is estimated that China will become the largest importer of fuel oil by 2015. Its energy consumption is growing by over 8% per annum inline with its GDP growth. It is not in China's interest that America should have puppet governments in oil rich countries like Iraq and Saudi Arabia, which together constitute over 26% of world supply. Iraq was the second largest exporter of oil after Saudi Arabia before imposition of economic sanctions after first Gulf war.

China's reaction to invasion of Iraq can be at best qualified as neutral. But this stance can change if it feels threats to disruption in its energy supplies. China has started laying groundwork for stronger diplomatic ties with middle and far eastern countries. It is one of the largest trading partners with America and has also been a large foreign investor in US government treasuries. It reinvests its trading surplus back into American economy financing her budget deficit. This makes world financial markets vulnerable to Chinese moves that could create havoc on bond markets if they dump their holdings in a short period of time.

Muslim world usually blames Western Societies for its evils. Since America is a dominant player in the western world it bears most of this anger and hatred. Western countries have secular governments while individuals adhere to Christian faith. Some biased commentators find it easy to call current war on terrorism as a clash of civilization or simply put war between Christianity and Islam.

These are misplaced conceptions. Evils of Muslim world are resulting from failure of their own governments and policies. America has taken it upon itself to introduce democracy in these Muslim countries by linking economic aid and trade to introduction of freedom of expression and maintaining good human rights record. In some extreme cases like Iraq and Afghanistan, it has decided to use military force to change regime and then engage in nation building.

It is clear from the aftermath of Iraq war that it is extremely difficult for any power to engage itself in war or nation building alone. Human and economic capital required to carry this enterprise is too high. Forming alliances and signing international treaties are still best approach to solving bilateral conflicts as well as to bring change to depressed societies. If America could engage in a cold war for 45 years with a European power they should have shown similar patience in dealing with a rogue state and its dictator Saddam Hussein. He was an oppressive ruler but he did not pose any serious threat to United States that demanded immediate action. There were other alternatives available to handle that problem.

It is in long term American interest to have closer ties with Middle East. Its past strategy of supporting kings and dictators may work in short term but in long term it becomes target of increasing hatred among the oppressed people. Best approach to bring change would be to help them bring change themselves. There are various platforms available including but not limited to Gulf Cooperation Council (GCC), Arab League (AL) and Organization of Islamic Cooperation (OIC). America should work closely with these organizations to change their charters to address social, economic and political structure of Muslim countries. Current charter of OIC is outdated and needs serious reconsideration. It provides cover to these oppressive rulers. US should provide financial and intellectual support to these organizations to monitor democratic and human right conditions in their member countries.

It is in the interest of terrorists to increase gulf between people on religious bases. There is a media war between Arab and Western media to present war on terrorism in different light. By labeling terrorist as Islamic Western media is promoting their message of hatred and increasing probability of a religious war. A terrorist has no religion. They are mentally sick people who are made to believe they will ascent to heaven by blowing themselves and killing innocent people. Quran clearly states that suicide is an unforgiving sin. Terrorist mastermind will always have abundance of willing recruits until there is political and social oppression in these countries. Killing one terrorist does not achieve eradication of terrorism. To kill the monster you have to cut its head by liberating people from oppression. As The New York Times columnist Thomas Friedman, put it in his interview with Charlie Rose on PBS "we have waged a war against terrorist. Not terrorism." Instead of throwing good resources after the bad it is better that Bush administration should rethink its strategy and give more consideration to multilateral platforms like GCC and OIC. It is better to collaborate rather than deciding for them unilaterally.

Background: Term "coalition of the willing" was coined by US State Department after it was evident that larger European partners France and Germany were not willing to lend support for war in Iraq. It was a coalition of 46 largely smaller countries of Europe and Asia. Condoleezza Rice, a close confidant of President Bush and National Security Advisor in his first term, became Secretary of State when widely respected Secretary of State Collin Powel resigned. Media reports suggested that General Colin Powell asked to be relieved after he was made to present questionable evidence on Iraqi WMD program to get support from UN Security Council. That evidence damaged his image as a promoter of peace.

Bush 2nd term: a review of foreign policy
(March 29, 2005)

It is believed that American Presidents set agenda for their four years term during first 100 days of their inauguration. Soon after taking oath for second term, President Bush started to unfold his foreign policy through carefully choreographed actions. Dominant foreign policy theme of State of the Union speech, delivered on 2nd February 2005, was introduction of democracy for oppressed while continuing pressure on countries considered a hurdle to American interest in Middle East like Iran and Syria. He advised autocratic rulers to introduce democratic reforms in their societies. His speech was followed by Secretary of State Condoleezza Rice's visit to Israel and Palestine to pave ground for resumption of stalled Middle East peace process. This was followed by President Bush's visit to European Union. Soon thereafter Secretary of State left for a tour of South Asia preceded by an announcement to sell arms to India and Pakistan. While first term was dedicated to fighting war against terror, it seems, second term will be dedicated to shift long term strategic focus from Middle East to South Asia.

It is evident that all pieces are in place for a two state solution to Middle East peace process. All players are in place to pursue this solution. Israeli Prime Minister, Ariel Sharon has got an authorization from his parliament to pull out from Gaza and West bank.

New Palestinian Prime Minister Mahmoud Abbas seems to be willing to adopt a conciliatory attitude towards solving the issue by considering the two states solution. Even a formula is devised for the administration of sacred Al-Aqsa mosque. Only thorny issue remaining is return of refugees, which can tilt balance of power in favor of Arabs in democratically elected Israeli parliament. It is a genuine fear that has to be addressed before they can arrive at an amicable mutually acceptable solution.

America has allocated over 700 million dollars for economic aid to Palestine that will play a critical role in achieving stability in the region. Syria is forced to pull out of Lebanon, which will further remove them from meddling in Palestine conflict. It is about time that Organization of Islamic Cooperation (OIC) calls a special meeting to discuss these developments and form a unified strategy to solve this issue once and for all. In last 50 years, this is probably first time when there is a probability that peace will finally be achieved. Muslims should remember that Prophet Mohammad (PBUH) signed his first defense and peaceful coexistence agreement with Jewish tribes around Medina. So there is religious precedence available for Palestinians to create understanding and harmony among diverse communities.

From President Bush's recent visit to Europe it is evident that the administration is serious in rebuilding bridges with its Atlantic partners. Major EU powers, France, Germany and Spain, realize that they have to play an increasingly independent role in international politics. This approach is given a boost with introduction of an EU foreign secretariat. Europe's policy independence was in full display during negotiations with Iran on nuclear non-proliferation as well as allowing defense export to China despite American reservations. European leaders understand that they have to tread a fine line between balancing their own interest in Middle East as well as maintain cordial relations with America. EU seems to be capitalizing on anti-American feeling in the region to its favor. Europe realizes that for a foreseeable future they have to rely on Middle Eastern oil for their energy needs and cannot afford to allow America to control two of three largest oil reserves giving them a strategic monopoly.

It is expected that EU constitution will be ratified by member states, which will result in formation of a legislative assembly and appointment of a President for a fixed term. These developments show emergence of Europe as a political, economic and social entity providing a counter balance to American influence. It is expected that NATO will be dissolved to form a new alliance to in tune with new world order in the aftermath of 9/11.

It seems South Asia will be a focal point of American interest once Palestinian problem is solved. American policy is focusing on India and Pakistan as allies to contain rising economic, political and strategic profile of China. Recent announcement of arms sales to these countries is an indication of a move in this direction. India can be a counter balance to Chinese dominance while Pakistan can provide a necessary pressure point to contain Indian ambitions. America would prefer to use its economic power to create a web around India and China. Through Afghanistan and CIS states, America can maintain its pressure on Russia, which is increasingly eager to bring its neighbors back into its fold as client states.

Pakistan, for its part, has to reevaluate its options and realign its long-term strategy. It is clear, both from history as well as common sense, that Pakistan should improve its relationship with India. First step in this direction is to gain access to Indian consumers through a trade pact. Second initiative could be a reopening of discussions on Kashmir with an open mind and form a new road map to solve this problem. Secretary level discussions are already on course but leaders on both sides are still fighting a media war, which can derail the process any time. Indian objections to stop US arms sales to Pakistan can result in some loss of good will. The question in Pakistani minds is that if India has signed a peace treaty with China, why does it need new arms? There is no other country in the region, which has had a thorny relationship with India but Pakistan. This creates a natural fear of a possibility of another conflict. Pakistan should consider strengthening its ties with EU, as a new emerging power, while maintaining its good relations with China.

The power imbalance created by the terrorist acts of 9/11 and subsequent American actions have still not created a new world order. The pieces are moving to acquire a long-term equilibrium. There are indications that EU, China and Russia will emerge as counter balance to American influence. On the other hand, America will shift its focus from Middle East to South Asia and create a staging ground to counter balance the expanding influence of India and China. Israel realizes this changing shift and would like to solve the issue with Palestine before they lose US support. In the broader Middle East, America will continue using democracy as a sword to get oil from autocratic rulers.

Bush 2nd term: Doctrine of global democracy
(May 11, 2005)

American President Bush made his first ever visit to Russia to mark 60th anniversary of Germany's surrender to Allied forces, which comprised of Russia, US and UK. Bush's itinerary included visits to Georgia and Ukraine to rebuff Russian ambition to establish its authority over their former USSR member states. These stops were meant to highlight the failure of communism and to emphasize the establishment of democracy as a central theme of American foreign policy. US aid and other initiatives are tied to the progress of democracies in countries seeking funds.

This is not the first time in human history that a country has taken initiative to dictate its philosophies to be adopted by the rest. In past centuries, weapons and armies were used to subjugate a nation while today trade sanctions and diplomacy is used to achieve those same objectives. Famous Egyptian Pharaoh, Khufu, circa 2575-2465 BC, was so influential that emperors from states far and wide would send emissaries to seek the alliance with the King and protection from other states. When Alexander came of age and became the ruler of Macedonia, he wanted to explore the world and impose his will by creating a unified world under Macedonian rule. In the last millennia, British, Portuguese and Dutch empires occupied colonies in the name of spreading economic prosperity to these culturally rich but economically poor Middle Eastern, African and Asian countries. In the 20th century, Hitler tried to create his own kingdom of Aryans in Europe by marching on Poland, France and Russia.

Not only rulers with armies and weapons aspired to create global influences, religions and philosophers had their own ambition of universal domination. Christian and Muslim religious leaders sought ways to spread their theologies that ultimately resulted in the Crusades that lasted for almost 200 years, consuming countless lives. Philosophers contributed to this ambition of a unified world by promoting ideologies and theories in managing human societies.

First such effort was Plato's "Republic" which used individual characteristics of justice, courage and honesty to be extended to a society in creating a state governed by these principles. Nicolò Machiavelli created his own body of work "The Prince" to advise rulers in controlling their societies. If "Republic" is a society's guide to establish an equitable system of government, "Prince" is a guide for autocratic rulers to suppress their people. Voltaire's Socialist ideas became an inspiration for French Revolution of 1795. Karl Marx's communist philosophy entailed that a state should be the arbiter of goods and property among citizens. Marx became a leading light for Russian Bolshevik Revolution of 1918. Once established, Russia wanted to impose communist philosophy on its neighboring countries creating the Union of Soviet Socialist Republic (USSR).

But all these efforts failed in one way or another resulting in a social vacuum that gave rise to anarchy and ultimately widespread human misery. Basic definition of democracy is "government by the people for the people". If we consider this definition to be valid then Mr. Bush needs to amend his ambition of global democracy by seeking approval from people of each country before it is imposed on them through military or economic intervention.

No one denies that democracy is effective in furthering equality among citizens and giving them a chance to enjoy fruits of progress of a civilized society. But it is also a fact that each culture has its own traditions that cannot be ignored in implementing democratic values. If democracy is considered an intrinsic part of human nature then an outside intervention is not needed to impose it on a society.

If Mr. Bush is serious in promoting democracy, first step should be to withhold economic support for autocratic rulers. President of Pakistan General Pervez Musharraf has broken his covenant with the nation to relinquish his military uniform and only keep civilian role of the President.

Instead of pressuring Musharraf to deliver on his promise, America has continued its economic support thereby defying its own commitment of promoting democracy around the world.

This duality of America is a prime reason for its damaging image in countries affected by her aggression. Instead of supporting movements for democracy she has been supportive of autocratic rulers. These suppressed societies become breeding grounds for terrorists and other anti social elements. Instead of waiting for the situation to become worst to the extent that Western intervention would be required, democratic countries should provide support to home grown reform movements.

America, traditionally, has been an open society with free flow of capital and labor across its boundaries that resulted in its unprecedented economic prosperity. This openness is a consequence of deep adherence to democratic values developed over 200 years of its history. But 9/11 changed all this, forcing lawmakers to adopt policies, like Patriotic Act, to convert America into an increasingly closed society. This has resulted in intellectuals migrating to Europe instead of opting for America. In past, it was this intellectual capital of immigrants that has helped her maintain technological lead over other developed countries. With rising phenomena of out sourcing to India and China it is even more important for America to maintain this technological advantage. It is responsibility of each citizen to protect their homeland from intruders and sabotages but closing society will only damage the American Dream that has survived for almost two centuries.

Democracy has proved to be a more successful philosophy as compared to socialism or communism. But it should be adapted to each country's culture and tradition.

Socrates and Bush
(September 13, 2006)

This week we are commemorating fifth anniversary of 9/11 terrorist incidents, a horrific but historical event that is still affecting the course of the 21st century. It started a major shift in American policy from that of economic and diplomatic efforts to a carrot and stick policy to promote its interests. It was a starting point of dividing the world between "us" and "them". "Us" being nations who acquiesce to American pressure to implement its definition of democracy, justice and human rights. On the other hand "Them" are people most probably of Islamic faith who refuse to accept current state of affairs in their countries and who have decided to embark on an armed conflict with their own societies as well as Western powers who are considered supportive of these governments.

Like Korean symbol of Yin and Yang it is always a struggle to define what is just and unjust. Same is true for Good and evil. These are important questions of our time. In his speeches President Bush has emphasized that America is in a continuing struggle against the evil forces. To define good and evil; just and unjust we reproduce a dialogue between Socrates and a person named Thrasymachus while sitting in a group from Book 1 of Plato's Republic.

Socrates:"Then I will repeat the question which I asked before, in order that our examination of the relative nature of justice and injustice may be carried on regularly. A statement was made that injustice is stronger and more powerful than justice, but now justice, having been identified with wisdom and virtue, is easily shown to be stronger than justice, if injustice is ignorance; this can no longer be questioned by any one. But I want to view the matter, Thrasymachus, in a different way: you would not deny that a state may be unjust and may be unjustly attempting to enslave other states, or may have already enslaved them, and may be holding many of them in subjection?"

Thrasymachus: "True and I will add that the best and most perfectly unjust state will be most likely to do so."

Socrates: "I know that such was your position; but what I would further consider is, whether this power which is possessed by the superior state can exist or be exercised without justice or only with justice."

Thrasymachus: "If you are right in your view, and justice is wisdom, then only with justice, but if I am right then without it."

Socrates: "Would you have the goodness also to inform me, whether you think that a state, or an army, or a band of robbers and thieves, or any other gang of evildoers could act at all if they injured one another?"

Thrasymachus: "No indeed they could not"

Socrates: "But if they abstained from injuring one another, then they might act together better?"

Thrasymachus: "Yes"

Socrates: "And this is because injustice creates divisions and hatreds and fighting, and justice imparts harmony and friendship; is not that true, Thrasymachus?"

Thrasymachus: "I agree"

Socrates: "I should like to know also whether injustice, having this tendency to arouse hatred, wherever existing among slaves or freeman, will not make them hate one another and set them at variance and render them incapable of common action."

Thrasymachus: "Certainly"

Socrates: "Yet is not the power which injustice exercises of such a nature that wherever she takes up her adobe, whether in a city, in an army, in a family, or in any other body, that body is, to begin with, rendered incapable of united action by reason of sedition and distraction; and does it not become its own enemy and at variance with all that opposes it, and with the just? Is not this the case?"

Thrasymachus: "Yes, certainly"

Socrates: "We have already shown that the just are clearly wiser and better and abler than the unjust, and that the unjust are incapable of common action; nay more, that to speak as we did of men who are evil acting at any time vigorously together, is not strictly true, for if they had been perfectly evil, they would have laid hands upon one another; but it is evident that there must have been some remnant of justice in them, which enabled them to combine; if there had not been they would have injured one another as well as their victims; they were but half-villains in their enterprises; for had they been whole villains, and utterly unjust, they would have been utterly incapable of action. That, as I believe, is the truth of the matter, and not what you said at first."

It would be a blessing that Bush Administration finds a Socrates among them who could provide guidance in these turbulent times. It would be comforting that extremist learns from history that violence is an unjust approach to struggle for a just cause. We have examples from Pakistan's founding father Mohammad Ali Jinnah and South African leader Nelson Mandela that freedom can be gained through peaceful means.

Sadly although Socrates won the argument but Thrasymachus proved right that injustice can be stronger than justice. Socrates was condemned to drink from a chalice of poison for his views that were considered a danger to society and State.

US-Pakistan Relations

Background: Pakistan, with a long border with Afghanistan, was asked to provide supply route for NATO and ISAF forces at the start of Afghan war. Military dictator General Musharraf motivated to gain international legitimacy for his unconstitutional rule agreed to American terms of engagement without conducting a detailed strategic review with his corps commanders, diplomats or political allies. It was evident, as far back as 2004 that as Afghan war produced increasing numbers of dead and maimed soldiers there will be growing pressure on Pakistan to do more. Increased frequency of CIA operated drone strikes to kill terrorists produced large number of civilian casualties conveniently called collateral damage by American establishment. These attacks were deeply unpopular pressuring the government to withdraw its support for US operations. On the other hand war in a neighboring country produced wave of terrorist attacks inside Pakistan. Pakistanis blamed their policy planners and elected representatives for succumbing to American demands to do more without giving due considerations to their own national interests. Diplomatic efforts came under strain as trust deficit grew and policy makers made errors in understanding each others interests.

US Pakistan relations: a historical perspective
(April 8, 2004)

US granted a most favored nation status outside NATO to Pakistan. It is considered recognition of her commitment to the global war against terrorism. As a trusted ally Pakistan has furthered American interest in the region for over 5 decades.

This special relationship dates as far back as 1954 when Pakistan became member of Southeast Asian Treaty Organization (SEATO) sponsored by America and supported by other western countries. Relationship got a further boost when in late 1950s Pakistan allowed use of its air bases for U2 spy flights for surveillance over USSR during the missile crises. Later Pakistan played a pivotal role in helping to normalize Sino-US relationship. In early 1970s then Secretary of State Mr. Henry Kissinger secretly flew to China from Pakistan for the first diplomatic contact with the Chinese ruling party. This event became a precursor to economic ties between these two countries. China today is one of the leading trading partners of America and largest investor in government securities.

In December 1979 USSR when invaded Afghanistan, Pakistan became a front line state in containing expansion of communism and to thwart longstanding Russian ambition to reach warm waters of Arabian Sea. Initially America was non-committal to curtail communist expansionism under Carter Administration. These policies changed by the surprise win of Republican Presidential Candidate Ronald Reagan. America decided to provide Pakistan with necessary economic and military aid to finance Afghan resistance. At the time Pakistan was ruled by an authoritarian military regime of General Zia ul Haq.

Although US pressed upon him to democratize the country but it was not a top priority item on the agenda. Democracy could wait as long as Zia ensured provision of training grounds for Mujahedeen under the tutelage of American military experts.

This war ultimately resulted in break-up of USSR into 13 independent states and an end to the cold war. Throughout 1990s America lost interest in the region and left Pakistan on its own to deal with proliferation of small arms from lawless Afghanistan as well as curtail expansion of growing drug trade and plan return of Afghan refugees to their homeland. It was a daunting task for a nation that was struggling with its internal political and economic issues.

American-Pakistani relations were put on a back burner because there was no major interest that could be served. All that changed after 9/11. Pakistan was considered a close ally of Taliban regime in Afghanistan and thus was asked to help with pressuring them to demolish terrorist infrastructure and training camps. It was beneficial to Pakistan as well which was concerned with infiltration of extremist ideologies, promoted by increasingly fundamentalist Taliban regime, into North West Frontier Province (NWFP). NWFP has a majority Pashtun population that shares similar cultural and linguistic ties with Southern Afghani people. Some of these Afghan mujahedeen have settled in these areas and established family ties among local tribes. These homogenous cultural and linguistic bonds made it impossible to weed out local from foreign people. In one recent missions Pakistan army has laid siege to those areas and arrested suspected terrorist by risking destabilization of a restive federally administrated tribal region (FATA).

Despite decades of bilateral relationship, American media are filled with images of people on Pakistani streets chanting anti American slogans. The question arises why people would consider a geographically far off country as its enemy and source of its political and social decadence. In meetings with American officials authoritarian governments use this fear tactic of rising fundamentalism to delay introducing democracy in their country. But reality is blurred behind political motive of the few.

Pakistani nation has lived under authoritarian rule for most of its history including 1999 coupe of General Pervez Musharraf.

These rulers have tried to mellow American insistence of introducing democracy by providing support for its interest in the region. America has found it easier to deal with the authoritarian rulers who are indifferent to public pressure when making decisions. It stipulates that unpopular policies will force political leaders to make choices that are not in American interest. That notion is faulty.

After Saudi Arabia, America has largest number of expatriate Pakistani population. There are close to 750,000 Pakistanis living in America and are engaged in her economic progress. Expatriate Pakistanis living in America send about 15% of foreign remittances. America is a large trading partner consuming over 30% of Pakistan's export and a source of private investment. Pakistanis are moderate people who are more interested in strengthening their political institutions and society. If fundamentalist elements were popular they would have been controlling majorities in Senate and National Assembly. But in reality they have formed government in a smaller NWFP province, which has borders with Afghanistan, and the election results could have been easily influenced by Afghan elements present there. These facts should be considered by American policy makers to improve bilateral relations.

Economic and strategic interests of both nations are aligned. It is common belief among Pakistanis that America abandoned them at various juncture in its history. Luke warm American support during the wars of 1965 and 1971; non-compliance of India to UN resolutions to solve the Kashmir issue; and non-acceptance of its nuclear program are some examples. Assigning a most favored nation status is a step in right direction but it can not produce better understanding until it is coupled with broader interaction on cultural, political and economic levels. Pakistan can learn from American democratic experience and establish institutions that suit its own social structure. It is in continued American interest to have a strong ally in volatile South Asian region. The choice is clear.

US-Pakistan relations: a friend or a foe
(March 4, 2007)

In last few weeks there has been debate in American media, about sincerity of Pakistan in fight against terror. Questions have been raised about efforts of Musharraf government to help control cross border infiltration to prevent resurgence of Taliban in Afghanistan. It was expected as Democrats took control of the US Congress that they would conduct a review of American policy in Iraq and Afghanistan. Pakistan, with Musharraf at the helm, was the first country to sign on to become a front line state in fight against terrorism. This alliance has now become a target by Democrats like every other part of Bush foreign policy. Real question is whether it is in American interest to pressure Pakistan for more than it can offer.

South Asia and Middle East are going to be focus of international attention for sometime to come. For many obvious reasons, it is home to two aspiring super powers i.e. China and India with huge armies and nuclear arsenal; it is home to an aspiring oil rich Muslim country Iran that understands frustration of Muslims with both Western powers and militant Islam; it is a region where America is deeply mired economically and militarily i.e. in Iraq and Afghanistan; it is in close proximity to a sleeping giant Russia that is nostalgic about its status as a super power as it overcome its economic morass supported by rising oil and gas revenues. In all this turmoil and uncertainty there are only few friends that have stood with America through thick and thin. This minority of friends include Pakistan, Jordan, Egypt, and Saudi Arabia which have risked their own integrity and sovereignty to help in her fight against terrorism. Imagine a strategically important region where America looses two of these friends because politicians in Washington doubted their sincerity. This sure isn't a pretty picture.

After 9/11, from nationalistic point of view Pakistan should have remained neutral considering social and political strain it would encounter especially when these terrorist are labeled Islamist.

With almost 95% Muslim population it certainly risked igniting emotions among the populace. It provided an avenue for Islamist political parties like Jamat-e-Islami (JI) and Jamiat Ulema Islam Fazal (JUI F) which has substantial presence in parliament to gain public support. Despite these political risks President Pervez Musharraf agreed to work with America without any precondition.

As time passed America kept asking for more and government of Pakistan tried their best to deliver whether it was tipping off British authorities to foil a terrorist plan to sabotage transatlantic flights or helping apprehend Al Qaeda operatives including notorious Khalid Shaikh Mohammad. Government of Pakistan went so far as to initiate a military operation against extremists in North Waziristan reportedly losing close to 500 soldiers. Government even suffered embarrassment when American army fired missiles into Pakistani territory on two occasions killing many civilians including some suspected terrorist.

Pakistan by its social character is a moderate country which is evident from popularity of Western culture, food and movies. These moderate has become a target of a small minority of fundamentalist element in the last two decades.

These elements became resourceful as a direct result of religiously motivated Afghan war against Russian occupation. Once that war was over those same Mujahedeen became a problem for Pakistan by targeting its society through sectarian violence, bomb blasts and suicide attacks. Under disguise of transit trade, Afghan warlords brought drugs, Kalashnikov and money laundering to Pakistan through their contacts in North Waziristan with whom they share same ethnicity and culture.

Fundamentalist elements, in Pakistan, were further augmented by lack of government focus on providing primary education to children through secular schools. These children were instead enrolled in narrowly focused Islamic madrassas (Seminaries) with no supervision by regulators. This produced a generation of brain washed young men with no special skills to earn a decent living.

It is worth while to note that North Waziristan region lies in a province governed by coalition of religious parties called Mutahida Majlis-e-Amal or MMA.

In this back drop of external and internal pressure Pakistan has tried its best to deliver on promises made to United States. Instead of appreciating these efforts, newly elected American congress has slapped it with a bill HR1 imposing restrictions on military aid. Recent visits to Pakistan by Secretary of Defense Mr. Robert Gates and Vice President Dick Cheney were reported as getting assurances from President Musharraf for more results. Americans should understand it is not possible for Pakistan to monitor a thousand miles long mountainous border with its limited resources when Kabul keeps blaming it for their own failure.

Solution to the current rise of Taliban and Islamist fundamentalism does not lie in military action. Presence of NATO forces will always be considered occupiers by proud Afghans. In short term a coalition force can be formed comprising of India, Pakistan, Central Asian States and NATO. While long term solution lies in introducing reforms in education systems so that next generation of Muslims are intellectually stronger with a deep sense of their history, has an understanding of the spiritual and social responsibility promoted by their religion. These social reforms can not take roots unless America stops supporting autocratic rulers that abrogate constitutions and undermine building of stable political institutions. General Musharraf can not deliver more as his government does not have a democratic mandate rather he relies on military establishment and forming alliances with various undemocratic elements. Under his rule indices representing child education, law and order, social justice and poverty has deteriorated much more than ever.

A strong prosperous Pakistan is in strategic interest of United States. But it can not happen unless she starts supporting people of Pakistan for a better future instead of an autocratic ruler to gain short term benefits.

American aid should be allocated to reform education system especially primary education. American think tanks can help guiding political leadership of Pakistan in creating stable political institutions that can meet expectations of the nation.

As they say all politics are local. A poverty stricken and ill informed population can not consider America a friend when religious leader at the pulpit is labeling it as a reason for all their miseries.

US-Pakistan relations: sacrifices of Pakistan
(August 4, 2007)

American people are progressive, humanistic, and passionate about protecting their values. They are firm believers in equal rights for all despite their race, color, sex or origin. But when it comes to American government, it is increasingly dominated by war mongering policy hawks lead by Vice President Dick Cheney. Bush administration believes that use of force is the only way to protect their homeland from an invisible enemy although it has been endowed with impregnable natural barriers of Atlantic and Pacific oceans, on east and west coast respectively. Ironically war on terror is fought in Muslim lands including Palestine, Lebanon, Kashmir, Chechnya, Afghanistan, Iraq, Pakistan, Egypt and Saudi Arabia. In past America collaborated with local governments to bust terror networks. This has changed as they claim to have a legitimate right to strike inside countries where they perceive success is not forthcoming. Traditional diplomatic norms restrict any sovereign nation to strike inside the internationally recognized boundaries of another.

Although Bush administration denies that war on terror is an attack on Islamic civilization but all their actions point in that direction. First, after 9/11 America introduced Patriotic Act which gave unprecedented powers to FBI including detention of terrorist suspect without access to their lawyers for up to seven days. This was followed by American immigration imposing special registration on Muslim migrants with sole exception of North Korea. When people agitated they were told that all countries will be subjected to this rule but as soon as registration of Muslims was complete the program was suddenly discontinued under a pretax that it is ineffective. Third, America waged war on two Muslim countries Afghanistan and Iraq. Afghan war could be justified for harboring terrorist networks but war on Iraq was based on total lies. While engaged in Iraq, Bush administration at various times, have discussed options to attack Syria, Iran and Pakistan. It seems that America has not learned any lessons in Iraq despite losing close to US$ 450 billion in treasury and over 3500 dead while over 15000 critically injured.

America should realize that Pakistani nation is now reaching a point of total exhaustion from bearing the burden of her war on terror and killing many of their own countrymen to make them happy. For each Taliban leader that is killed there is a collateral damage of innocent people that include women and children. The loss of these lives is creating a group of people who will not rest until they take revenge from America and their allies. Throughout its history a large majority of Pakistanis have supported friendship with America but that majority is quickly turning into a minority. As public support vane for war on terror the politicians have to listen to their constituents and change their position from support to disengagement. In that case, if America decided to strike inside Pakistan it will be considered an attack and people can demand declaration of war with America and Afghanistan. No one in their right senses will want this scenario to emerge and policy makers should realize that they can not make unilateral decision to strike inside Pakistan.

In case a war like situation emerge, because of irresponsible actions of decision makers, there is a likelihood Iran will support Pakistan both financially and militarily. It will allow Iran to focus on gaining further ground in Iraq. Turkey has always enjoyed deep friendship with Pakistan going back almost 120 years since Indian Muslim formed a movement for preservation of Ottoman Empire. Recent victory of Islamist party AKP in Turkey could mean that Pakistan can count on Turkey for diplomatic support in multilateral organizations. Keeping in view the recent deterioration in US-Russia relations, there is a possibility that Russia will try to reemerge as a power by blaming America for damaging world peace and turn around European support away from it. China will be hesitant to allow growing American influence in their backyard after their interference in resource rich Iraq and access to oil reserves of Central Asian states. China might not come out openly in support of Pakistan but it will not refrain from bolstering military supplies to it. India understands that any damage to territorial integrity of Pakistan will not only agitate its 200 million strong Muslim populations but also severely hurt her economy.

America should understand that it is in Muslim character that as soon as an existential threat emerges whole nation unites against the larger enemy forgetting their internal conflicts. Pakistan is the second largest Muslim country with one of the strongest and most trained armed forces. Pushing Pakistan towards an open conflict will cost unimaginable loss both in terms of money, people and diplomatic relations. American law makers should learn to behave more like peace seeking diplomats rather than weapon yielding extortionist.

Friendship develops over a long time and vanishes within moments. Few years ago America declared Pakistan a most favored ally after NATO. In diplomatic terms it meant that America believed that people of Pakistan are true friends that have stood the test of time. But apparently that friendship has not lived up to their expectations. They are now talking about attacking Pakistan regardless how mildly one puts it. The fast change in position comes at a time when government of Pakistan has done more than their fair share of efforts to curtail terrorist activity. American citizen are afraid of a future terrorist threat while people of Pakistan live it on a daily basis with a tremendous loss of innocent lives. Action against terrorist is as important for Pakistan as it might be for the people of USA with or without their aid.

America fully understands history of fragile relations between India and Pakistan which went to war three times during their 60 years history. America acknowledges that Kashmir conflict can become a flash point for nuclear confrontation between the two nations. Despite these facts it has decided to sign a nuclear treaty with India without enough safeguards in place to ensure it will not be used for development of nuclear armament. This can become an impetus for arms race in the region as well as a direct threat to Pakistan. This is a material breach to security of a nation which has been designated as a most favored nation status after NATO by US.

In diplomatic nomenclature, that has developed over thousands of years, once there is substantial change in the attitude or position of a nation towards another nation it triggers renegotiations of all agreements. Considering recent change in American foreign policy it is time for Pakistan to rethink their support for war on terror.

First step government of Pakistan has to take is to understand context, definition and objectives of war on terror. Terror defined by America may not necessarily mean the same to Pakistan, its people, territory or geopolitical situation. For its own survival Pakistan has to fight extremist, sectarian and ethnic militancy. It is her fight for survival and would like to handle it on her own terms without interference from other countries. Many countries, like Spain, Italy and Canada, have already changed their position on American war on terror and pulled out their forces from Iraq.

It is required of a friend to be frank and candid when it comes to advice, help and guidance. American legislators are debating whether war in Iraq and Afghanistan has curtailed terrorist threat or fuelled it even more. Pakistan should act as a true friend and point out that war on terror can not be won through weapons. Throughout recorded history weapons have only produced misery for mankind. It is time for all nations to sit together and negotiate a lasting peace.

US-Pakistan relations: The Pakistani impasse
(October 12, 2007)

On October 10, 2007 US Congress's Armed Services Committee held a hearing to understand political situation in Pakistan. It does not bode well for Pakistan that this hearing was conducted by armed services committee instead of foreign relations committee. This suggests that policy of preemptive military strike inside Pakistan has broader appeal inside US Congress. Witnesses invited to the hearing included among others Hussain Haqqani, a scholar from Carnegie Center for international Peace. Congressional panel asked probing questions to get an insight into political situation of Pakistan and to formulate future approach towards it. American scholars presented a dooms day scenario with fewer chances of success. Mr. Haqqani, a Pakistani scholar, on the other hand emphasized that long held American approach to support military dictators has to be blamed for current crisis. He advised congressmen to focus more on providing assistance to ensure provision of basic social needs including healthcare, education and job creation. As an intellectual with political ambitions Mr. Haqqani used this platform to lobby for ascension of Benazir Bhutto as a Western friendly liberal who might be a better alternative to a military ruler.

On October 11th Najam Sethi, editor of The Friday Times, in his op-ed piece in The Wall Street Journal advised American policy makers that formation of a military-civil coalition government by General Pervez Musharraf and Benazir Bhutto is their best bet in prevailing environment. Sadly he remarked that free and fair elections might not be in American interest as it might give religious parties greater political powers. This could result in Pakistan pulling out from deeply unpopular war on terror leaving America alone to tackle with issues in the region. Same scenario is witnessed in Turkey, Algeria and Palestine where Islamist parties have gained popularity among voters to gain parliamentary majority in recent elections.

For large part of its history Pakistan is ruled by military rulers who were supported and aided by successive American administrations for one or the other reason. It is obvious that a soldier will always aspire to have best weapons rather than consider farm equipment for an agricultural society. American has feed this greed for best weapons by selling billions of dollars of military equipment. America lost his credibility with Pakistanis by suspending US AID program in 1990s which was supporting projects in social sector. And recently Amnerica signed a nuclear treaty with India despite strong reservations from Pakistan that it could tilt the balance of power in the region and result in an arms race.

A policy focusing on individuals can not produce deep rooted friendship between any two countries. America has openly supported coalition of Benazir Bhutto and General Musharraf. This has further tarnished its image in Pakistan as it is no secret that previous Benazir governments have been engaged in corrupt practices. Armed forces of Pakistan have been a symbol of unity for the nation but they have lost credibility among its own people because of their continued operations in North Waziristan under American pressure.

America can either continue to support proxy rule through their puppets or facilitate formation of a government elected by people. Popular leaders will have a better chance to go back to their constituents seeking help to fight extremism. History shows puppets do not command mass support and eventually fail jeopardizing the strategic interest of their allies as well.

It is quite apparent that in the foreseeable future Pakistan will continue to play an important role for the US in the region. This demands that America takes a long term view of her relationship with Pakistan and instead of relying on military cooperation develop grass roots level contacts with local politicians and policy makers through exchange of delegations. It should consider a free trade agreement with Pakistan which could provide much needed economic boost to alleviate poverty. To counter infiltration of conservative religious seminaries America should provide help in development of modern education system.

Almost three quarters of Pakistan's population rely on agriculture which lacks capital investment in modern farming. America could reach out to rural masses to initiate a farming revolution that will not only uplift economic well being of the poor but also create a positive image for it. In last few decades cultural exchanges between America and Pakistan has been nonexistent. These cultural exchanges could create better understanding between these nations.

Pakistan faces internal and external threat to its solidarity as well as a young population struggling with poverty and unavailability of opportunities. Extremism is still on fringes but wide spread poverty can fuel its spread to all of Pakistan. We have to take a long term view and offer a better ideology to the nation nurturing our deeply routed values of family, dignity and mutual respect. Failure is not an option this time.

US-Pakistan Relations: tunnel vision
(November 1, 2009)

In last one year, Pakistan has not attracted as many foreign tourists as it has US State Department big Whigs. American Special Envoy Holbrooke is there almost every other week. Senate foreign Relations Committee Chair Senator John Kerry was there recently to shed light on the provisions of Kerry-Lugar-Bergman bill. And this week the most influential of all of them former first lady and current Secretary of State Hillary Clinton was there for a much talked about visit.

Despite all these high profile visits it seems that gulf between the two nations is widening rather than abating. Reasons are both historical and current. Historically Pakistan blames America for abandoning it during 1965 war with India and responded slowly to curtail Indian interference in East Pakistan in 1971 that resulted in succession of Bangladesh. In current era it blames America for imposing a proxy war on it costing innocent lives in drone attacks.

US-Pakistan might have experienced bumps in their long relationship but Pakistanis must remember that a lot of their economic progress relies on Americans. It is home to one of the largest expatriate Pakistani community which is close to 750,000 by some estimates; US universities enroll one of the largest number of Pakistani students after UK; US health care industry employs over 15000 Pakistani doctors; American consumers purchase an estimated $3.5 billion worth of Pakistani merchandize out of her total exports of US$ 17 billion; and Pakistani Americans send over $1.6 billion in foreign remittance every year.

These facts should make Pakistan realize that America is a strategic partner in trade and geopolitics. Based on its importance, it is imperative that both government and opposition political parties should have a unified foreign policy position. Both Republican and Democratic Parties of America have agreed on a joint policy towards Pakistan as demonstrated by formulation of the Kerry-Lugar bill by Democratic Senator John Kerry and Republican Senator Richard Lugar.

In their pronouncements Pakistani opposition leaders should refrain from using vocabulary that is undiplomatic and that can damage long term bilateral relations. An important relationship should not and can not be defined by one bill or one administration.

Friendship does not mean agreeing all the time nor does it mean that one party dictates and other accepts. It means speaking with an open heart and mind to share ideas and form joint strategies to promote mutual interests. Pakistan must try to convince Americans that Afghanistan is a regional problem and all stakeholders in the region should be invited to the negotiating table. Pakistan must demonstrate that it is a country of moderates who are entangled in a web of extremism that is not entirely of their making although they did make some decisions in past that seem unwise in hindsight.

In early 1970s, Pakistan had opened doors of cooperation between America and China that did not had diplomatic relations. Pakistan can once again play that role by bringing Iran and America to a table to sort out their differences and reduce tensions. Iran has borders with both Afghanistan and Iraq that makes it even more important that these two countries should talk. European Union is not a right platform for this. A regional conference involving Iran, China, India, Russia, Pakistan, Afghanistan and America could achieve many objectives including agreements on Iran's nuclear program and stabilization of Afghanistan & Iraq.

No country can expect to grow economically if it faces terror threats on a daily basis and whose neighbors are hostile towards it. Economic growth requires peace, stability and continuity. Pakistan has weak political institutions, ineffective law & order and narrow industrial base. If Pakistan wants to achieve long term prosperity it must allow its democracy to flourish, modernize its police and educate its masses.

Pakistani nation has shown its resilience and sense of unity under conditions of duress and crisis. All it needs now is an able leadership that makes nation building their top priority.

US-Pakistan Relations: Views are not news
(November 20, 2009)

Prominent American journalist Seymour Hersh wrote an article in The New Yorker magazine raising questions about safety of Pakistani nuclear weapons program. After reading that article the question that immediately came to mind was "what's American foreign policy position towards Pakistan?" because after trade, security is the next big item on bilateral diplomatic agenda. It is common knowledge that there is strong nexus between American policy makers and prominent journalist. When policy makers need favorable public opinion then influential journalists are instructed to promote it in their op-ed pieces. If we accept validity of views expressed by Mr. Hersh to be those of Senior US administration officials then it is evident that diplomacy between these two countries is failing miserably and that is more dangerous than nuclear weapons falling into hands of terrorists.

Other disturbing view that is expressed in the article is equating religious practice with fundamentalism. If a soldier or an officer gives up alcohol or visits mosque regularly then he is presented as a danger as there might be an extremist streak in his soul.

Third disturbing item is that US State Department has relinquished their lead to US Defense Department on South Asian affairs which traditionally should be their domain. Professional soldiers are trained to wage good wars and use weapons as means of achieving peace. They can not be expected to engage in developing mutual understanding, diplomatic negotiations and security pacts.

Most damaging piece of the article is presentation of Pakistani senior officials and army generals as only interested in goodies rather than protecting the sovereignty of their country. This view is not entirely Mr. Hersh's fault our policy makers have not been able to articulate their position in any other language but dollars and cents.

But if money is made an integral part of diplomatic relations then it should not be expected that goodwill will remain after money is spent. Then America should not label blame that Pakistanis don't have a better view of them as there is always a hangover and headache after a good night out.

Mr. Hersh repeatedly mentions that Pakistani officials expressed reservations that Americans might share their secrets with India. He did not however mention any reference to General Stanley McCrytal's report which states that growing influence of India in Afghanistan could act counter to American interests in the region. Mr. Hersh also did not report that US officials gave any assurances to alleviate these concerns of sharing information with India. This indirectly validates Pakistani position.

America as a superpower has interest in South Asian region which is understandable. But the question she has to ask is what will be the driving force of their foreign policy to maintain and safeguard her interests. During cold war most favored approach was containment. It seems in this post cold war era, to fight with rising tide of stateless actors, most favored weapon is drone.

The problem with drones is that it might achieve a short term objective but in long term it creates more potential terrorists from among relatives of those innocent civilian deaths that are labeled as collateral damage. On the other hand, errors are bound to happen when foot soldiers stationed in foreign lands are expected to make split second decision whether a person approaching them is a friend or a foe.

During my visits to Pakistan and my meetings in America, I have asked one question from people of influence, what is American interest in Afghanistan? Most common response I got is to fight terrorist. But if that is true then it is a civil law enforcement issue. This work is responsibility of Federal Bureau of Investigation (FBI) and other civilian law enforcement agencies in America.

A strong government with credibility in Afghanistan should be able to control terrorist criminals. Military presence in Afghanistan has produced a geopolitical power imbalance that is creating security anxiety in Iran, China and Russia. It is highly unlikely that these countries are sitting idle while America tries to entrench itself in the region by twisting arms of Afghan and Pakistani governments.

Withdrawal of American forces will be the deepest blow to promoters of extremism. American media has tried to play the card of division in Iraq, Afghanistan and Pakistan but they have failed to achieve that objective. America can not afford to achieve control of hearts and minds through their drones and technologically superior soldiers. They should rather promote their values of equal opportunity, freedom of expression and liberty. This is a more powerful message which was deployed during struggle against communism.

As for Pakistan, they made a wrong choice of losing the status of non-alignment when they succumbed to American pressure to break all rules of diplomacy and accept terms dictated by Secretary of State Colin Powel. Now they are viewed with suspicion by their neighbors as a satellite of America which creates a security risk of its own.

Additional Comment: Article of Mr. Seymour Hersh can be found at the following URL:

http://www.newyorker.com/reporting/2009/11/16/091116fa_fact_hersh

US-Pakistan Relations: Diplomatic reset
(June 18, 2011)

Since its inception Pakistan's foreign policy has been dominated by paradigm of security which provided military establishment an upper hand in its execution. Recent failures of security institutions have initiated a debate that civilian leaders should be allowed free hand in formulating foreign policy. This is probably second time in Pakistan's history, first it was 1971 after separation of East Pakistan, that military establishment is on the defensive and does not enjoy mass support for its interference in non-military functions. Key questions to address in foreign policy development are what are our national interests? What is our domestic situation? And what is our regional role? In short term Pakistan should seek to reduce tensions with its immediate neighbors, strengthen alliances with strategic partners and seek membership of economic blocks. In long term, Pakistan's foreign policy should be interplay of three objectives i.e. economic growth, domestic security and promotion of peace in South Asian region. In light of this strategy it is important to reevaluate our key relationships.

Current phase of US-Pakistan relations started after 9/11 terrorist attacks when America took an aggressive stance against Afghanistan and Iraq for harboring terrorism. It is now clear that Military President Pervez Musharraf, who needed international recognition for his government, accepted US terms of engagement without in-depth consultations with the politicians, diplomats and security experts. There is much speculation about a secret deal between Pakistan and US to allow drone strikes on terrorists inside its borders. Although there is no significant evidence of such agreement but in its absence, American drone attacks will be classified as acts of war against a sovereign nation which has far greater consequences. Collateral damage caused by drone attacks and unilateral action to kill Osama bin Laden has considerably damaged American image as an ally among Pakistanis.

Despite setbacks it is an important relationship to maintain and grow. America provides important diplomatic support in multilateral institutions like IMF, WTO and United Nations.

America supplies a significant portion of military hardware to Pakistan as well as economic aid. Pakistan's relationship with America at best can be termed as transactional rather than strategic. A long history of diplomatic relationship has not transpired into cultural, social and intellectual interactions. In absence of this human factor the relationship will always be oriented towards short term interest rather than a true alliance of friends based on mutual trust, respect and national interest. Pakistan must reconsider its strategic priorities with America and seek greater cooperation in fields of student exchanges, cultural development, encourage foreign direct investment rather than aid and emphasis on technology transfer.

China is not only a neighbor but considered an all weather friend of Pakistan. After assassination of Osama in Abbottabad, China came out strongly in support of Pakistan and recognized its contributions in war on terrorism. China is backing permanent membership of Pakistan in Shanghai Cooperation Organization (SCO) which will not only help her economically but reduce some of the security fears it has. Despite international pressures China has provided Pakistan nuclear power plants and missile technology.

Military cooperation has resulted in joint developed of fighter aircraft JF-17. That plane was successfully inducted into Pakistan Air force as well as secured orders for 150 planes from other countries.

It must be pointed out here that although China has stood with Pakistan in times of peril that does not mean that she will subordinate her national interests for Pakistan. A look at China's foreign policy initiatives suggests that it is seeking to resolve its border conflicts with India and has advised Pakistan to resolve Kashmir issue amicably. China has not objected to inclusion of India in SCO which is an indication that it recognizes her regional role.

China has economic interest in Afghanistan and Central Asia. Pakistan provides a good logistical route to access these natural resources as well as provide a trade route to these new markets for its merchandize. While developing this important relationship, Pakistan must inform America that it is not at the cost of their interests as it is not a zero sum game.

In last decade, India has gained world wide recognition for opening up its economy, resolve internal conflicts and emerge as an important contributor in multilateral organizations. Russia and USA has announced their support for the Indian candidacy as permanent member of UN Security Council. Pakistan has to understand that reducing tensions with India is in its own self interest. Pakistani diplomats must take into account that India fully understands that its policy towards her is keenly watched by its 200 million strong Indian Muslim community. Pakistan should improve its trade ties with India while maintaining active negotiations to resolve Kashmir, Sir Creek and access to water issues.

Afghanistan has traditionally been a supporter of Indian position in multilateral organizations. Their historic relation goes far beyond 1947 when Pakistan came into existence. India has provided economic aid to Afghanistan to the tune of 1.2 billion dollars and is willing to offer more. On the other hand, Afghanistan appreciates that its economic survival is based on its friendship with Pakistan. Corner stone of Afghan-Pakistan diplomacy should be to negotiate a security agreement which formally recognize the Durand line as an international border, non aggression against each other and military cooperation. This agreement should be followed by a bilateral free trade agreement.

Iran-Pakistan relationship should be modeled after Turkish-Iran model whereby both countries enjoyed peaceful coexistence for over 360 years through recognition of borders and increased trade. Iran could be a major energy supplier as well as a market for Pakistani textiles and other merchandize.

Pakistan should focus inward to grow its economy, improve quality of life of its citizen, strengthen internal security and build strong state institutions. These objectives can not be achieved until her foreign policy is realigned to reduce tensions and improve relations. A senior diplomat once defined their strategy as "we have only two categories of countries. Friends and potential friends".

Background: In 2008 presidential elections it became clear that American people were tired of Iraq war especially since economy was faced with a recession producing high unemployment and rising government debt. Democratic Party candidate Barack Hussein Obama and Republican Party candidate Senator John McCain contested on the platform of opposing and supporting the war respectively. This article was written a week before people went to vote.

Obama Administration: What should be US foreign policy?
(September 26, 2008)

New American Administration will be elected on November 4th when voters will elect their 44th president. Other than economic recession, challenges faced by the incoming administration will be realignment of foreign policy with war in Iraq at the center of the debate. American foreign policy is largely driven by three main interests. First, America believes that ideals of human liberty and freedom should be promoted in the form of democracy and free markets. Second, America wants to maintain its economic growth by ensuring access to markets, uninterrupted supply of energy and natural resources. Third, America believes that security of its people and homeland is contingent upon preemptive actions around on non-state organizations like Al Qaeda.

Ideals of human liberty and freedom are not political objectives but rather values that are promoted by all religions including Christianity and Islam. These noble ideas are the basic premise of creation and make it a mainstay of human society. This means that societies should be eager to participate and join hands with America in protecting these ideals. This can only be achieved if she is able to maintain respect of a true leader without a strong bias towards its own interest or allies.

Accepting Palestinian right of return and abandoning support of autocratic rulers would be two important steps in this direction.

Similarly, bringing change within a society requires patience and perseverance rather than resorting to a quick fix. Military intervention to remove an autocratic regime at the cost of innocent lives does not bring social change required for emergence of a stable society. It would be wise for America to adopt a policy of engagement and negotiation to promote ideals and resolve issues. This will earn her the respect it deserves as bastion of liberty, freedom and equal rights.

Exponential rise of oil prices and its negative impact on American society has driven the point home that energy security is important for economic growth. Sending militaries in Middle East to ensure steady supply of oil can not solve this issue in long. China and India with close proximity to Middle East are eager to out bid anyone for this resource. On the other hand Russia is playing this card to its advantage by exerting influence on energy rich Central Asian states to develop a pricing and supply mechanism. America should realize that they can solve their energy problem by adjusting their life styles giving up on gas guzzling SUVs for smaller cars while at the same time making investment in research and development of alternate greener energy sources.

For last eight years an important focus of American foreign policy has been securing lives and property from terrorist threats. America is gifted with natural barriers in the form of Atlantic and Pacific Ocean to prevent any direct military threat to its home land. To further augment this defense America formed North Atlantic Treaty Organization (NATO) with its Western allies. This cold war era edifice could become a new flash point with reemerging Russia if membership is extended to Georgia and Ukraine with American support.

After the break up of USSR in 1991, Russia needs a neutral buffer zone between its bounders and Western Europe with which it fought many wars over centuries. Expansion of NATO should be reconsidered by the incoming administration if they would want to avoid emergence of another cold war. This NATO expansion would force Russia to reinvigorate their long forgotten WARSAW pact with some new friends and allies.

Other important corner stone could be to reestablish credibility of multilateral platforms to resolve issues. It has become apparent that ignoring UN to pressure Saddam regime was a foreign policy mistake resulting in tremendous loss of goodwill, treasure and lives. America should redouble its efforts to put UN reforms on fast track so that it becomes an effective organization in solving international issues. One such step would be reconstitution of Security Council to bring it more in line with new world realities. UNSC should be reconstituted to add more permanent members and offer observer status to Organization of Islamic Cooperation (OIC).

America needs to redefine its meaning of a terrorist by removing her emphasis that somehow Islamic faith has religious edict in support of inhuman acts. A faith can not attain a global following if it is not driven by truth and human values. By labeling terrorists as Islamic implicate whole Muslim world as suspects until proven guilty. A terrorist is a criminal with no real understanding of Islam or any other faith. The recent monk movement in Burma shows that it is not religion but political injustice that forces peaceful people to take an extreme position. Redefining terrorist will not only help America regain its lost respect among Muslims but will inspire other governments to cooperate in this fight without fearing a backlash from masses. A bomb going off anywhere is immediately labeled as Islamic terrorism without carefully considering evidence. This negative perception of a large innocent majority creates a moral dilemma for people which ultimately results in sympathizing with an underdog that is looking for a popular support. A terrorist in most situations is a product of poor governance and bad politics.

Resolution of Arab-Israel conflict, occupation of Kashmir, Iraq war and withdrawal of NATO forces from Afghanistan would help improve American image and contribute towards world peace. America has military presence in Germany, Korea, Japan, Iraq, Oman, Bahrain, Saudi Arabia and Afghanistan. Maintaining these military bases creates an impression of imperialism that turns popular opinion against them.

Use of soft power through economic, cultural and diplomatic relations would go a long way in ensuring lasting security.

If prime reason for a governments' existence is to provide good life for its community then American government is failing miserably. Economic meltdown can be blamed on foreign policy. It is now apparent that America could have avoided invasion of Iraq as it took away valuable resources from local economy. It will be a mistake for incoming president to change the label of war from Iraq to Afghanistan. Instead, objectives of eradicating terrorist could be achieved by supporting local governments to fight it through indigenous efforts.

America is the last best hope for humanity to achieve peace. Stakes are too high for the world. We can all hope that sensibility will overcome emotion and a new approach will be adopted. Political satirist Jon Stewart said it all when he commented in one of his programs that America will always be threatened by 19 people, referring to 9/11 hijackers, who want to commit harm but in eradicating those 19 it can not have an unfavorable opinion among rest of the world.

Background: Immediately after inauguration President Barack Hussein Obama appointed former CIA analyst and counter terrorism expert Bruce Riedel to prepare an extensive review of Afghan war and provide strategic options available. There were media reports that US military planners were seeking a surge of 30000 forces to contain Afghan insurgency while the President preferred to commit a smaller number. The Riedel report, released in March 2009, blamed Pakistan for supporting Afghan Taliban. The report also suggested that Taliban leadership is operating from southern Pakistani city Quetta.

Obama Administration: Afghan War- Cat on a tin roof
(December 2, 2009)

Cat is finally out of the bag. After protracted deliberations President Obama announced his Afghan policy in a speech to West Point Cadets on December 1st, 2009. In first part of his speech he defined that mission in Afghanistan is "disrupting, dismantling and defeating Al Qaeda and its extremist allies". In the same speech he announced withdrawal of American forces by mid 2014. He said without doubt that Al Qaeda leadership is based in Pakistan. Combining the two elements could mean that war will be fought in the desert and hills of Pakistan for next eighteen month.

For quite sometime Obama Administration officials and American media has proclaimed that the leadership of Al Qaeda and Taliban have shifted to Quetta from Afghanistan. The question that comes to mind is Why Quetta? During Soviet occupation mujahedeen were recruited and trained in Federally Administrated Tribal Areas (FATA). This means that Taliban not only know that terrain but also have deep friendships and family relationships in that area. This defies the logic that Quetta is their place of choice for a command center.

Choice for Quetta should be taken in a different perspective. America has long standing interest in the region as it gives them a leverage to have influence on oil rich Central Asian States as well as keep an eye on China, Russia and Iran.

American strategic planners build scenarios for 25 to 30 years horizon. They knew from the beginning that Afghanistan is hostile to foreign occupation and a large presence there will be costly in life and treasure. In 2001 they initiated Afghan campaign with a relatively small force to overthrow Taliban regime to gain a foot hold. This foothold was important to find a permanent base for long term.

Baluchistan is suitable for American interests for many reasons. First it is a vast area with a relatively small population of only 11 million as compared to 34 million in Afghanistan. It is largely desert and plains which are easier to control than hills and mountains of Afghanistan. It has an established port that could be used for logistic support. It will enable America to monitor sea trade going out of Iran. To prepare infrastructure to support separatist elements America allowed India to establish consulates along Pakistani border in Afghanistan. Pakistan has blamed these consulates for providing resources for escalation of separatist sentiments in Baluchistan. These separatist might be more willing to welcome American bases in return for a support to their separatist agenda.

One might argue that America and other Western countries have publicly stated that maintaining territorial integrity of Pakistan is one of their prime objectives. But history tells us a different lesson. During World War I Britain assured Arab separatist that Arabia will be left united if they supported them against Ottoman Turks who allied with Germany. After the end of war those resistance leaders were assassinated and Arabia was broken into small states that form much of Middle East today. In World War II Britain gave assurances to Poland that their territorial integrity will be ensured after the end of war while at the same time they were negotiating a secret deal with Russia to allow it to absorb large parts of Poland. These are just two examples from a long history of broken promises.

There is a misconception in Pakistan that India is disappointed with American announcement to work with her.

This is a mistaken view; India is fully on board with this strategy and was taken in confidence during visit of Indian PM Manmohan Singh. America knows that historically Afghans have had good relations with India. These relations have strengthened during Karzai government because of an Indian aid package of over a billion dollars for reconstruction efforts. On the other hand, Taliban feels let down by Pakistan when she decided to provide logistic support for NATO forces in Afghanistan and initiation of counter terrorist campaign in FATA. This will help India gain friends in Taliban and forge an alliance with them. This will be a strategic asset if American decides to form bases in Baluchistan.

These developments might look bleak from Pakistani perspective but there are many options available to counter this development. First Pakistan should quickly put an end to their operation in Waziristan and mend any broken ties with their Pashtun tribes. Second, Baluchi population understands that their tribal Sardars are more interested in their own financial benefits rather than improving their lives. Baluchis will never support presence of foreign forces on their land and seek separation from Pakistan. This sentiment was demonstrated when America announced inclusion of Quetta as a probable drone attack target. They do feel let down by Pakistani governments which can be corrected if moderate Baluchi leaders are engaged in preparation of a wide ranging Baluchistan package. Third, Pakistan has to engage with its friends in the region especially China to create an alternative platform for the resolution of Afghan situation. Pakistan must resist temptations to become part of any initiative promoted by UK or EU. Participation in it will give a signal to other stakeholders in the region that Pakistan's interest lies with the West.

Superpowers make designs for their own interest but realities on the ground move faster than anticipated. Pakistan will be facing a rough ride in next eighteen months but she has the capacity and ability to emerge out of it unscathed. All it needs is the unity among masses that could pressure hands of proxy rulers to refrain from making deals with their own personal interest in mind.

Background: By the end of 2010 President Obama had announced pull out of American forces from Iraq and gave a schedule of drawdown from Afghanistan. To improve relations with Muslims, he made a historic address in Cairo on 24ᵗʰ June 2009 titled "A New Beginning". It became start of the emergence of new Middle East.

Obama Administration: America going forward
(November 9, 2010)

Last week President of United States Barak Obama visited India and announced its support for her candidacy as a permanent member of UN Security Council. Earlier in October, it held a strategic dialogue with Pakistan which was dominated by military brass on both sides. American engagement with these nations is viewed with interest by international observers to gauge direction of her foreign policy in South Asia. Allocation of US$ 2 billion military aid for Pakistan without any significant announcement of a civilian part indicates that security priorities are still a primary focus.

American foreign policy rests on three pillars, purchasing power of American consumers; destructive potential of American weapons and appeal of American values of freedom, liberty and free speech promoted. These are promoted through her diplomatic dominance of multilateral institutions UN, WTO and World Bank.

During cold war Union of Soviet Socialist Republics (USSR) provided a counter weight to America on military & diplomatic fronts while lacking an economic clout. This impediment was removed when USSR was dismantled and disappeared. This resulted in a new world order in which America would run free with her international dominance. Peak of this power was reached, immediately after 9/11, when America decided to ignore multilateral institutions to impose war on Iraq and Afghanistan. These wars demonstrated wrath of its weapons but in the process also exposed their limitations and weaknesses.

Appeal of American values was tested when it was know that case for Iraq war was based on a pack of lies. Human right violations in handling of Iraqi prisoners of war further eroded ethical base of military operations. Erosion of Economic power was a corollary of huge budget deficits produced by ever growing war expenditure. This resulted in curtailed purchasing power of consumers further dampening American influence.

If American power is waning then what will be the world order in coming decades? Chinese leaders in their media interviews have down played its ascension as a superpower to provide a counter weight to America in a bi-polar world. China has taken a back seat to international conflicts in Afghanistan, economic sanctions on Iran and Middle East peace process further demonstrating its inward looking policy. Despite becoming second largest economy in the world, Chinese leaders find their hands full in dealing with large portions of their populations still below poverty line. An urbanized emerging middle class is challenging social and political status quo. Brazil, India, Russia & South Africa, other members of BRICs countries, are all struggling with their own internal issues in managing their fast growing economies.

This inability of other powers to act on a global platform is an opportunity for America to rationalize its policies to maintain its position of a sole power.

Election of Mr. Obama, as first minority President, was a big boost to American image as a country with equal opportunity for all. Since Obama administration took oath, in January 2009, American foreign policy is driven by improving its international image especially among Muslims. President Obama's stance on approving ground zero mosque and his speech in Cairo ware parts of this effort. Nobel Committee's award of Peace Prize to President Obama was West's efforts to put him on a high pedestal to end wars. After over 10 years of direct military operations, it seems that it is moving towards an environment of proxy wars through its allies and friends. Sale of American weapons to Saudi Arabia and Pakistan will help maintain military influence in these countries.

Third element of foreign policy is strength of economy. Economic recovery is contingent upon reduction of budget deficit, reduction in unemployment and growth in domestic demand. After November 2010 mid-term congressional elections, the expectations are that Republicans will emerge as a majority party in congress and Senate. Despite this control of both houses it might be good politics for Republicans to approve tax hike proposed by Obama Administration to help in deficit reduction. If these measures fail they can blame it on Democrats in next presidential elections. Ending wars will help diverting resources to local stimulus package which will help in creating more jobs.

In light of our proposed scenario, America will start withdrawing its troops from Afghanistan next year, as previously announced by President Obama. This withdrawal does not mean it is abandoning the region rather the instrument of influence will change from weapons to proxies and diplomats. Rising influence of India in Afghanistan; influence of Indian-American in US administration; American refusal to include Kashmir on its Indian agenda; and civil nuclear deals is evidence that US is promoting India as its partner in the new South Asian order.

China may not want to play a role in world politics but it can not allow growing Indian influence in its own backyard. It will be wise for Pakistan to bring China to the table to find a viable solution of Afghanistan and keep itself relevant in the region. Pakistan should adopt a position of non-alliance and non-interference while spearheading objectives of regional peace and stability. This will help its international image, provide resources to uplift economy create more jobs, and improve internal law order and rebuilding of the infrastructure.

America needs a safe passage for its troops and equipment through Pakistan for which consent of military establishment will be a key factor. Announcement of 2 billion dollars of US military aid is to make them happy. In short term Pakistan can benefit by earning transit fee but in long term peace in Afghanistan would translate in emergence of Pakistan as a stable nation and economy.

End of war in Afghanistan is an opportunity to increase focus on putting our house in order by strengthening democratic institutions, resolving provincial issues and creating a stable economy. But to achieve all that requires a sincere, focused and capable leadership. Next elections are in 2013 that will be an opportunity for Pakistani voters to take it more seriously and elect leaders that can lead by example.

Background: This article was writing while US Presidential election was in progress. On media there were discussions of Red and Blue states; democratic and republican divide; conservative and liberal struggle.

American Society: Democracy- What democracy?
(June 28, 2004)

When tuning to a TV channel, whether in Pakistan or America, one word that is mentioned most often is DEMOCRACY. Democracy enables politicians to affect our lives in a most profound way. Democracy is defined in Webster's dictionary as: "a: government by the people; especially rule of the majority; b: a government in which the supreme power is vested in the people and exercised by them directly or indirectly through a system of representation usually involving periodically held free elections." If you refer to the Encyclopedia Britannica it is defined as: "literally, rule by the people (from the Greek demos, "people," and kratos, "rule"). A form of government in which the right to make political decisions is exercised directly by whole body of citizens, acting under procedures of majority rule, usually known as direct democracy." Now lets us examine how this concept is implemented in real life by considering two extreme examples one from America, which presents itself a bastion of democratic values, and the other Pakistan, which has struggled in establishing democratic institutions throughout its history.

In American form of democracy two majority parties namely Republicans and Democrats nominate their candidates to run for the office of the President, Senate and Congress. President is top elected official who exercises executive powers to make strategic and policy decisions that has to be ratified by lower and upper houses of Congress. President can use his power of veto to forestall a bill or a resolution.

President appoints around 4000 officials who run government commonly referred to as an Administration. Presidential and Congressional elections are held on a fixed date which is first Tuesday of November according to a schedule laid out in the constitution.

President is elected for 4 years and can run once for reelection for a maximum two terms. Each state is awarded electoral votes for each congress and senate seat. These Electoral College votes are allocated to a candidate who acquires 50%+1 vote in a particular state. The winning candidate has to acquire 50%+1 out of the total 538 electoral votes which comes out to 270.

American Senate is composed of 100 members with a quota of two seats for each State. Terms of senators are staggered so that every two years 33% senators seek reelection. These senators are elected for a term of six years through direct elections. Senators do not have term limits. Some US Senators are serving the nation for over 30 years. American Congress, lower house, has 435 members based on population estimates of US bureau of census. Each state has at least one member in the House. Congressmen do not have term limits but they have to seek reelection every two years.

It is expected that Congressional Representatives will support or oppose a bill based on their party affiliations. In some cases they vote contrary to their party position by gauging sentiments of their constituents through polls conducted by various media and non-governmental activist organization.

This system has inbuilt flaws which can result in political deadlock and undemocratic characteristics. This system is dominated by two political parties i.e. Republican and Democratic Party. This makes it prohibitively difficult for a person who may be qualified but does not want to use platform of the two parties. Theorists argue that during general elections the whole population could accept or reject a candidate, which nullifies effect of a faulty nomination process.

But what if there is more than one qualified candidate from a party who could serve their community. This approach of party nomination for highest executive office is a cause for division among the nation.

Elected representatives have to make compromises to maintain support from party members while making a decision for the whole nation, which is against tenet of democratic theory.

Why can't there be election for a President on a non-party basis since he has to lead the whole nation not just people from his own party.

Other fault is election by Electoral College vote while a winner could have lost in popular vote. This fault is magnified in close elections as we saw in November 2000 when Democratic Party presidential candidate Al Gore secured majority of popular votes nationwide but still lost to Republican Party candidate Mr. Bush based on Electoral College majority. Argument in favor of Electoral College is promoted by smaller state that wants to maintain their influence at the top through it. In absence of such mechanism they will lose out to larger states like New York, Texas and California which can substantially weaken the federation. Absence of Electoral College will create a bias for the president to tilt more towards states with higher number of electoral votes. One proposal debated by political scientist is to create a condition that certain percentage of State Electoral College votes are allocated to a candidate that secure nationwide majority rather than State winner take all method used now.

A democratic government has two roles to play. Their first role is to work as a custodian of national resources to manage them efficiently for betterment of people at large. It has to ensure there is equality in distributing the wealth of the nation. The other role is to draft legislation that could provide a level playing field for all citizens. In current democratic system in America there is minimal referral to the nation on matters of national interest, which is against tenet of democracy. In an ideal democratic system policy decisions should be referred to people for an approval. Getting ratification from Congress alone may be efficient but does not constitute approval of the majority of constituents.

This system can achieve some level of legitimacy if representatives communicate with voters to explain to them pros and cons of a pending policy decision and then let them decide in an election if they are for or against that policy. This system is implemented in a limited manner by city administrations when they need consent for issuance of a municipal bond or to undertake a major project like light rail project in Houston.

One argument against instituting national voting on policy is that once mandate is given to Representatives it is not necessary to go back frequently to voters for decisions for lack of resources. With advancement in technology it is now possible for governments to go back to the population to get their consent with minimal cost. Theses costs will still be much smaller than what America has spent for war in Iraq.

Pakistan is at other extreme of a democratic spectrum. It is a parliamentary form of government where members of National Assembly are elected by citizens in a direct party based election for a five years term. Members of the assembly then elect a Prime Minister, usually from a majority party, as Chief Executive of the Government. Prime Minister in turn selects his/her cabinet from among assembly members to run affairs of government. Legislative body is divided into a bicameral lower and upper house of National Assembly and Senate respectively. Each province has equal number of seats in senate whereas in national assembly seats are allocated based on population. Senators are elected indirectly by provincial assembly members for a term of six years. Head of state is President elected by an electoral college comprising of National and Provincial Assembly members.

Pakistan's democratic problems emanates from both lack of democratic tradition as well as an obsolete system. First and foremost problem is non-democratic nature of political parties. Second Prime Minister has to get a vote of confidence from national assembly, which results in horse-trading. Thirdly a weak judicial system does not ensure free and fair elections. Fourth non-democratic institutes with their own vested interest, for instance military and civil bureaucracy, influence out come of the election.

Background: Hurricane Rita is the fourth most intense tropical cyclone in American history. It happened within few months of Hurricane Katrina which devastated city of New Orleans and claimed over 1826 lives. Performance of city officials and Federal Emergency Management Agency (FEMA) was widely criticized for their slow response in providing relief and containing lawlessness. When Hurricane Rita hit Galveston and Houston city, once again city administrators were held responsible for chaos and mismanagement.

American Society: Hurricane Rita- lessons in chaos management
(September 26, 2005)

Scare of Hurricane Rita was one of those events that totally paralyzed 4th largest city of America Houston and it's surrounding areas. Fortunately, city was spared devastation that a hurricane of Rita's magnitude (category 3 according to US Federal Emergency Management Agency-FEMA) would have caused had it hit port of Galveston directly. But it did demonstrated cracks in administration in handling emergency situation at city, state and federal level. It was second time in a month, first with hurricane Katrina, when there was no coordination between government departments to ensure effective management of a heightened public state of fear.

It was obvious in all this mayhem that there was lack of coordination between various mayoral offices with their counterparts in State government. It has to be defined who will be incharge when a State of Emergency is declared so that all other administrators can coordinate with that official and his staff. Since emergency situations arise in a particular geographic area the most suitable person is Mayor of the city. Mayors are much more familiar with ground realities of their region than any other entity sitting in a state or federal capital. He/She should be the point man in all communication and actions. We have seen this scenario work effectively in the incidents of 9/11 when New York Mayor Rudy Giuliani rose above the situation and did not even allow governor to interfere in operations.

A Mayor should be given extraordinary powers, when a State of Emergency is declared, to be able to activate state and federal agencies required according to nature of the situation. It means that mayor's demand for a resource from another agency should be met without delay. In terms of legality of these powers, a Mayor can send request for grant of extraordinary powers from the Governor through a written request explaining reasons for such action. In case surrounding areas are also affected, mayors can form a mayoral committee and choose one person among them to lead the efforts.

Most large cities have divided their administrations into various districts represented by district Councilmen elected by people. When it was known that Rita might hit Houston these district councilmen should have initiated command centers in their districts to feed information to central mayor office about situation in their areas. These councilmen should have sent police to provide protection to gas stations to prevent vandalism and unrest. Many gas stations only have a staff of one or two persons at a time and are not equipped to handle panicked customers. Many gas stations decided to close, although filled with gas tanks, for fear of vandalism that added to panic and created artificial scarcity of gasoline.

Media did little to calm panicked residents. Each channel presented its own weather expert with over 12 different tracks for the storm, which is fine. What was worrisome was that at the end of each presentation they would say something to the effect "No roadwork in country can handle a mad rush of people". Such dramatization of facts by news media was done over and over again. Facts, of course are of great importance in such times but highly charged news could also endanger lives. Media channels, striving hard to heighten the drama, and to beat each other at it, broadcasted different messages instead of a unified message. To avoid this, when a state of emergency is declared, Mayor should form a media council to broadcast one message from all channels to reduce conflicting messages to residents. Media council can decide content and presentation of this emergency broadcast without interference from government officials.

Disaster in New Orleans by Hurricane Katrina was partly from the storm but largely from failure of levee system, which flooded the whole city. In Houston, various bayous present danger of flooding certain areas but there is no way a storm alone can disrupt the whole city life. Evacuation should have been more planned with people in flood zones instructed to evacuate first before others. Historical flood data about various zip codes is handily available to prepare an such plans. I heard a certain councilmen repeating after each call during news broadcast to evacuate city even if they were not in a flood zone. This kind of irresponsible statement was largely responsible for chaos on the roads.

Other failure observed in New Orleans was that people were out of water and food for many days. A similar situation was experienced in grocery stores in Houston where people started hoarding food sufficient for weeks and months creating a food crisis. Storm and flooding is only one form of a disaster there could be other incidents when city life is disrupted including terrorism. City should prepare a database of all major food and grocery stores and designate some of them as relief centers in case of emergency. These food stores should be provided protection by the army or local law enforcement officials. Supplies should be sent to these stores for distribution to people.

Last, but not least, is behavior of citizens. Largely, people were in good spirits and helped each other. In such crisis situations, people should get a few days worth of supplies so that there is some left for others. Stores should self impose rationing of essential food supplies when government announces a state of emergency.

Humans can not command nature to behave in a certain manner but they are certainly capable of devising systems and procedures that ensure that humanity does not suffer severely from these disasters. There is no perfect system but we learn lessons from each new experience and improve on it.

Background: Each year United States attracts large number of immigrants from around the world. America not only encourages legal immigration but also allows them to become naturalized citizens with full rights defined in the constitution. This social acceptance is termed as "the American Dream" which means that there will be no discrimination against any immigrant based on their race, religion or color. There are numerous rags to riches stories of immigrants. Apart from legal immigration there are a large number of illegal immigrants crossing long border with neighboring Mexico. According to some estimates there are an estimated 11 million undocumented immigrants. According to PEW Hispanic Center 56% of undocumented immigrants are Mexicans, 22% from other Latin American countries, 13% from Asia, 6% from Europe & Canada and 3% from rest of the world. In each election cycle immigration reforms is on top of manifestos of both Republican and Democratic parties but no viable solution has been found. Scope of this social problem is enlarging considering that children of these illegal immigrants are facing consequences of the actions of there parents.

American Society: impact of immigrants
(April 30, 2006)

In the year 1519, a small number of Spanish invaders, around 176, landed on shores of Mexico with an objective of plundering riches of the land. They faced an army of close to 10,000 too confident in their superior numbers but finally succumbing to weaponry of Spanish with help from local dissident tribal leaders. Since that day cultural mix of North America changed forever. European powers ruled Mexico until early 1810 when it was liberated from clutches of Spanish colonial power. American States of California, New Mexico, Arizona, and Texas were part of greater Mexican territory before they were annexed in a Mexican-American war from 1845-48.

Plundering of almost three centuries took its toll on culture of Mexico forever changing psyche of its people. It is now slowly emerging from this deep slumber and reclaiming its cultural heritage. Release of a Spanish language American anthem is a sign of that emerging trend. This has become a controversial issue even prompting American President to disapprove it. But this is a natural progression of a dynamic country.

Spanish-speaking immigrants from North and South America have changed cultural mix of America. Only recently, Spanish overtook African-Americans as the largest minority group in America. They will get further boost to their voting power if 11 million illegal immigrants get a right to citizenship debated in a reform bill. This will give them enough electoral power to influence policy decisions. Due to language barriers and low literacy Hispanics have traditionally participated in farming, construction, janitorial and landscaping services. This is going to change as these immigrants educate their next generation to rise on economic ladder. Proliferation of Hispanic TV broadcast, radio channels and newspapers suggest this rise in economic power.

If America wants to prevent increasing migration from its Southern neighbor, Mexico, it has to develop a multi-pronged strategy. First, it should encourage its industries to increase their investment in Mexico to create jobs. It should provide incentive to American farming industry to hire people on temporary work permits with the condition that these workers return to their homelands after the expiration of these permits. For Mexico remittances from America is one of the largest source of foreign exchange, approximately US$ 25 billion last year, which is even more than their oil production. As long as Mexico relies on these remittances it would not have an incentive to prevent border crossings. America should help Mexico find new markets for its exports to earn foreign exchange.

As far as Pakistani immigrant community is concerned, it has thrived in America starting from low paying jobs at gas stations, grocery stores, and limousine/cab services. Pakistanis are preferred for these jobs because of their English language advantage over Hispanics. Gradually, they have started moving upwards by owning those same stores and employing the next wave of immigrants from their homelands.

This scenario is changing by three emerging trends. First, as Hispanics overcome the language barrier and gain more confidence in their abilities, they would like to come out in the front from the back.

Secondly, the Patriotic Act will put Pakistanis at a disadvantage with the scrutiny of Muslim license applicants. And lastly, next generation of Pakistani-Americans, born and raised in America, is not interested in inheriting the gas station or 99 cents stores from their parents. They are moving to other business segments like technology & banking or seeking career in multinational corporations.

If Pakistanis want to maintain their economic profile, they must start thinking about their future in America. They should form a nationwide chamber of commerce to lobby with policy makers. Pakistanis should form investment groups to help young entrepreneurs to enter new industries. Indians have successfully created The Indus Entrepreneur (TIE) forum to provide a platform for Indian entrepreneurs. Few years ago Pakistanis created The Organization of Pakistani Entrepreneurs of North America (OPEN) to help technology start-ups but the bursting of technology bubble badly hurt its efforts. It is now time to reconstitute OPEN or create some new organization to help young Pakistanis in realizing their dreams. American-Pakistanis can form joint ventures with companies in Pakistan, not only to diversify their risks but also to improve the competitive edge for Pakistani products.

Times are changing fast around the world. Pakistani immigrants have to unite behind a common cause and prepare long term strategies to ensure a safe future for their coming generations.

Background: Anti-Muslim sentiments were on the rise because of labeling of terrorist as Islamic. Communities in many States are hesitant to allow building of mosques in their neighborhoods. Nine Zero Cultural center in New York and Temecula mosque became centers of national debate. I was one of the speakers at city hall hearing that considered approval of a mosque project in Temecula, California.

Speech at Temecula City Hall hearing to approve building of a mosque
(January 23, 2011)

Honorable members of the city council and fellow citizens

My Name is Abdul Quayyum Khan Kundi, I am a business owner in consumer technology sector.

When I was preparing my speech for today the question I had was, should I prepare a defense for building of a mosque or for continuation of the American Dream.

I decided to prepare an appeal for the later as it is a much nobler cause.

In recorded history of mankind there has been many great nations including Romans, Byzantines, Egyptians, Ottoman, British and in 20th Century United States. One common characteristic of all these nations was openness towards other religions and cultures. But sad fact is that most of these nations eventually faded into the dust bin of history. Common factor in their demise was eventual closeness of their societies to accept diversity of cultures.

United States in 21st century is faced with this dilemma of whether to continue with its American dream that attracts thousands of new immigrants to this land of opportunity or close their doors to certain religions and cultures.

The case in front of you today is a microcosm of that larger struggle. Your rejection of building this mosque and cultural center will hardly affect lives of people who are already living without it. But it will struck a nail in the heart of American Dream in persuasion of which many members of Muslim community came here leaving behind their childhood friends, parents and even wives and children.

Last week President Obama in his press conference with President Hu of China said: "We have some core values as Americans about universality of certain human rights like freedom of speech, freedom of religion and freedom of assembly that transcends cultures." I believe he truly represented America.

When I arrived in United States in January of 1998, I took a sub-way train ride in the great city of New York. After that ride of 15 minutes I sat in a park and thought for an hour which one of those fellow riders was an American. I saw Chinese, Indian, Korean, African America, Vietnamese, White and Arab. The whole world was there and that is the greatness of America. It is a place where people come to shine and in the process make this country great. And to get that shine they risk everything.

It is up to you today to decide if American Dream is still alive or it is on a death bed. I hope and pray that it survives as it is the shining star which inspired Martin Luther King to say "I have a dream".

Section IV:
Islam, Muslims & the West

Arab Spring: Muslim world- where are we heading?

(June 1, 2004)

Majority of Muslim countries have autocratic rulers while national assets are plundered by a handful of their cronies. Libya is ruled by a revolutionary authoritarian, Indonesia is reeling under corruption of Suharto era bureaucracy, Egypt has not seen change of power since Anwar Sadat was assassinated in 1980s. Much of the Arab world is in a strong grip of Monarchs who rule with medieval era principles. South Asia, which includes Pakistan, is ruled by military dictators for large part their history. If we look closely we can see similarities in social structure of most of these countries that supports continuity of these exploitative regimes. There is small group of people who maintain a strong hold on political power while another group are retaining power of the pulpit and define religious percepts biased towards their own twisted agenda. A band of industrialists have monopoly on wealth of the nation by providing support to these groups. Coalitions of these three despite their small numbers dictate destiny of the vast majority of population.

If we consider democracy as cure for all evil then we should give it a chance to prosper in the Muslim world. Establishment of democracy was one of pretexts for war in Iraq to create an example for other nations in Middle East. But democracy can not gain wide acceptance until the person sitting on the pulpit is sold on this concept. Resistance offered by Muqtada al Sadr in Iraq is one example to learn from. During renaissance in Europe similar struggle for power existed between Pope and the monarchy. Monarchy derived its divine entitlement to rule through endorsement of the church. As Europe became a colonial power and controlled vast dominions of non-Christians a need arose to separate religion from government in order to rule these colonies. Priests resisted erosion of their political power but were gradually phased out from affairs of government although it was not without bloodshed.

Economic greed was prime mover in expansion of the West in 18th and 19th centuries. Earlier in Islamic empire, on the other hand, religion became prime mover to expand into new territories. A consultative form of government, in early days of Islam, was later converted to a monarchy called Caliphate which exerted influence on Muslim states throughout Asia and Middle East. All rulers were required to get endorsement from the Caliphate who derived his power by acquiescence of religious scholars. Concept of Muslim umma was derived from common religious beliefs without giving thought to nationalistic tradition and culture. When caliphate was disbanded at the end of World War I, most of the Muslim states were colonies of Britain, France and Netherlands. These colonial powers ruled by accentuating religious differences between various sects notably Sunni and Shiite. They also created a ruling class by allocating to them property and revenue collection rights.

After World War II when these colonies gained independence, in a last ditch efforts to retain control, departing imperial powers installed their proxy rulers from among their chosen elites. That establishment is still surviving in one form or the other in most of the Muslim countries. Religious leaders who were left out in this power sharing felt betrayed and exercised their power of the pulpit to start movements against these governments. West provided support to authoritarian rulers to control masses against exploits of the religious leaders.

As percentage of younger population grew they were increasingly disappointed with their rulers. Muslim countries are rich in one or the other mineral resource. Arab world controls almost two third of known oil reserves. This national wealth was exploited for benefit of the few, which contributed to frustration of these youth. High unemployment, growing incidence of human rights violation and corruption became hallmark of Muslim countries. This disenfranchised youth became breeding ground for the exploits of religious leaders who were waiting to regain their political control lost during independence movements.

Recent control of parliaments by Islamist parties in countries like Indonesia, Turkey and Bangladesh is a sure sign of revival of religio-political parties. In Pakistan Mutahida Majlis-e-Amal (MMA), which is a combination of many small religious parties, has gained substantial number of parliamentary and provincial seats in general election in October 2002. Although they did not get a majority to form a government at federal level but they did form government in North West Frontier Province (NWFP).

Renaissance of the Muslim world can only happen if leaders make efforts to establish political institutions which give masses voice in formation of policies. Democracy in present form or any other form that suits local culture should be instituted. Governments should exercise greater control on curriculum of religious schools or madrassas, which has become breeding grounds for promotion of extremist ideas. Religious leaders use mosques as a power base to spread propaganda against government and established order. Awareness campaigns needs to be initiated to better inform people on religious exploits from the mosque. Corruption should be curtailed and merit established. Religion is universal, in the name of religion nationalistic tradition and values should not be lost. If West is interested in achieving global peace it should stop support for exploitative governments who violate human rights. It should share their democratic experience with rest of the world instead of seeking support from authoritarian rulers for short term gain.

Arab Spring: State of Muslims
(May 22, 2006)

Since 9/11, Western media and society at large seem to be at odds with Muslims. Every now and then there is an article published in a prominent newspaper citing causes of malice in Muslim societies. West wants to fix the Muslim world, just like it has wanted to correct every other civilization before ours, by imposing its homespun remedies. America considers democracy to be solution to all that ails the Muslim world while Europe feels freedom of speech is answer to all problems. Muslim leaders, aligned with West, are recommending their own solutions on somewhat similar lines; General Musharraf promotes enlightened moderation while Saudi monarchs support *Wahabi* conservatism. But no one seems to have the perfect answer to this dilemma of bridging gap between West and Islamic world.

Organization of Islamic Cooperation (OIC) has 57 member countries, which can largely be termed as the Muslim World although a large number of Muslims also reside in other countries as minorities. Only handful OIC member countries have functioning democracy. Three largest countries, by population, Indonesia, Bangladesh, and Pakistan have struggled with maintaining democracies. Despite controlling almost half of world's oil reserves Muslim world has large segments of populations living below poverty line. None of these countries can be termed as fully industrialized except for Malaysia and Turkey to some extent.

As we have witnessed Danish cartoon debacle, Muslims are quick to blame West for all its problems. Although West in the past have taken advantage of these countries by colonizing large parts of Africa & Asia or engaged in slave trade. Today West maintains its control on many parts of the world through proxy rulers and dictators. But real virus among the Muslim world is its own misunderstanding of the meaning of religion and the social system proposed by it.

Islam is the youngest religion among prominent religions of the world i.e. Christianity, Hinduism and Buddhism. All these religions have struggled with their own problems of mixing politics with religion. For many centuries Christian Clergy maintained political control until French revolution, which became benchmark for separating church from government. Once this was achieved it was much easier for people to become less emotional about rejecting religious taboos that made their societies conservative and orthodox. Once church lost its political power it had to struggle to maintain its importance. This irrelevance in society forced clergy to gain deeper understanding of the spiritual meaning of their religion to serve their communities.

Al-Qaeda and other terrorist organizations, with which Western media is so fascinated, are not religious but political movement that derives its appeal from largely impoverished Muslim youth by presenting West as an enemy and source of their misery.

They have used universal appeal of religion to cut across boundaries to gain recruits. Al-Qaeda has single handedly damaged the spiritual appeal of a peaceful religion that has never happened before in its history. Their political movement has brought more misery to the world of Islam than the damage it has inflicted on West.

In spiritual terms, it is imperative for each individual to seek truth about life, creation, unity of God and purpose of existence. But this is a quest that should be left to an individual to decide which path he/she wants to choose. Greek philosophers believed that after earning subsistence level earnings people should spend rest of their time with family and quest for knowledge. Christianity, Hinduism and Buddhism have all transformed over centuries. Followers of most of these religions look towards their preachers for spiritual guidance while they are busy running their daily lives which is governed by secular laws.

On the other hand poorly trained clergy in Muslim societies define spiritual meaning of their religion. They lace spiritual content with cultural taboos and politics, which has no relevance to actual message of the faith. This amalgamation of religion with politics has been a deadly combination when it is in hands of clergy that is trained in narrow science of theology. Only a handful of these clergy truly understand depth of the faith and its comparison with other religions. These clergy pressure governments to draft constitutions from religious tenets. Since most of Muslim countries are either dictatorships or kingdoms it is in the benefit of these rulers to control minds of the people through these clergy like in medieval Europe few centuries ago.

The worst thing that has happened in the Muslim world is appointment of mosque imams that have limited knowledge of the spiritual side of the religion. In order to keep their jobs these imams prefer to keep their audiences engaged in following a strict code of tradition through symbolism of dress and appearance rather than mentoring to be more spiritual. These Imams secure funds for their establishments from their disciples by presenting fearful scenarios of an afterlife if they fail to support spread of their particular message. A mosque is a community center where people gather to pray, network, share life experiences and comfort each other. At the appointed time of the prayer a person from among those present can come forward and lead the prayer. In order to maintain mosques administrators should be hired who can take care of maintenance of the place, its cleanliness and safeguard its assets.

A board should be established that certify Muslim scholars that can be hired by parents to tutor young children in matters of faith. These Muslim scholars should be well versed in all other religions, as well, so that they have clear understanding of spiritual side of religion in general and Islamic spirituality in particular. I sent a translation of Quran to an atheist European friend and asked to comment on it. The feedback was that it is as simple as a story book while Bible is complicated. This should sum up message of Islam for everyone. It is a simple religion made complicated by Imams of the mosque.

It is imperative for Muslims to resolve this conflict of religion and politics to come up with a form of government that is more in tune with advancement in science, technology, and economics. Islam does provide means to achieve this through Ijma or conference of Muslim scholars to debate, argue and formation of consensus. But Ijma is difficult as infighting between various schools of thought has resulted in numerous sects with each prophesying they are true bearer of the religion and rigid about accepting views of others. Although Sunni and Shiite are the two majority sects but even in those two sects there are various shades that don't agree with each other.

One positive outcome of 9/11 is the initiation of a debate among Muslims to take a second look at their societies and find solution to their problems. Next generation of youth that are going through this debate will be better equipped to manage their affairs and bring positive change.

Background: Israel started bombings of Hezbollah strongholds in Lebanon on 12th July 2006 which continued for 34 days. Israeli response was out of proportion to Hezbollah missile attacks and was condemned around the world. This war produced heavy casualties on Lebanese side including 500 Hezbollah Militia and 1191 civilian deaths while on Israeli side 121 soldiers and 44 civilian dead. Israel was held responsible for attacking a UN compound resulting in deaths of 5 officials.

Arab Spring: War & Peace
(July 28, 2006)

It seems that precarious balance between Israel and its neighbors is once again broken. Western media blame Hezbollah for breaking peace by ambushing Israeli soldiers killing some and kidnapping two. Israel retaliated with full force by bombarding Beirut for last 16 days and entering Lebanese territory with an objective to strike at the strongholds of Hezbollah. Skirmishes between Israeli militia and Muslim organizations have been going on forever without any real break. Israel has repeatedly bombarded Palestinian and Hezbollah positions during last 10-15 years killing many activist as well as civilians. Muslim resistance organizations are no match for military might of Israel. They have to resolve to gorilla tactics to retaliate against occupation of their territory and to get release of their prisoners held in Israeli jails. Figures are daunting, there are so far 1691 Lebanese killed while 165 Israelis lost their lives. Israel has so far sent 2000 air sorties to destroy already weak Lebanese infrastructure.

American diplomatic response to this conflict has been controversial. It is first time she refused to push Israel for a quick ceasefire. State department officials have in fact supported Israeli advancement into Lebanese territory. It serves two purposes. First, it takes attention away from Iraq war and provides a source to uplift public support for the administration. Secondly, it helps America to use Israel as a front line state to fight Muslim activist organizations in Middle East.

America has been quick to blame Syria and Iran for supporting Hezbollah thereby making them party to the conflict. This conflict helps Bush administration in gaining voter support in the upcoming congressional elections by validating their case for fight against terrorism.

International response has been mixed. Russia, France and Germany have condemned the aggression of Israel. United Nations Secretary General Kofi Annan has criticized bombing of Beirut and destruction of UN observation post.

Muslim countries in their official response are divided as always. Countries with significant American influence like Saudi Arabia, Jordan and Egypt have made Hezbollah responsible for this conflict. But most surprisingly institutions like Organization of Islamic Cooperation (OIC) and Arab League have not been able to become part of negotiations for a cease fire. OIC has only conducted an ambassadorial level meeting which issued a weakly worded communiqué to ask Israel to cease hostilities and allow initiation of humanitarian aid for civilians affected by this conflict.

So far there has been no emergency meeting of heads of Muslim states to form a united front to address this crisis in Middle East. Mostly Western countries have called a meeting in Rome without adequate Muslim representation to address this situation. OIC and Arab League should have been made part of these negotiations. Ourcome of that conference naturally was a failure.

Another dynamic in play here is that Muslims have lost trust in their governments to represent their interest in domestic and international affairs. They consider their governments to be non-representative, exploitative and agents of the West. Western media has continually questioned validity, ethics and moral values of Islamic faith labeling terrorist as Islamic terrorists. This has further alienated masses who are beginning to consider radical organizations as guardians of their faith against western aggression.

Militia organizations like Al Qaeda and Hezbollah understand this dynamic very well and use it to their advantage to gain finances, recruits and geographical protection. Since there is no Muslim country strong enough to stand up to military might of America and Israel, Muslims largely feel that gorilla fight is their only option to respond to armed aggression in their lands. They have seen this scenario play out in Afghanistan, Iraq and now in Lebanon where Hezbollah has withstood sophisticated armory of Israel.

A lasting peace can not be attained unless everyone agree that we have a serious crisis at hand which can quickly convert to a global war. It is a dangerous strategy by West to try to divide Muslims in Shiite and Sunni sects. They might be able to do that at the government level but masses understand this play and are united as one *Ummah*. Each passing day in Israel-Lebanese war is creating deeper support for Lebanese among Muslim populations. This could ultimately result in upheavals in countries with authoritarian rulers considered proxies of the west and introduction of more radical governments. This will result in more conflicts throughout the region.

Wars do not solve any conflicts. They are only used to vent anger and frustrations building up for decades. In the end peace is always attainted by sitting around a negotiating table to reach a compromise that is equitable and just. Israel's efforts to build walls and buffer zones will not ensure its security unless its neighbors see her as a friend and partner.

Background: On 18th December 2010 street protests started in Tunisia after a street vendor Mohamed Bouaziz self-immolated when police ill treated him. This became a precursor to a wave of uprising against dictators in Egypt, Libya, Bahrain, Yemen, Morocco and most recently Syria. These street agitations resulted in removal of long time dictators Husni Mubarak in Egypt, Maummar Gaddafi in Libya, Zine el Abidine Ben Ali in Tunisia and Ali Abdullah Saleh in Yemen. These developments were popularly termed as an Arab Spring.

Arab Spring: Awakening of the Muslim world
(February 12, 2011)

It seems that everyday newspaper brings news of a new uprising as masses are rising up against dictators in the Muslim world. First it was Tunisia and now Egypt. The next in line are Yemen, Jordan and Morocco. Syria and Saudi Arabia seems stable right now but no one knows for sure what storms are brewing under calm surface of the sea. Question we need to ask is what will be the outcome of these uprisings? How will it affect the Muslim *Ummah*? And what is historical perspective for it.

Degree of independence of any nation is an interaction of three factors freedom of thought, thriving economy and military strength. Freedom of thought is prevalent when there is a freedom of speech, freedom of assembly and the right to choose leaders without interference from domestic and foreign interests. Economic freedom is manifested through equal opportunity for all, equitable imposition of taxes, efficient government and containment of corruption. Military strength results from the indigenous development of weapons technology that provides a sustainable deterrent against adversaries.

From this perspective United States is independent in two of the three but relies on foreign money to finance its budget deficit which considerably weakens its economic independence.

China on the other hand lacks freedom of thought which can become a reason for uncertainty and anxiety among the masses but it has attained military and economic independence to some extent.

South Korea, Japan and Germany lost their freedoms of maintaining armies but retained freedom of speech and economies. None of the Muslim country is fully independent based on this formulation except Malaysia and Turkey which enjoy a degree of freedom in thought and economy.

Present situation in Muslim societies has to be understood from perspective of history. By the end of 19th century most of the Muslim world was colonized by European powers i.e. British, French, Italian and Dutch. Britain controlled Egypt, current day Pakistan, Malaysia, Palestine, Transjordan, Iraq and Arabia (which included Saudi Arabia, Yemen & UAE). French controlled Algeria, Morocco, Tunisia, Lebanon, Mauritius, Syria and parts of Libya. Ironically methodology to control these colonies was derived in large part from systems of government of Mughal Empire in India and Ottoman Empire in Middle East. This system contained division of community on ethnic & linguistic lines, development of an elite class that was loyal to the Empire and introduction of a police force that was utilized to squash an uprising before it becomes a major problem. To dampen spirit and initiative of local populations Colonial powers destroyed freedom of thought by forcefully imposing their cultures on their dominions.

At the end of World War II, these European powers were totally destroyed economically and militarily. It was not possible for them to hold on to their colonies when resources were needed to rebuild infrastructure in their own countries. Instead of withdrawing altogether they devised a mechanism to retain strategic and economic interest through the support of their loyal elites to the position of power.

To ensure control these autocratic proxy rulers were provided safe heavens from prosecution, by local populations, in the form of citizenship. Their sons/daughters were educated in Western universities and their wealth was invested in foreign stock markets and banks. This created a system of mutual interests where decisions of these dictators were inclined to provide economic benefits to their benefactors in the form of mining concessions, preferential treatment in government procurements and oil drilling rights. National wealth earned from export of oil & other commodities were spent in equipping armies with foreign weapons subjecting them to outside dependence on spare parts and ammunition in times of war. These economies were mismanaged by rewarding cronies that produced corruption resulting in bad governments which were unable to meet fiscal deficits. Economic independence was lost when these deficits were financed through foreign aid and sovereign debt from multilateral banks controlled by the West. To ensure longevity of their rule freedom of thought was curtailed through censorship and right of assembly thereby damaging prospects of emergence of a stable popular social order. This meant that for masses independence never became a reality.

Muslim world is rich in natural resources that are important raw materials for any industrialized nation. But none of the Muslim country developed their own technology to exploit these natural resources which would have created technological independence, added value to their exports and created jobs for local populations. Cars we drive, computers we use, TVs we watch, and internet & cell phones we so much yearn for are developed and sold to us by foreign countries.

Most Muslim countries rank low in literacy rates, higher in poverty rates, low on women rights and ripe in sectarian and ethnic divisions. Current turmoil in Muslim world is the first round of revolution. It will hardly change the status quo since there is an absence of ideology and availability of indigenous leadership to steer masses on the path of progress. Most likely scenario to emerge from this is rise of another Hosni Mubarak who will rule for next thirty years. Real change means to empower each individual by providing them access to education, provide everyone an equal opportunity to succeed and treat everyone as equal in eyes of the law. We have to better manage our natural resources to be self-reliant and develop indigenous technology through local innovation and scientific research. This requires an ideological uprising which has been lacking in current struggles in Tunisia and Egypt.

Islam & West: Desecration of Quran
(May 18, 2005)

In its May 9th, 2005 issue Newsweek reported desecration of Quran at Guantanamo Bay. Muslim Holy book was flushed down toilet as a psychological tactic to force inmates to cooperate during interrogations. Later this story was retracted by the magazine. No one knows if this story is credible but it does raise questions about state of American society, emotionalism of Muslims even about fictitious incidents and quality of journalism in West.

America is a capitalist society where everything is measured in dollars and cents. Whether it is a prenuptial agreement or taking care of aging parents, economics rules all decisions. This capitalist ideology spills over to religious beliefs and traditions of the society. American filmmakers have made comedies on life of Jesus. Late night comedy hosts Jay Leno and David Letterman dish out sarcasm on American Presidents on a daily basis. There is nothing sacred in a society that considers economic benefit as an ultimate end. People who are investigating at Guantanamo Bay are representative of this society. American educators need to reevaluate their social structure and devise curriculum that develops respect for the foundation of a society: religion, faith and respect for elders, especially parents. In absence of these founding stones, possibility of these kinds of incidents cannot be ruled out.

Quality of journalism has deteriorated noticeably in last few years even in some revered institutions like The New York Times and CBS News. Competitive pressures to out perform each other strains resources of news organizations which sometimes result in serious errors costing not only lives but also property. We have heard of plagiarism by a reporter of The New York Times and then there was an unsubstantiated story of President Bush's record at Texas Rangers and now this Newsweek error, which has resulted in loss of human lives.

Muslim world has always suspected Western media to be biased, presenting only their side of the story. This changed considerably in last few years when Arab world countered this media bias by creating news networks like Al-Jazeera. In the Newsweek debacle, Al-Jazeera played its role in igniting emotions of Muslims without coordinating their story with Newsweek. It is a demonstration that conflicting media views could result in serious social conflicts.

There is no doubt that desecration of Quran is something Muslims should not ignore. But real issue for Muslims is implementing true spirit and teachings of Quran in their societies. There is not a single Muslim country that can be presented as an Islamic model to the world practicing love for peace, kindness towards mankind and equality of all men regardless of their race and creed. Autocratic men rule a large number of Muslim countries. These men promote emotional appeal of religion through Imams of mosques to maintain grip on their societies. Imams understand power of the pulpit and use it to provoke people in taking extreme actions that result in loss of innocent lives.

This power was in full display when blood was spilled for an error committed by irresponsible journalism. We forget that Prophet Mohammad (PBUH) forgave woman who used to throw trash on him everyday. Correct approach was to put diplomatic pressure on American government to prosecute perpetrators of this crime. Guarantees should have been sought that these events are prevented in future. But instead, we yet again reacted emotionally by resorting to violence that claimed 16 innocent lives.

If we want others to respect Quran as a holy book, we have to demonstrate its teachings in our lives by exercising it in trade, society and justice system. Throughout history traders spread message of Islam by demonstrating a way of life taught by the Quran and adopting qualities demonstrated by Prophet Mohammad (PBUH) in his Sunnah. Those followers of Prophet Mohammad's (PBUH) exemplary life style had a profound effect on people they interacted with resulting in many conversions to Islam.

Today's preachers are professionals who are paid for their services which result in a conflict of interest. In order to retain their control on minds and souls of the people, these Imams, instead of explaining finer points of religion use emotionalism and oratory qualities overshadowing the true message. We have forgotten that Prophet Mohammad (PBUH) was a businessman, a statesman, as well as a messenger of God. It is true for other Sahaba who had a profession to earn their livelihood instead of relying on financial support from mosque. Since mosques are financed through charitable donations from community members, these Imams strive to increase their sphere of influence, which creates professional jealousy between them resulting in armed conflicts among sects in extreme cases.

Mentoring of spirit is very important for spiritual development of an individual. But it is important that in choosing a mentor it is ascertained that they have acquired in-depth knowledge of theology as well as practical aspects of human society. If we want to develop our societies, we have to rethink how our religious institutions are organized as well as develop syllabus of madrassas on modern lines. We cannot expect an Imam trained in conventional madrassa to appeal to a person who has completed his masters in science or acquired a PhD. We have to create a council of community elders to conduct prayers in mosques instead of appointing a salaried Imam who is then more concerned to maintain his job then to focus on the spiritual meaning of the prayers.

As a Muslim it is prime responsibility of each person to explore truth by using his or her intellectual capabilities. A deep understanding of faith only happens when a person strives to find meanings through his own personal exploration. Until we take this individual approach to understand Quran and demonstrate it in our daily lives, we cannot expect to avoid desecration of Quran by those who don't believe in it anyway.

Background: During October and November of 2005 Paris was subjected to a series of violent protests spearheaded by youth from mostly North African immigrant families. This raised concerns about compatibility of Islamic culture with West and whether rising numbers of Muslim immigrants is altering social fabric of Europe. Subsequent events like publications of Prophet Mohammad's (PBUH) Cartoons in a Danish newspaper and remarks of German Chancellor Angela Merkel that "This [multicultural] approach has failed, utterly failed," specifically pointing at Muslim immigrants raised emotions.

Islam & West: Muslim Immigrants in Europe
(November 28, 2005)

Riots in Paris, France, have been a topic of much debate in international media and forums. Governments and policy makers are revisiting their immigration and naturalization policies to ensure they are not faced with the same dilemma in their countries. Netherlands faced a social crisis when a citizen of immigrant descent murdered the television producer Van Gogh in broad daylight for his anti-Islamic views. It is important for immigrant communities to analyze such events and take corrective action to prevent the same crisis happening to them.

France, like England and Netherland, has been one of the imperial powers with colonies around the world. As England took hold of South Asia, France, an archrival, focused its attention on North Africa, gaining control of Algiers, Nigeria and Morocco. Being part of French dominions, citizens of these countries were granted special immigration rights, which resulted in a large African Muslim population that is estimated at almost 11% of the total population of 60 million.

These French citizens are forced to live in ghettos spread across outskirts of Paris. Predominantly Muslim, these populations have over 60% unemployment rates three times that of national average, with no opportunity to socially blend with larger French culture.

As a culturally rich nation with almost a thousand year history, French have tried to hold on to their culture; jealously guarding against integration of other cultures into its own. Although first generation immigrants in France lived as second-class citizens, second generation, born and raised there is not willing to accept this discrimination.

French economy is in a deep recession, which has further fuelled divide among various social classes and raised ethnic tensions. France's immigrant children feel an identity crisis; feeling no real association to either their parent's culture or to the country they are born in. This combination of lost identity and lack of economic upward mobility created a social time bomb waiting to be ignited. An error of judgment by law enforcement authorities sparked anger when police killed two young men, mistaking them for criminals fleeing from a crime scene.

Another social time bomb waiting to explode is in Germany where Turkish immigrants, even after almost three generations are not fully integrated with main stream. They are at lowest economic and social level. It is only a matter of time when young Germans of Turkish descent take a clue from French riots and pursue same tactics to claim their rights from the society they live in.

America on the other hand is considered a melting pot where people from all over the world migrate to avail economic opportunity without any prejudice of race, color, creed, sex or religious preference. This is what is classified as an American Dream. Founding fathers realized that America should always get fresh ideas and foreign blood to keep itself vibrant. They ensured this through Declaration of Independence and Bill of Rights in the American constitution giving equal rights to all citizens born or naturalized who pledge their allegiance to the country regardless of their heritage. After over 200 years success of this American experience can be credited to combination of right policies, acceptance of diversity without bias and equal economic opportunity.

All this, however, changed after 9/11 when policy makers decided to depart from tenants of American Dream and vision of the founding fathers by taking away civil liberties in certain clauses of Patriot Act, in the pretense of a precaution to prevent terrorist acts. Patriot Act will become permanent at the end of this year. There are already discussions of creating a nation of two classes of citizens. Children born to certain classes of immigrants will not be given equal citizen rights. If these bills are passed, it will be a final nail in the coffin of American Dream, and one that will adversely affect its image of being a beacon of equal rights. With legitimization of discrimination and without equal opportunity to all, social structure of this country will be severely weakened. Scientific circles are already worried about departure of intellectuals to their native countries or other immigrant-friendly countries. Founder of Intel, Gordon Moore, in an interview suggested in good humor that America should staple a Green Card to each PhD degree awarded to a foreign student.

It is important for all immigrant communities to be politically active especially in registering and casting their votes. They should form political action committees to identify best candidates seeking office and form lobbying organizations to promote their policy choices. Immigrant communities can improve their situation in their adopted homeland by having a political voice.

Globalization means less immigration but politics prevent this vision to be realized. In today's world the globe is increasingly divided along ethnic and sectarian lines. People migrate to seek greener pastures for their future generations and explore avenues to improve their lot. Migrants cannot afford to sit idle on the sidelines; they must get involved in the political process.

Islam & West: Prophets Cartoons
(February 15, 2006)

Our world in 21st century is a place of swift communication where news travels many times around the globe within a day's time. This communication bridge has made it possible for people of all cultures to interact with each other at a pace that was unimaginable until few decades ago. This communication revolution has made world a global village realizing centuries old desire of mankind to be close to each other. Like all other revolutions this one also imposes certain level of responsibility on participants i.e. to be cognizant of other's feelings and place limits on infringement on other's privacy. Recent incidents related to publishing of Prophet Mohammad's (PBUH) cartoons in an obscure Danish newspaper and subsequent riots in the Muslim world to express their anger is a good example of responsibilities imposed on societies by this communication age. This demonstrates how a single incident can fuel a chain reaction perpetrated by people with ulterior motive on each side. Before we analyze this incident let us first narrate how all this came to pass.

On 30th September 2005 Jyllands-Posten, a small Danish newspaper, published 12 cartoons of Prophet Mohammad one of which portrayed him as a terrorist while another had a caption that heavens are running out of virgins for suicide bombers. Head of a local Muslim organization promptly protested about publishing these cartoons but received no attention. He then approached ambassadors of some Muslim countries including Egypt and Saudi Arabia. These ambassadors requested Danish government to seek an apology from the newspaper but it refused to act citing Freedom of Speech/Press as a state policy.

When local organization failed to muster support for an apology they traveled to Egypt to show these pictures to the Muslim clergy there to seek their support. From there the issue became a political one and exploiters saw an opportunity that it could be used to their advantage. Rest is history.

We all saw the whole Muslim world gripped by demonstrations by agitated crowds; banning of Danish product in some countries as protest; and subsequently Saudi Arabia and UAE suspending their diplomatic ties with Denmark and called their ambassadors back. Europe in a show of solidarity stood behind Denmark and went so far that French and German newspapers published those same cartoons.

Ensuing debate from these incidents is revolving around two main themes, namely, Freedom of Speech and state of Muslim societies. Freedom and rights of individuals in a society are two conflicting philosophies. In dealings between individuals it is easy to create an understanding but when it comes to societies the issue becomes more complicated. For instance, a person may decide to be nude inside his home, which might be acceptable to his/her companion or friends. But as soon as that person steps out on the street, individual rights become subservient to community rights. In a utopian society a person can claim to have right on his body and has freedom to choose how to adorn it. But in real world there has to be a delicate balance between individual's self-assumed rights of expression and the rights awarded by a society to its members. The issue becomes even more complex when definition of these individual rights gets varying interpretations by different cultures and religions in a global village.

According to famous western philosopher Kant, knowledge and reason fail when it comes to acceptance of faith. Faith transcends all logic and reason offered by science. We can argue about validity of one's faith as compared to the other. But as long as there are followers of a faith in a society we are bound to respect it for peaceful coexistence and communal harmony. During a meeting with Dutch journalist in Houston, in October 2005, one of the points discussed was why western media call a terrorist an "Islamic terrorist" and in the process play to the advantage of those few that has kidnapped a peaceful religion for furthering their political agenda. Broad consensus in the meeting was that it is a valid point and should be considered while preparing news about terrorist events.

Now appearance of Prophet Mohammad's (PBUH) cartoon shows that image of Muslims at large as terrorists is deep rooted in psyche of the western mind. Though literacy level of western countries, as compared to Muslim countries, is much high yet they decided to reprint cartoons in solidarity with Danish newspaper without giving due consideration to feelings of a large section of the world that adhere to Islamic faith. Role of American news media was commendable which has shown greater respect for sentiments of Muslims. They conducted open debates on the issue while not showing those cartoons, appreciating sensitivity of the issue.

Other side of the coin is state of Muslim societies. Attitude and behavior of orthodox Muslim clergy is of double standard. At one hand they are intolerant of point of views of other religions and on the other they do not openly condemn killing of innocent people by terrorists in the name of religion. These orthodox religious leaders have no real understanding of Prophet Mohammad's life, which on many occasions showed deep respect for other faiths. Prophet Mohammad (PBUH) did try to convey message of God to everyone but never used any suppressive means to seek their conversion. Even when Mecca was conquered, he pardoned all those who conspired to assassin him. During many centuries of Muslim rule, especially during Mughal and Ottoman rule in South Asia and Europe, people of various faiths lived in total harmony with equal rights to all. Anger demonstrated by Muslims is not a religious matter rather depicts social decline of societies with a large population of young people. These youth are devoid of proper Islamic education and hence fall easy prey to manipulative clergy.

It goes without saying that Muslims around the world have a right to protest against indignant representation of our beloved Prophet Mohammad (PBUH). But there are many peaceful means available to protest instead of resorting to violence. Muslim societies should ponder as to why they feel exploited by western civilization even though they are almost 30% of world population. Instead of pointing a finger outside, we need to look inward.

One positive effect of this incident is the initiation of debate on both sides of the spectrum to find a common ground. We need to continue this debate to find out where we differ. Once we understand each other better we can expect to live with harmony by agreeing to disagree. If we fail this could be another in a series of events fueling clash of civilizations.

Islam & West: How would Prophet (Pbuh) feel?
(February 20, 2006)

After publication of indignant cartoons of Prophet Mohammad (Pbuh) in an obscure Danish newspaper the Muslim world is gripped in a continued state of terror and violence. Ironically agitations are more prominent in countries with authoritarian rulers like Pakistan, Afghanistan, Egypt, Syria and Nigeria to name a few. Conspiracy theorist explain this phenomena that these agitations are politically motivated by rulers to convince West they need continued support from them to keep religious fundamentalist at bay. Anthropologist on the other hand suggests that these agitations are a demonstration of frustration of populations oppressed by dictators and reeling under never ending poverty. Instrument used in these agitations is the clergy who are always in look out for a way to show their control of masses to further their orthodox religious agenda. Let us take a look at life of Prophet Mohammad (Pbuh) to see how correct these clergy are in prophesying their understanding of the faith and true message of the Prophet.

Biographers of Prophet Mohammad (PBUH), whether Muslim or non-Muslim, agree that he is one of the greatest person to inhabit this world. His message of Islam is the fastest growing religion. This message must have some appeal to attract large number of converts every year. He was raised by his uncle Abu Talib who was one of the Bedouin tribal leaders in Mecca. As a young adult he was hired by a widow Khadija (RATA) to take care of her trading business. This means that he must have enjoyed good reputation in the city as well as shown good business acumen. This implies that he must be conversant with business practices related to accounting, merchandising, sales negotiations and settlement. Message from this is that it is important that a person has to be involved in seeking livelihood besides spending time on spiritual elevation.

If we look at lives of our current day clergy and religious leaders only a handful of them are involved in gainful employment. Most of them make their livelihood from donations given to mosque.

This is a departure from the *Sunnah* to use religion as a means of personal gain. This economic interest from mosque creates a conflict of interest in promoting true message of Islam. In order for an Imam to be successful he has to make his mosque a success which in return means to attract large number of people to it by playing on their emotional psyche. One way is to play on people's fear of an after life for their sins here on earth.

As a young man Prophet Mohammad (PBUH) was not comfortable with pagan religions. For almost fifteen years, He would go to a nearby mountain and spend parts of nights there to meditate and find true meaning of life. We must try to emulate the state of mind of a young person who has no formal education. We have to understand the psychological development he must have gone through while sitting alone in a cave reflecting on life and its meaning. We see similar experiences in lives of other great people of human history like Buddha, Moses, and Jesus who spent countless years developing their spiritual self before announcing it to the world. It was a journey through depths of the soul that our current cadre of religious scholars is totally incapable of. How many of our religious leaders have meditated for even few years to find spiritual enlightenment? This is another departure from *Sunnah* of the Prophet.

When Prophet Mohammad (PBUH) announced his message to the world no one doubted that he is true but he struck at the heart of their faith, which is not an easily digestible idea. As he kept preaching he made enemies who became bloodthirsty creating a risk for his life. As a practical realist as soon as Prophet realized his life could be in danger that could in turn jeopardize propagating his message. He decided to accept invitation of people of Medina to migrate there to mediate their conflicts as an arbiter as well as promote his message of Islam.

This shows that despite being a Prophet with powers at his command he pursued a realistic and prudent path. If we look at attitudes and speeches of our clergy after publishing of the cartoons we can see that they abandoned this *Sunnah* of the Prophet for their own personal political and religious views.

These religious leaders exploited a situation that could have been handled peacefully without resorting to violent agitation costing human lives and property.

In Medina Prophet Mohammad (PBUH) quickly gained a large number of followers. But even with this fast growing community he felt that he needed to act swiftly to ensure their safety from aggression of Meccan's who were still pursuing to capture and kill newly converted Muslims. Prophet Mohammad's (PBUH) proceeded to sign a peace and mutual defense agreement with Jewish tribes in the region. This was a brilliant political move by the Prophet who in a single stroke of pen gained strength against much stronger aggressors. This shows that Prophet Mohammad (Pbuh) was not averse to signing pacts and agreements with non-believers. This is evidence that he understood that there will always be non-believers in the world but mutual coexistence is important for the well being of mankind. In today's Muslim society non-believers feel pressured and discriminated. This is another departure from *Sunnah* of the Prophet. Throughout thousand years of Islamic Empire, it was an open society with equal opportunity for all, low tariff and excellent educational institutes.

After victory at Mecca Prophet Mohammad (PBUH) gracefully pardoned all those who conspired against him. He is said to be home sick in Medina, as he loved Mecca deeply, but he still decided to return to Medina to be with people who accepted him when everyone in Arabia rejected his message. This shows that a person should be dedicated and sincere to his adopted homeland regardless of where he was born. To follow *Sunnah* Muslim immigrants have to protect their adopted countries but at the same time continue their efforts to improve relations between West and Muslims.

It is understandable that Muslims around the world are deeply wounded by publication of Cartoons in the Danish newspaper. Resorting to violence to protest these cartoons is a departure from *Sunnah* of the Prophet. If we really want to agitate we need to pursue education, economic independence and social reforms in our societies.

Background: *Samuel P Huntington, a well known political scientist, wrote a book titled "The Clash of Civilization and Remaking of the World Order" to refute theory of a post cold war era presented by Francis Fukuyama in his book titled "The End of History". American wars in Muslim majority countries of Iraq and Afghanistan were compared with Huntington's theory of war of civilizations.*

Islam & West: War of Civilizations
(August 8, 2006)

Collapse of Soviet Union (USSR) elevated America to the position of sole superpower. This status was expressed in promotion of a New World Order by President Herbert Walker Bush. This doctrine manifested itself in gulf war after Iraqi occupation of Kuwait in August 1990. America quickly built a coalition to force withdrawal of Iraqi forces and impose sanctions to prevent further aggression. After ascension of Bill Clinton to Presidency, the new administration got more involved in internal affairs and concentrated less on the international agenda. Inauguration of President George W Bush shifted foreign policy towards unilateralism by reducing involvement in international institutions like United Nations, international courts and Kyoto Protocol for protection of environment. Final piece of this new approach was put into play after 9/11 when America decided to rely on its own military strength to invade Iraq to impose its version of democracy on Middle East.

Many political pundits have referred to this new environment as war of civilization, a theory presented by Samuel Huntington. Ideas presented in the book about violent struggle between civilizations, defined in cultural terms, have been denounced by many scholars especially from Muslim world. But prevailing situation in the world requires analysis of this hypothesis. First step is for all stakeholders to realize that there is a bloody war underway between various cultures to impose their values on others. Unless we accept this reality we will not be able to negotiate a lasting peace.

Major players in this war are Muslim world on one side and West comprising of Western Europe and America on the other. China is benefiting from this by forming alliances with countries in Africa, South America and South East Asia.

In presenting case for war on terrorism American leaders has repeatedly emphasized that Islamic terrorist are attacking values of the West. They have doubted that Muslim countries are willing to accept democracy as a form of government as Islamic faith is not compatible with it. They have expressed reservations about theological content of Islam as a peaceful religion. Western Media has emphasized in their press reports that terrorists are driven by Islamic ideology undermining humanistic appeal of this faith.

We should try to understand today's situation in historical perspective. As Western influence rose in 17th century they started colonizing smaller and weaker Muslim states in Africa, Middle East and Asia. Once subjugated to a foreign influence it started a debate among Muslim masses to find cause of their failure. This resulted in a two divergent approaches. One group blamed corruption of rulers and departure from orthodox practices of Islam.

This group aspired to reestablish rule of *Sharia* as it was in the times of first four rightly guided caliphs. They emphasized to get rid of amendments made to *sharia* law after first few centuries of its introduction. While the other group promoted nationalist ideal to overthrow shackles of colonization. They rejected creation of pan-islamic *Ummah* and relegated religion to be a subject of individual persuasion. Quran accepts validity of separate cultures living in harmony under one system. According to Quran Chapter 49 verse 13;

"O mankind! We created you from a single (pair) of a male and a female, and made you into nations and tribes, that ye may know each other (not that ye may despise each other)."

During struggle for independence the later group won out and lead movements in different parts of the Muslim world.

By mid 20th century independence was achieved by these nation states but centuries of foreign rule had deprived masses of necessary skills to manage their societies. It was like a caged bird with clipped wings was suddenly allowed to get out and fly. Result was devastating. Most of these countries were not able to create stable political, social and economic order that could lead masses towards a better life. Since West still needed access to natural resources so they maintained their influence through proxy elite class.

Inefficient governments produced disenfranchised masses that increasingly looked towards religious organizations to provide some relief and direction. This resulted in creation of largely religio-social organizations which later took increasingly political role. Organizations like Jamat-i-Islami (JI) in Pakistan and Muslim Brotherhood in many African states refused to accept validity of a nation state and emphasized that Islam mandates creation of a pan-islamic ummah. Iranian Islamic revolution of 1978 and Russian invasion of Afghanistan in 1979 provided a potent breeding ground for these pan-Islamic philosophies.

In last decades of 20th century, Afghan struggle against a communist superpower became a struggle of Islam against an infidel power. Volunteers from all over the world participated in this war. America, with its own agenda in mind, provided necessary training and equipment to this Islamic militia. Russia, weak internally, succumbed to this volunteer force and was forced out within a decade. America could have played a positive role in reconstruction after the departure of Russians but instead suddenly lost interest and left this Islamic militia to its own design.

When these Afghan war volunteers returned to their home countries they became members of their local religious organizations who started an increasingly armed conflict with their Western influenced rulers. This extremely radical element needed another enemy to fight and West provided a potent target. These religiously motivated organizations formed a way of coordinating their efforts infused by the concept of one *Ummah* fighting their Western exploiters.

This phenomenon has created an internal tug of war where a small ruling minority is aligned with West whereas the large majority is alienated by it and manipulated by religious parties. In his book Mr. Huntington has predicted that Muslim world will align itself with China to win its struggle with West. Reality may be otherwise, despite many differences Muslim and Western values have many commonalities emanating from believing in one God, acceptance of Jesus as a Prophet of God and morality in social behavior. Their major difference lies in exercise of political power. On the other hand Chinese civilization is totally alien to Muslims and their atheist lifestyle is an uncompromising characteristic for them.

Key to create a lasting peace between these two warring civilization lies in realizing that Westminster style democracy is not a universal order and those other philosophies of government can also achieve the objectives of equality, tolerance and freedom of speech. West should recognize that Islam is a major civilization with its own unique culture and set of values. Western media should stop labeling terrorist as Islamic terrorist thereby irritating a large majority of mostly youth who then become sympathetic to terrorist militia outfits.

It is important that international institutions like UN should give due representation to the Muslim voice by inducing a permanent member to UNSC from the Muslim world. Without this representation a major civilization is left out of having a say in international conflicts where interests of their co-religionist are at stake. Both Pakistan and Turkey are in good position to assume this role with help from West.

For Muslim world solution is in creating institutions that respects each unique culture while strengthening common values offered by Islam. To achieve this objective EU provides a good working example which has members with diverse cultures but still found a common ground to achieve social, economic and political unity.

Organization of Islamic Cooperation (OIC) should be reconstituted to become more influential in helping its member states in introducing reforms in politics and economics spheres. First step in achieving this objective is to amend charter of OIC so that it can formulate a constitution acceptable to all members. Instead of appointing a Secretary General elected by Foreign Ministers Conference, a President should be elected based on votes awarded to each member state either on their populations or size of their economy. OIC should create a foreign relations secretariat to represent Muslims in multilateral organizations instead of participating as an observer in the current structure. OIC should form linkage with other multilateral institutions like EU, UN, NATO and OECD to initiate dialogue on better relations between their respective member states. OIC should be accepted as arbiter of representing Muslim opinion in resolution of conflicts with non-Muslim states including Middle East or right of self determination of Kashmiri people.

World is in a state of flux since two cataclysmic events. First breakup of USSR demolishing long established balance of power. The other was events of September 11 when America was attacked by terrorists. This charged environment can only be normalized by initiating a dialogue at all levels and respecting views of others. Until we embark on this course of peace and reconciliation the war will rage on claiming more lives with each passing day.

Islam & West: Neo-imperialism
(October 25, 2007)

After end of cold war there has been a debate in American policy circles about next threat to national security. There seems to be agreement between neocons and liberals that extremist elements in Muslim societies, from Sudan to Indonesia, might create problems for West. To deal with this West decided that they did not need a cold war because there was no military power that could stand in front of their weaponry. To prepare public opinion to support their agenda, research papers are published by propaganda machines that highlight verses of Quran in a twisted manner. Today there is an article in The Wall Street Journal written by an intellectual Stephen Prothero, Professor of Department of Religious Studies in Boston University, in which similarities are presented between Prophet Mohammad (PBUH) and Somali pirates. The point presented by this author is that during his time in Medina Mohammad (PBUH) and his followers engaged in piracy to fund their religious enterprise.

But there seems to be a disagreement on approach to handle extremism. On one side are conservatives lead by Henry Kissinger and Richard Perle who believe in preemptive strike at rouge Muslim states like Iraq and Afghanistan to curtail extremism at grass roots level. It is a reported fact that in 1991 neocons wrote a letter to President Clinton to start a preemptive strike against Iraq to prevent them from acquiring WMD. President Clinton was able to contain ambitions of this neocon group by focusing more on improving the American economy and improving quality of life of people. President Clinton's approach is now questioned by these conservatives who blame 9/11 attacks on his indifference to handle Al-Qaeda after first attack on World Trade center in 1993.

Liberals, on the other hand, lead by former President Carter and his National Security Adviser Zbigniew Brzezinski believes that negotiations at multilateral platforms are the only viable means to achieve greater cooperation between West and Muslim countries.

Liberals believe that fear of military action is a better instrument than the action itself. In their view it is important to resolve long standing grievances of Muslim community particularly solving Palestine and Kashmir issues. They point to the success achieved in cold war through a policy of containment while dealing with Soviet Union. It is unfortunate that traditionally liberal Democratic Party's presidential hopefuls are marching to war bands and commenting they will pursue preemptive strikes inside Pakistan and Iran at their discretion. It is a set back to pro-peace leaders Carter and Brzezinski.

After events of 9/11, neocons were able to exert greater influence on American policy makers, media and mould public opinion to pursue preemptive military action against a state even in the absence of a direct provocation or threat from her. Britain, a close ally of America in Europe, has experience in dealing with Muslim populations through their former colonies in sub-continent, Africa and Middle East. British understand that best approach to subjugate large number of people by a small force is to ensure divisions on ethnic, sectarian or even social lines. But divisions can not occur unless there is widespread hatred among different sections of community. Prolonged violence prepares people's psyche to accept divisions to regain normalcy in their communities.

Clandestine operations play a pivotal role in promotion of division in an occupied territory. Nature of these operations is such that governments have to give unusual financial and operational liberty to the field force. These largely independent operators create an action plan taking hint from broader policy approach adopted by their governments. These plans sometimes include working with both fighting factions to ensure widespread chaos and damage of social fabric. We are probably witnessing the same environment in Iraq where all kind of forces are at play. It will be foolish to think that energy hungry China and dignity seeking Russia will stay out of Iraq to allow America to take control of second largest oil reserves in the world without at least maintaining some kind of intelligence presence.

Evidence that West is pursuing the approach of divide and contain is demonstrated in policy research prepared by think tanks and academics. Presidential hopeful Senator Joe Biden has presented plans to break Iraq into three units with or without a confederate structure. In case of Pakistan, an analyst writing for a defense journal in a 2006 article sketched future by predicting break up of the country in probably three or four pieces. Similarly, recent bill to classify Turkish action against separatist Armenian's, almost a century ago, as a holocaust could be construed as a signal to Kurds to legitimize their separatist claims as a nation. Media classification of Iraqi national insurgency as Shiite and Sunni is an effort to create ethnic division in a society which was non existent even during dictatorship of Saddam Hussain.

In light of this theory recent comment by Benazir Bhutto that she is targeted because of her ethnicity indicates that she is becoming an instrument of division instead of unity. She has fueled ethnic divisions by naming Chief Minister of Punjab being responsible for the bombing attacks on her in Karachi. She has appealed to international community to investigate these events inviting them to interfere in domestic affairs. UN resolution to condemn Karachi bombing incidents as international events rather than a domestic crime should ring an alarm bell for Pakistani foreign policy planners. This could mean that UN might use this precedence to authorize, if situation arises, a preemptive strike inside Pakistan because of presence of international terrorism and inability of local government to deal with it. This is termed doctrine of responsibility which is now promoted by UN.

Sometime complex issues are solved through simple measures. West's hands off approach to allow Muslim societies to develop their home grown democracies could curtail the rise of extremism. In short term there might be disturbances and disputes but in long run it will enable modernization and liberate them from conservative forces.

Additional comment: Link to Stephen Prothero article in Wall Street Journal

http://online.wsj.com/article/SB124054446854951883.html

Background: *Western media labeled terrorists as Islamic terrorists subjecting tenets of Islam under microscopic scrutiny. It was a fact that most of the alleged terrorists were followers of Islamic faith and their actions put moral pressure on 1.25 billion Muslims around the world. Western media blamed Muslim moderates for their inaction to criticize terrorist acts. This letter was written in this backdrop and published in USA.*

Islamic Ideology: An Open Letter to a Terrorist
(August 22, 2004)

Mr. Terrorist

I have been reading about your activities in world media. Each terror incident has made me think which Islam you have been following. So I decided to talk to you through this letter to elaborate certain values promoted by our religion.

For Muslims, like you and me, basic tenants of religion are out lined in Quran, the divine book, and then demonstrated in life of Prophet Mohammad (PBUH). Any actions deviating from that cannot be called Islamic in its essence. I would like to quote few verses from Quran to highlight some of these teachings.

Al-Jathiya (45:14): "All those who believe, to forgive those who do not look forward to the Days of Allah: It is for Him to recompense (for good or ill) each People according to what they have earned."

Al-Furqan (25: 63): "And the servants of (Allah) Most Gracious are those who walk on the earth in humility, and when the ignorant address them, they say, "Peace"".

Al-Imran (3: 128): "Not for you (but for Allah), is the decision: whether He turns in mercy to them, or punishes them; for they are indeed wrong doers."

An-Nisa (4:29): "O ye who believe! Eat not up your property among yourselves in vanities: But let there be amongst you Traffic and trade by mutual good-will: Nor kill (or destroy) yourselves: for verily Allah hath been to you Most Merciful!"

It is a word of God that a person should not kill himself. Neither can he assume the role of a Judge to decide to punish those who do not conform to Islamic teachings. It is a matter between God and its creation. No one has the authority to intercede for Him.

Prophet Mohammad (PBUH) led his life portraying teachings of Quran. He made peace pacts with Jewish tribes. He never gave orders or waged a war against any person or tribe who disagreed with him on the message. Even people who attempted to physically harm him he never retaliated against them in vengeance.

You have forgotten both the teachings of Quran and Prophet Mohammad (PBUH). You are following criminal gang leaders who have misguided view of both the religion and its teachings. They are settling their personal scores in the name of Islam.

Your actions are killing both Muslims and non-Muslims alike and giving bad name to the religion in the process. They are asking you to commit suicide attacks against innocent people when both Quran and Hadith make clear that suicide is prohibited especially to further a political agenda. Here is what Mohammad (PBUH) advised his disciples:

"He who commits suicide by throttling shall keep on throttling himself in the Hell Fire (forever) and he who commits suicide by stabbing himself shall keep on stabbing himself in the Hell-Fire."

You have been promised a place in paradise for killing yourself in the name of the God when the God says in his own book that taking ones life is prohibited.

You blame West for dilapidating condition of Muslims when actually you are yourself to blame for that. If you believe Western civilization support despot ruling your country then you should form political reform parties. You should convince people to support it to over throw these dictators and install a system that provides a just and prosperous life to the community.

This struggle for betterment of the community, by bringing political change in your country, is a much more noble way than blowing yourself to kill innocent people. By killing yourself you are creating a bad example for younger generation and distorting the image of Islam as a peaceful religion.

You have chosen a path that is in conflict with basic tenants of Islam, which is a message of tolerance, love and peace for all mankind. Islam advises you to first take care of your parents, then your neighbors and relatives and then the community at large. You leave your whole family in disarray by indulging yourself in actions that bring shame and agony to them. You should use your energies to help your community and your country in becoming a model society by waging a peaceful struggle against inequality and injustice. You have examples in the world like Nelson Mandela who sacrificed 27 years of his life in a prison cell to fight against a strong apartheid government.

You blame America and other western countries for supporting Israel in occupying Palestinian territory. But Israeli atrocities are nothing but a demonstration of weakness in Muslim world to stand united in support of Palestinians to convince international organizations like United Nations to impose sanctions against her.

We are a community of over 1.25 billion people which is almost a quarter of world population. We have abundant supply of natural resources in our countries. We have established one of the largest empires in the human history. But your actions are destroying all those good values we have acquired over centuries. If you want all of us to get out of this slump you have to say no to people who are asking you to kill. Killing never brings understanding or helps achieve objectives.

As a brother I would ask you to question wisdom of your terrorist leaders about sincerity of their efforts, ask them to explain to you how can murder be justified under any circumstances?

Your Muslim Brother.

Islamic Ideology: Secularism and Islam
(November 26, 2010)

Secular governments, hallmark of many Western democracies, believe that God has no place in affairs of state. This concept of God less state in secularism is similar to communist rejection of religion as an institution. Proponents of Secularism think that it is a fair and just solution to manage religiously diverse societies because spirituality is an individual concern.

During middle ages, from 5th to 15th century after collapse of Eastern Roman Empire, Europe was engulfed in a conflict of cultures and needed an ideology to unite people. Christian church with its universal appeal cut across national lines and provided an alternative institution to create a community. As it grew in influence endorsement of Church became mandatory for a Monarch to legitimize their rule. This political endorsement by a religious entity created frictions with rulers which turned violent on many occasions. Rulers legitimized their political power by emphasizing that Christian religion does not provide a code for managing affairs of state. This lack of theological basis and constant struggle for power between a temporal and spiritual authority created an environment conducive for separation of these rights. At beginning of modern era, French revolution introduced concept of a nation state governed by people's representative without any endorsement from Church for its legitimacy. Over last three centuries America and Europe have refined this philosophy of a secular form of government with democracy and capitalism as its vehicles.

While Europe was engulfed in violent conflicts, a new religion emerged in Arabia called Islam. Islamic concept of government emphasizes that as a creator absolute sovereignty reside with God. Humans, as vice regent, can rule a community with a limited authority to make laws. In Islam concept of Monarch or King is unacceptable. A ruler is elected by consent of people which laid foundation of popular democracy and direct elections. This was a relatively modern concept in 6th century when rest of the world was ruled by Kings.

Islam presented this idea that a ruler should stay in power as long as he does not break covenants of religion and enjoys support of the community. Islamic concept of government looks down upon succession through inheritance and prefers that personal character being the sole criteria to choose a leader. In an Islamic society a candidate would not seek public office rather people would choose a person they feel is most suitable for the post. That is an advance concept even today and addresses dilemma of conflict of interest between personal and national interest. American Presidential system comes quite close to Islamic form of government.

Islam grants absolute executive authority to rulers but at the same time clearly states that they will be subjected to higher standards of judgment in after life. Rulers are required to appoint a group of people, called a *Shura*, to advise him. It is widely perceived that members of *Shura* have to be experts of *sharia* or religion edict but reality is that it should comprise of technocrats who are experts in matters of government.

Unlike Christianity, in Islam there was no concept of institutionalization of Church or appointment of religious leaders that could influence people's political choice. This liberated people from a divided loyalty between a temporal and spiritual authority. In general, Islam does not differentiate between a person's dual role of an individual and as part of a larger community.

From 6th to 15th century, Islamic empire expanded to include most of Middle East, Spain & Turkey in Europe, parts of Central and South Asia, and North Africa. As this community grew, and included people of diverse ethnic backgrounds, it became necessary to create a cadre of religious scholars to educate these new converts about Islamic way of life. Intentions were good but, like Christianity, these scholars used pulpit of the mosque to start influencing political, social and scientific views of people. This eventually led to curtailment of open inquiry and narrowness of religious percepts. While Christianity found solution in Secularism to curtail political influence of the Pope, in Muslim capitals *Mufties* started exerting their political influence.

While Islam was in demise in 17th century, Europe embarked on a renaissance and an industrial revolution that was accredited to their adoption of secular ideology. End of cold war in early 1990s was considered triumph of secularism and its validity as a common good for all. Throughout its history, as was experienced by communist states, secularism has struggled with controlling religious impulses of decision makers that governed. President Bush, though head of a secular state, sought guidance from a higher father to start invasion of Iraq. In pure secular society abortion should not be a debatable question but it has been at forefront of presidential campaigns. During President Obama's election campaign many questioned his religious orientation which demonstrates that even in a secular government religion of a person is important for an electorate. Similar struggles have been experienced in Netherland, Sweden and France where expressions of religion have been widely criticized. In Islam there is no ambiguity as it is a mandatory requirement that the person elected to public office is a person of faith.

Some political thinkers question viability of an Islamic system of government in a religiously diverse society. Quran clearly states that there is no compulsion in religion and each person has to find his/her own faith. A Muslim citizen has to obey laws of the land in which they are a minority and defend their country against any kind of aggression. They are required to agitate only when they are discriminated against or refrained from practicing their religion. Similarly, a non-Muslim in a majority Muslim country is ensured safety and practice of their religion.

Islamic economic system can be termed as capitalistic with the only exception that interest as a financial instrument is prohibited. In Islamic society capital that is in excess of a person's need has to be reinvested in a new venture through equity participation. This not only creates employment through formation of small enterprises but engages the investor as an active participant rather than a passive receiver of a fixed share.

Private property is considered sacred in Islam and no one, even state, has the right to confiscate it except when a criminal or civil court orders it. To reduce income inequality wealth tax in the form of zakat is imposed which has to be distributed to the poor as a social safety net.

In 21st century, West is faced with a challenge to rethink effects of secularism on their societies. West may be rich in terms of quality of material life but they are faced with a spiritual dilemma resulting in suicides, broken marriages, and children raised by single parents. These will ultimately affect creativity, innovation and passion to succeed. Islamic societies on the other hand have to take power away from theologians to empower each individual to seek knowledge, elect their leaders without coercion and have a direct spiritual connection with God.

Islamic Ideology: Freedom of Expression
(July 16, 2011)

Freedom of expression can be unsettling if used without paying attention to the choice of medium or grasp of the context of intended message. Socrates had to drink from chalice of poison for his dissenting social views. Galileo was incarcerated for suggesting that Earth revolves around the Sun. For politicians, words are an important tool to convey their vision and appeal to the electorate. Struggle to define acceptable boundaries of expression is as old as human society. Secular democracies of West pride themselves for the freedom of expression it grants to its citizens. These freedoms are not limitless but are restricted through adherence to a constitution that applies to all citizens by fair application of law. Boundaries of these expressions have been continuously expanding as new technologies of communications evolve and advancements are made in understanding human psyche.

Western obsession with individual liberties has produced ever expanding boundaries of acceptable social behavior. For instance frequent use of curse words, open mingling of homosexuals and minimalist dress have become norms without any social reprisal. Larger question is what are limits of freedom of expression that does not damage social, moral and spiritual fabric of a society? What should be the code of conduct in a diverse society? And where does Pakistani society stand in this time of competing ideologies and values?

Dilemma faced by West is acceptance of a political system that has no room for divine interference and strictly believes in secular evolution of species. Ironically majority adherent of this system accept existence of God in their daily practice of religion. This unbridgeable paradox has created a conflict between individual and collective behavior.

At community level social limits are defined by human instincts that get accepted through democratic process of majority vote for example gay rights.

A concern with this approach is that human behavior is evolutionary and can be easily manipulated by various internal and external influences. Process of evolution has pushed human intellect to develop new methods of organizing society and create technologies to improve quality of material life. But it is nurturing of the spiritual being that has been ignored by this process of change.

Culture plays a significant role in defining boundaries of social behavior within a geographic territory. For instance Asian cultures are highly hierarchical and look down upon free expression without consideration for time, place and audience. On the other hand Western cultures are individualistic and grant equality regardless of age, education or social status. It is wrong for West to assume that their values have universal application without regard for other cultures. For instance in West it is not unusual to make jokes about Prophet Issa (PBUH) (Jesus Christ) but when they apply same standards to allow publishing of caricatures of Prophet Mohammad (PBUH), it resonates strongly with Muslims. This unilateral definition of freedom of expression not only creates stress but in some instances can create frictions resulting in violence.

Contrary to culture, religion on the other hand, especially monotheistic religions Islam, Judaism and Christianity, promotes social behavior mandated by divine sanction. In this approach boundaries are largely fixed and immovable. Although Judaism and Christianity have subordinated their religious teaching to secularism, Muslim societies continuously strive to impose those limits on social behavior. This issue becomes complex when members of Muslim society are illiterate in Quranic teachings and rely heavily on orthodox *maulvis* for interpretations.

Most of the *Maulvis* are graduates of unregulated madrassas that do not include scientific, social and economic concepts in their curriculum to have broader understanding of spiritual matters.

Presence of multiple schools of thought with varying interpretations of Quranic percepts add further to complexity. One drawback in most Muslim societies is absence of think tanks to undertake research on Quran and *Sunnah* i.e. the life of Prophet Muhammad (PBUH). This becomes a recipe for disaster as women and minorities are most affected in a society where there is no clear understanding of their rights and privileges. A starting point could be inclusion of complete Quranic translation, in local languages, in secondary or higher school curriculum.

Pakistan has become a breeding ground for exploitable extreme religious and ethnic views. Religious and political leaders seem to use inflammatory views to gain shortsighted benefits of votes or legitimacy. These views are then flashed on television screens and make headlines in newspapers without much regard for their editorial content or its affects on masses. Disenfranchised and disoriented youth becomes fuel for these views and gets consumed by it leaving a terrorized community in their wake.

To function as a normal society we have to take action at various levels but first step starts with self. As individuals we have to read Quran in totality from start to finish in our native language so that we get a first hand experience of its message. Second step could be that we condemn all expressions of divisions regardless of our political, religious or ethnic orientation. At community level we have to start raising our voice against abusive language or personal attacks by sending signed petitions to media outlets and their advertisers. It is about time that religious schools are regularized and their curriculum approved by ministry of Education. Last step could be rejection of all those politicians through an electoral process that promote divisions and raise emotions in the name of ethnicity.

A nation is a collection of individuals that are cognizant of their roles and responsibility towards each other. We can not sit idly by assuming that our politicians, imams, judges, generals and bureaucrats are some alien force imposed on us. They are part of the nation and we have to tell them what we expect from them.

Islamic Ideology: Islamic Social State Vs Capitalism
(November 2, 2011)

Capitalism is economic manifestation of secular democracy. In its ideal form a capitalist society should have free markets, no price control, no regulations, no barriers to entry or exit, and free flow of capital. This idealistic view of capitalism was never in practice but was credited with rise of West. In early 1990s after collapse of communist Soviet Union, it was aggressively pushed for universal adoption as part of the new world order. In early part of 21st century, failure of West to contain their economic recession has stalled this effort. On the other hand Arab spring has taken everyone by surprise and the question that comes to mind is whether this movement would produce an alternative Islamic economic model.

Classic definition of Capital is land, labor and equipment. It is interplay of these three resources that define an economy. In 20th century land and labor was provided by colonized regions of Asia, Africa and South America while technology and equipment was the domain of West. After the end of World War II exhausted imperial powers had to reluctantly allowed independence of their dominions. Since prime mover for colonization was economic a two pronged strategy was adopted to maintain their control i.e. introduction of a global corporation and support autocratic proxy rulers.

Like the Frankenstein's monster global corporations did not had allegiance to any one nation but rather were driven to achieve higher profits for their investors. Growth in profitability could be achieved in one of the two ways. First, reduce per unit cost through pursuing economies of scale by building ever larger factories & automation. This made it impossible for small guys to compete and forced them to go out of business severely affecting local economies. Second, relocating plants and equipments where labor was cheaper or raw material was in abundance.

This started a process of relocating manufacturing to low labor cost countries in the process imparting some of the industrial knowledge to emerging economies like South Korea, Japan, Brazil, India, China and Singapore.

In a truly capitalist world there should be free flow of labor across borders. It is ironic that it was these capitalist societies that introduced, for the first time in human history, a visa regime creating barriers to free flow of labor. A brain drain from third world to developed world enabled them to staff their companies with best talent without spending a dime on their education. This created an imbalance in distribution of humanity seeding an impending ecological disaster. Africa which was plundered for last two centuries for its natural and mineral riches was left with a large population, no infrastructure or organized societies to cope with famine and food shortages. On the other hand Europe is faced with declining populations. It is estimated that nation of Estonia will disappear from the face of earth by 2050. Asia is experiencing rising populations that are eager to migrate to Europe, Australia and America which can accommodate many more people.

In a free world there is no place for most favored nation (MFN) status or need for a GATT agreement. Nations can impose a uniform tariff on all imports rather than discriminate based on the origin of goods. Imposition of favorable terms has become a political instrument to meddle in internal affairs of other nations or to pressure them to accept a certain definition of human rights. Islamic concept of trade requires free flow of goods across border and respect for intellectual rights.

Islamic concept of economy requires minimal interference from state to impose restriction on movement of labor or capital. An Islamic state is required to maintain a balanced budget. Taxes should be kept at a level so as to finance the functions of a government that are limited to border security, internal security, provision of justice, ensuring equal rights of citizen and development of basic infrastructure.

In an Islamic society social services like Education and Healthcare are responsibility of non-governmental organizations (NGOs) created and run by wealthy and professional individuals. These NGOs are required to be non-profit, self-sustaining operations where rich pays higher price for the services while poor are subsidized or even given free service. It is a concept practiced by Sindh Institute of Urology (SIUT), Shaukat Khanum Memorial Hospital (SKMH) or Lahore University of Management Science (LUMS). In a Muslim society there is no concept of a retirement age. A person is expected to be a productive member of the community as long as they have the physical and mental ability to work although it is expected that their performance will deteriorate and their function change with age.

Individuals have complete liberty in investing their capital in whichever manner they see fit and have complete control of their property without any conditions imposed by state. Individuals are required to be active investors in businesses rather than seek a fixed return in the form of an interest. This is a concept similar to venture capital industry in America where wealthy individuals not only offer capital but advice to start-up companies. Islam does not look down upon accumulation of wealth. Instead it defines wealth as one of the blessings of God and a test for individuals to manage it wisely for the benefit of themselves and society at large. Islam does look down upon exhibitionism, consumerism and waste while encourages modesty in daily life. It prefers wealthy individuals to engage in active participation in charity by not only giving money but also engage in its decision making. To reduce income inequality Islam imposes a social tax in the form of *zakat* that is mandatory and must be distribute to poor segments of the society.

As capitalism loses its universal appeal it is an opportunity for Islamic intellectuals to offer an alternative that is more natural, equitable and social.

Islamic Ideology: Concept of an Islamic social state
(November 14, 2011)

In West and most of the Muslim world there is a wrong perception that struggle to establish Caliphate is mandated by Quran. Reality is far from that. There are many verses which points to formation of local governments while there are none that mandate a Caliphate. *Ummah* itself is not a political concept but rather a social one where people from diverse cultures share a set of common spiritual and social values. That is the reason we find common cultural traits in food, clothing, family rituals and celebrations of Muslim countries around the world. Islam does emphasize that Muslim communities should collaborate and cooperate with each other to gain strength economically and militarily. Many Pakistani political party manifestos include establishment of an Islamic social state. If this is the objective then it is very important to understand what it entails and how society will look like if we achieved it.

First order of business to establish an Islamic Social state will be to change the current Westminster form of parliamentary system to an American style Presidential system which is quite close to an Islamic form of government. Islam emphasizes election of individuals who then have executive authority to run state in consultation with a **shura** comprising of professionals with knowledge of government, administration and law. In Pakistan, we don't have to write a new constitution rather introduce amendments to existing one will achieve this objective. In Turkey ruling AKP party in the leadership of Recep Tayyip Erdogan made it part of their election manifesto that a presidential form of government will be introduced through constitutional amendment. In Pakistan many leading politicians have already expressed their preference for a Presidential system.

Majority of Muslims go to great lengths to tell the world that Islam is religion of peace. But in reality essence of Islam is justice. Peace and harmony are an outcome of a just society.

Promotion of justice is an active persuasion while peace is more passive approach to society. In an Islamic state introduction of an affordable and efficient system of justice is one of the top priorities of state. Procedures for discharge of cases should be such that decisions does not cost so much that it is not affordable or take so long that it is a hindrance for people to seek justice. Independence of judiciary is important. State has to ensure that life and property of judges are protected as well as implement their verdicts without delay.

In an Islamic state security policy will be oriented towards defensive rather than aggressive posture. This should become corner stone of Pakistan's foreign policy position to initiate negotiation to sign non-aggression and non-interference bilateral agreements with its neighbors and focus more inward than outward.

Prophet Muhammad (PBUH) in his last hajj sermon to *Ummah* clearly stated that in an Islamic state there will be no preference given to anyone based on their ethnic identity. Quran makes it clear that God, the ultimate sovereign, does not differentiate based on ethnicity among its creation to bestow its blessings on them. Quran does not mention that punishment of Shirk or Kufar is awarded in this world rather that it is a sin judged on the Day of Judgment which in a way is an opportunity for an individual to find the truth. Quran mentions that people were divided in tribes and nations to be identified rather than discriminated or preferred. In an Islamic social state everyone will be allowed to practice their cultural heritage without any discrimination or hindrance from the state. At federal level decisions will be taken only considering well being of people. In this scenario provinces will be created not on ethnic lines but administrative basis as preference is given to well being of individual citizens. In the same vane quota system has to be abolished and only merit should be the basis of all appointments in state and private enterprises. Similarly, Islam recognizes that non-Muslims are full citizens of state and have the right to practice their faith without recrimination from State which has to ensure safety of their prayer places.

Very first verse of Quran iqra was to encourage acquisition of knowledge of life, universe and spirituality. Islam looks down upon ignorance and mandates that everyone should seek knowledge which means that state should ensure that adequate educational institutions are available throughout the country. In Islamic state religious seminaries will be required to provide education in science and technology. As centers of learning and prayers mosques will be required to hire religious scholars that can provide spiritual enlightenment to the people. These religious scholars should be educated not only in science, social sciences and anthropology but also aware of the spiritual difference between Islam and other religions.

Quran does not differentiate between men and women in terms of their participation in society. Islam encourages that all members of society regardless of their gender should participate to establish a just and equitable society. Islam acknowledges that women have much higher responsibility than men because of their critical role in development of a nation as mothers. But this domestic role does not preclude them from pursuing a career to express their talent and exercise their capabilities. In an Islamic state role of women has to be recognized as full participant. This was evidenced from lives of Khadija (RA) and Aisha (RA) who took active roles in business and politics respectively.

Many Muslim countries are now realizing true meaning of a social state and embarking on reformation. Turkey, Malaysia, and Indonesia are good examples from which other countries can learn. Pakistan seems to be waking up to its true potential as freedom of speech is encouraging debates to create greater understanding of our religion, history and social values while at the same time destroying dogmas.

Section V: World & Regional Affairs

Background: In 20th century world powers were engaged in two major wars (First & Second World War) that not only cost million of lives but shattered economies of many countries. After World War I, it was agreed at the Paris Peace Conference to form a league of nation which was formally inaugurated on 25th January 1919. Charter of this organization was to prevent wars by adopting doctrine of collective security and disarmament. The idea was championed by American President Woodrow Wilson but he could not muster enough votes to get it ratified by US Senate. At its zenith League had 58 members but it could not prevent World War II and was ultimately dissolved in 1946.

Mistakes learned from failure of League of Nation helped alliance powers to reconstitute a world body called United Nations. Allied powers started discussions on creation of an international organization for peace and stability as early as 1941. After nearly four years of consultation a 111-article charter of United Nations was formally adopted on 25th April 1945 in San Francisco. UN system comprise of General Assembly, Security Council, Economic and Social Council, Secretariat, International Court of Justice and UN trusteeship council (currently inactive). General Assembly is open to all members and has annual sessions in which world leaders express their views.

UN Security Council (UNSC) is mandated with ensuring peace and security among member states. Security Council has fifteen members including five permanent members. These permanent members are America, China, France, Russia and United Kingdom. Non-permanent members are elected from general assembly through elections. Dual membership structure of UNSC has tilted balance of power in favor of permanent members who can block a resolution through veto. This exercise of veto allows world powers to safeguard their strategic interests but at the same time create a sense of inequality among other member states. Since its formation UNSC has not been able to prevent wars like Korean War, Vietnam War, Iran-Iraq War, first US war with Iraq to liberate Kuwait, US invasion of Afghanistan and Iraq.

Collapse of Union of Soviet Socialist Republic (USSR) ended cold war, elevating United States to the position of sole superpower. Although President Herbert Walker Bush successfully conducted first Iraq war by liberating Kuwait and gaining permanent bases in Middle East. He was criticized for not pursuing removal of Saddam Hussein from power. His failure to support Shiite and Kurd uprising in Iraq cost him re-election allowing Democratic Presidential Candidate Bill Clinton to win elections. President Clinton is credited with building a strong economy accumulating budget surplus year after year. He is criticized for ignoring foreign policy to safeguard American strategic interests.

Since beginning of 1990s intellectual debates were focused on defining the future of foreign policy. These intellectual debates were later credited to shape the Bush doctrine. In 1992 a group of neo-conservatives wrote a letter to convince President Clinton to attack Iraq to complete the unfinished business of removing Saddam from power. About same time political scientist Francis Fukuyama wrote his book "The End of History and the Last Man" presenting a theory that demise of USSR has demonstrated that democracy and capitalism are universal values.

Fukuyama's theory was countered by another political scientist Samuel P Huntington in his essay which was later expanded to a book "The Clash of Civilizations and the Remaking of the World Order". In this book Mr. Huntington proposed that although end of cold war could be attributed to triumph of democratic ideologies but it will not translate into end of conflicts. He suggested that future conflicts will be driven by cultural rather than ideological differences. In his book he proposed that future conflicts will occur between major cultural regions including West, Islam and China.

In 1997, Zbigniew Brzezinski former National Security Advisor of President Carter wrote a book titled "The Grand Chessboard". He proposed that Eurasian region will be next centre of global power struggle because of its mineral riches as well as access to land and sea routes linking Europe with Asia. He proposed that America has to create strategically placed assets in the region to protect its interest before Russia regains its national vitality dampened after the breakup of USSR. Mr. Brzezinski proposed expansion of NATO to include countries from Eastern Europe and former Soviet states with special emphasis to encourage Ukraine to become a member. He suggested that a cataclysmic event will be required to unite the nation to execute this strategy.

After terrorist incidents of 9/11, US got overwhelming support from UN member states to overthrow Taliban government in Afghanistan for harboring Al Qaeda. Later when they sought UN approval to wage a war against Iraq many members including France and Germany refused to provide support. In absence of UN mandate America decided to by-pass it and attack Iraq by forming a coalition of the willing comprising of Europe, Asia and Australia nations.

American unilateralism to pursue Iraq war without a creditable evidence of its Weapons of Mass Destruction (WMD) program or links with terrorist organizations raised questions about UN ability to implement its charter. In 2005, then Secretary General Kofi Annan, convened a World Summit to discuss proposals to reform UN. Many ideas were presented including increasing numbers of permanent members of UNSC as well as democratization of veto powers. India, Brazil, Japan and Germany have been active in lobbying for their candidacy of UNSC permanent seats.

While intellectuals were debating future of American foreign policy in seminars and academic sessions, US invasion of Iraq and Afghanistan resulted in loss of civilian lives producing widespread anger in Muslims. Many analysts suggested that these wars are an evidence of clash of civilizations proposed by Samuel Huntington.

Predicting future trends: World in 2025
(August 31, 2004)

In last three decades of 20th century world has changed a lot. Pakistan lost its eastern part, East and West Germany united after almost 4 decades, United Socialist Soviet Republic (USSR) dismantled into thirteen independent states proving communism as a failed ideology, East Timor gained independence from Indonesia, Hong Kong reverted from being a British colony to become part of China. Besides these positive developments some conflicts are still risking the world peace notably Israel/Palestinian conflict and India/Pakistan dispute over Kashmir region. American occupation of Iraq and volatile situation in Afghanistan has the potential to trigger global wars. For any government to form a foreign policy it is important to take a longer-term view to identify future friends and analyze balance of power between various countries.

Asia is the fastest growing region of the world. It is home to two most populous countries namely India and China. It is home to almost half the Muslim population. By year 2025 it is expected that China and India will become top two economies assuming that they will continue growing at the current pace of over 7%. To achieve this level of growth both these countries will be reforming their economies to attract required capital from around the world. They will be competing to ensure uninterrupted energy supply from Middle Eastern oil producers. China has already started strengthening its diplomatic ties with these countries. India-China will be investing heavily to equip their armies as well as resolve disputes with smaller neighbors like Pakistan. Emerging dominance coupled with presence of large number of immigrants from these countries around the world would make their cultures gain higher acceptance.

European Union will continue integrating its member countries to become a much more economically, politically and strategically cohesive power. It is possible that it may suspend membership of some countries because of their difficulties in integrating cultures and economies with larger European Union.

EU will increasingly look towards East for military and economic alliances. Russia, India and China will emerge as major trading and military partners for EU where by reducing the importance of NATO as a guarantor of its security. Because of an aging population it will rely heavily on labor pools from India, China, Pakistan and Bangladesh. Influx of these immigrants will drastically change cultural, social and political make up of Europe. Muslims are currently the fastest growing minorities in Germany and France, two large members of EU. This trend will continue which will bring these countries closer to Middle East, Asia and Africa.

Iraq crisis can result in redrawing of boundaries where it is split in three parts. Northern Kurdish region could seek autonomy and declare confederation with Turkish Kurds. Shiite majority could align with Iran to form a state. Southern Iraq with Sunni majority could align with Kuwait to create a new larger state. Movements for political reforms will get wide spread support among Middle Eastern countries and could result in toppling of monarchies and autocratic rulers in some of these countries. Likely candidates for leading these changes are Egypt, Libya, Syria, UAE and Jordan.

Missteps in Iraq and Middle East will cost America dearly in economic, political, diplomatic and social terms. American economy relies on influx of both intellectual and economic capital from around the world. Growing concern over security of lives and jobs will force America to adopt stricter immigration policies. This could result in lower number of intellectuals seeking employment there making a dent in the scientific edge. Continuing inward looking economy and emergence of other world markets would reduce infusion of capital in America.

Emergence of India, China and EU on the world stage would result in reduced American political influence in multilateral organizations. Diplomatic isolation from Europe and Asia as well as rising Latin American population, currently 21% of total population, will increasingly bring America closer to its southern neighbors especially Mexico.

In Americas both Brazil and USA are dominant countries with identical land mass and populations. Economically America is much stronger than Brazil. Brazil has been actively involved in influencing other South American countries to become part of an economic block sponsored by it. The struggle between these two giants will continue for dominance of South America.

If all these assumptions are true, Pakistan is heading for turbulent waters in coming decades. Our foreign policy should be driven by economic and social development instead of looking for a leadership role in Muslim Ummah. Squeezed between two large economies it is an opportunity for the country to create a road map for peace with its neighbors and gain access to these markets for its merchandize. High growth is usually accompanied with rising inflation and wages which is the case in India and China. It should not be difficult for Pakistani producers to export to these countries. Pakistan had rocky relationship with Russia. It is important for Pakistan to resolve past disputes and strengthen economic and diplomatic ties with Russia, which is also one of the largest producers of oil & gas. Russia exerts considerable influence over its past oil rich Union members like Kazakhstan, Lithuania, Uzbekistan, Azerbaijan etc. Pakistan produces a surplus number of doctors, engineers and scientists who can become a substantial earner of foreign exchange if she can sign a manpower export protocol with countries from EU like Germany, France and Italy. This will not only provide necessary foreign exchange but would help strengthen diplomatic and cultural ties with these countries. Biggest security challenge for Pakistan will be infiltration of extremist elements from volatile Middle East region. Pakistan should equip its first responders like fire Fighters, domestic intelligence and police to meet these challenges especially in densely populated cities like Karachi, Lahore, Rawalpindi and Peshawar.

Pakistan would require a visionary leadership in the next few decades to channel the ship through these turbulent times. If we fail we can become a destabilizing factor in the already volatile Middle East.

Predicting future trends: A quasi 3rd World War
(August 29, 2006)

Many American media outlets including guests on CNN and The Wall Street Journal op-ed writers have opined that world is on the brink of being engaged in a quasi third World War because terrorists are targeting all states and nations. Giving examples of terrorist acts in Spain, UK, USA, India, Afghanistan, Pakistan, France, Turkey, Africa and Middle East they emphasize, indirectly, that Islamic extremist elements are on one side and rest of the world is on the other. If we accept this, then this is a war of civilization- a concept presented by Samuel Huntington's in a book 'War of civilization'. For the sake of discussion, let's accept these arguments and believe that world is in a state of a Third World War. Now, let us analyze how this war is fought and what will be its implications.

America considered acts of 9/11 as a strike at its values of capitalism and democracy. Declaring herself as an aggrieved party, America being world's sole super power with unmatched economic and military strength, could not resist waging a war against an invisible enemy termed as Islamic terrorists. Since these terrorists did not belong to one country and were rather scattered in many different countries, this paved the way for an aggressive stance against Muslim populations at large. America's war on terror has expanded to Afghanistan, Iraq, Yemen, Sudan, Somalia, Lebanon and Pakistan, causing extensive destruction of life and property in many of these countries. And worst of all, the crisis in these countries has deepened and conflict has become more fierce.

In this new volatile situation, West a largely Christian society, is in armed conflict not with a particular state but with extremist Muslim organizations Hezbollah, Muslim Brotherhood and Al Qaeda. Since these organizations have no sovereignty but are operating hidden among masses of different nations, various methods are employed to curtail their influence.

First, there is the approach of military operations against states that are considered sympathetic to extremist elements. These include for now Afghanistan, Iraq, Lebanon and Iran.

Second, there is the tactic of pressurizing Islamic states Pakistan, Egypt, Saudi Arabia and Turkey, to weed out extremist elements from among its population. For their cooperation they are awarded economic incentives. Third is racial profiling of Muslim immigrants in Western societies through special registration, deportations and monitoring of religious places. Countries enforcing such actions include Britain, America, Germany and France.

In last five years, if we consider 9/11 to be starting date of this war, results are more troublesome than comforting. There has been a tremendous loss of civilian lives which is diplomatically disguised as collateral damage. States cooperating with West are increasingly in danger of being upturned by masses that are getting radicalized because of these extrajudicial killings.

Media's labeling of all terrorists as Muslims is fueling resentment for the West. Racial profiling is fostering radical sentiments among second and third generations of Muslim youth living in Europe and America. We have seen this in recent riots in Paris and terrorists acts in Britain. America has so far prevented this to happen because of its successful integration of Muslim immigrants in its society. But these integration efforts got a jolt when special registration was announced for Muslim immigrants and Patriotic Act was introduced which has allowed authorities, besides other things, to detain terror suspects for longer terms without court orders.

Usually a war ends when both parties are exhausted after incurring heavy loss of life and resources. We have seen this happen in two World Wars, US invasion of Vietnam, Russian invasion of Afghanistan and all other conflicts. This new war will be no different. Sadly, United Nations, which is bifurcated in two worlds, will not be able to play any role here and will be as ineffective as it has been to solve other conflicts.

Instead of resorting to armed intervention and racial profiling, West should engage with Muslims through its main organization, Organization of Islamic Cooperation (OIC) to reform troubling societies and states. Without this dialogue, peace will be uncertain with continuation of global conflict.

Predicting future trends: Cold War 2.0
(December 12, 2011)

The avalanche of 9/11 shattered delicate balance of power producing cascade of events that are now approaching an end and world is slowly moving towards a new equilibrium. It is important for Pakistan foreign policy planners to understand this diplomatic chess board positions, approach of players and strategic options available. A superpower has to demonstrate global reach in military, diplomatic, and economic capabilities; enjoy stable social order and have a vibrant culture. There is only one power that meets these criteria today which is United States of America (USA).

Russia, a previous era superpower, does not have global capability but its military operation in South Ossetia, in 2008, has demonstrated a resolve to safeguard its strategic interest and regional influence. Its economy is heavily reliant on export of natural resources and lacks depth in its manufacturing base. It has a long history of diplomatic experience in large parts of the world. Its Christian Orthodox culture is unique from Europe in language, dress, cuisine and rituals. Large segment of its population, about 80%, is Russian which provides a social uniformity. Potential for social disorder is present in discontent among people seeking freedom of speech and political liberalization as evidenced in recent election protests. Reemergence of Putin as likely President, for next 12 years, will give rise to an aggressive and nationalistic Russia. Despite an upward momentum Russia's leaders realize that it is not yet ready to assume the role of a global power.

China with its large population, vibrant economy, and entrenched culture is the most likely contender for a global superpower. But China lacks international diplomatic skills, presence in multilateral organizations, and understanding of other cultures. Militarily China is still at least three decades away from projecting a global reach. Rise in urban middle class is exerting social pressure on its existing government structures.

Chinese Communist Party (CCP) has started introduction of democracy for electing city officials but it is yet to be seen whether this is enough to satisfy people. At its current stage of development China understands that it can not assume the role of a global power. Its leaders realistically define China as the most developed developing nation.

Now if two likely contenders for a multi-polar world are not ready to stall American influence, then who can? The answer may lie in Russo-Chinese alliance. These two countries have collaborated during communist era and can learn from their past mistakes to be more effective this time. In last decade they have formed economic and political alliances. The only missing piece is a platform for military cooperation. It may not be too far off in the form of Shanghai Cooperation Organization (SCO) which is fast emerging to challenge the influence of NATO in South and Central Asia. Russo-China will have a global military reach and diplomatic influence to create an effective barrier to US influence. The new multi-polar world would thus be one versus one plus one.

In this new world some countries will play pivotal role of a bridge between these two power centers. These will be India in South Asia, Turkey in Europe, Brazil in South America, Saudi Arabia in Middle East and South Africa in Africa. These countries have growing economies, geo strategic location, and diplomatic goodwill for arbitration of disputes. Rest of the countries will feel increasing pressure to become a satellite of one or the other power center. Multilateral organizations like UN, WTO and World Bank will become platforms for resolving disagreements between satellites.

Announcement of American force deployment in Australia, approval by Afghan jirga to allow presence of US bases for 10 years beyond 2014, increased sanctions on Iran by West, Arab spring and NATO strike on Pakistani soldiers have accelerated hardening of positions for the emergence of second Cold War. For a cold war it is imperative that for each US advantage there is a balancing advantage available to Russo-China alliance.

In Europe, Russia has successfully stalled expansion of NATO to include Georgia and Ukraine. In Central Asia it has re-asserted its influence through security agreements with former USSR states and creation of Shanghai Cooperation Organization (SCO) to maintain its relevance to Euroasia.

West's emphasis on sanctioning Iran will move it into Russo-Chinese camp that will ease Chinese anxiety over uninterrupted supply of oil in return for a guarantee that Iran will not acquire nuclear weapons. This arrangement will provide a cause for continued presence of American forces in Middle East. Israel will be given up by America as a strategic partner in return for goodwill of Middle Eastern masses. Israel would move to Russo-Chinese side as a balancer of influence in the Middle East. US Secretary of Defense Leon Panetta's comment about Israel's diplomatic isolation gives an indication of US thinking. Palestinian bid for UN seat is another piece in US strategy. Israel's military cooperation with China and diplomatic alignment with Russia is an indication of shifting trends.

In South Asia, as America moves towards India as a strategic partner, it seems they have decided to push Pakistan into Russo-Chinese camp. Russia and China has gladly accepted it by endorsing Pakistani membership in SCO and providing diplomatic support after recent NATO attack on Pakistani check posts. Reduced US military presence in Afghanistan will be balanced by limiting supply routes through the north thereby creating a Russian influence on every US move.

It may hurt egos of Pakistanis but we must realize that in the grand diplomatic chess board we are a piece not a player. To become a player a nation has to have economic and military independence, social cohesion, and diplomatic reach. This leaves Pakistan with limited options. If it continues on its path of a security state then Russo-Chinese block would use it as a constant irritation for American presence in Afghanistan. The other option could be the path chosen by Germany, Japan, South Korea, Singapore and Malaysia. In this option Pakistan should focus inward to embark on a path of nation building.

South Asian Region: Options for Pakistan
(December 18, 2010)

Chinese Premier Wen Jiabao visited India and Pakistan to discuss regional and economic issues. During his visit to India, Chinese Premier signed 11 agreements with his counterpart most notable of which is the resolution of long standing border dispute as well as economic and strategic cooperation. In their statements Indian Premier supported China's claim on Taiwan whereas China supported Indian campaign for a permanent seat on UN Security Council. In the light of these events Pakistan has to reevaluate its foreign policy position and prepare a long term strategy for its survival as a sovereign state.

For centuries, the region comprising today's Pakistan has acted as a conduit for Buddhist monks to take silk route and pass through Peshawar to enter India to visit their Buddhist holy places. In recent times Pakistan became a close ally of China after its border clashes with India in early 1960s. Those ties were further strengthened during 1965 Indo-Pak war when America withheld its military support of Pakistan while China provided much needed weapons. Since then a substantial portion of Pakistan's military gear is of Chinese origin. China supported Pakistan's nuclear program as a counter balance to Indian influence. On trade front Pakistan remained a nominal partner. In recent years China extended cooperation in infrastructure and natural resources projects, like Sandak Copper Gold Project, Gawadar deep sea port and construction of a highway up to Peshawar. This is evidence of the fact that China sees Pakistan as its gateway to resource rich central Asian states. These infrastructure projects can help China market its products to these land locked nations. During Kargill conflict with India (in 1999) it was suggested in news reports that China pressured Pakistan to withdraw its forces to internationally recognized borders. For regional balance of power, China sees Pakistan as a counter balance to ambitions of India.

On the other hand China and India has experienced a paradigm shift in their relationships. During recent visit of Premier Jiabao it was evident that both countries realize they can benefit more by mutual cooperation instead of embarking on a colliding course. As a gesture of goodwill China has started showing signs of withdrawal in disputes between Indo-Pak. Bilateral trades have grown from $400 million in 1994 to over $13 billion in 2004. The industrial development of both nations does not overlap which induces greater cooperation. India is considered a powerhouse in services exports while China has become a manufacturing center for hardware. Combining these two industrial strengths can be a formidable challenge to other economies around the world. In dealing with India, China is using strategy of economic interdependence as well as maintaining relations with states like Pakistan and Sri Lanka to exert an indirect influence.

Economic interdependence has become a new strategic hurdle in preventing armed conflicts. After its defeat in World War II Japan, leaving its border security to the American forces, concentrated on increasing its economic power by focusing on exports creating a trade surplus. Those surplus dollars were then invested in US government securities.

At one point Japan was the single largest investor in US government treasuries investing over $ 229 billion or 34.9% of daily US borrowing. This gave a distinct strategic advantage to Japan to influence American foreign policy in Korea and China. China is following same strategy of economic interdependence becoming second largest investor in US treasures with almost $ 180 billion invested in last 12 months. Cheap Chinese products are largely responsible for maintaining low levels of inflation in US despite rising oil prices. China is recipient of largest foreign direct investment by American corporations.

For Pakistan these are difficult times. It cannot expect China to risk its strategic interest to provide support. America has shown more interest in strengthening its ties with India while using Pakistan as a launching pad for its war against terrorism.

Pakistan's relations are at best neutral with new Afghan government as well as with Iran. Russia and India has always enjoyed deep friendly relations through out its history after independence. Pakistan's relations with Saudi Arabia are cooled off after the evidence of their funding of Wahabi brand of madrassah's in Pakistan and financial support of orthodox religio-political leaders.

Natural course of action for Pakistan is to gain leadership role in Muslim world replacing Egypt as spokesman in multilateral platforms. It is in mutual benefit of India and Pakistan to Resolve Kashmir issue and create tripartite economic block with Bangladesh. As America gains better control of Afghanistan and Iraq through establishments of proxy government it will reduce its reliance on Pakistan as an ally against terror. During the reign of Shah of Iran, Pakistan enjoyed good relations with Iran and formed many cooperative organizations like RCD. But since the Iranian revolution of 1979 Pakistan has become victim of US/Iran diplomatic war and lost that friendship due to its siding with Americans during Russian invasion of Afghanistan. These relations are further strained by international pressure after reports were published that a Pakistani nuclear scientist sold technology to Iran. If Pakistan can resolve its differences with Iran then it can play a vital role in easing tension between America and Iran. European Union can at best be a trading partner and source of foreign direct investment. Russia has not forgiven Pakistan for its role in Afghanistan's resistance movement. But in this changing environment Pakistan should adopt a neutral stance on issues affecting Russian interest and then gradually improve those relations.

In this interdependent world economics plays an important role in geopolitical decisions. Pakistan's foreign policy is dominated by emotionalism instead of analyzing longer term trends and forming a consistent strategy. Attractions of Indian markets will always play against Pakistan to gain reliable friends that appreciates its position.

South Asian Region: Indo-American strategic alliance
(December 5, 2008)

Foreign policy is an imperfect social science with as many views and opinions as there are writers. Formulation of different scenarios helps in devising strategies for long term and channeling public opinion to support policy makers. Any foreign policy expert that does not consider history and culture of a region can not come up with a realistic scenario. Deployment of NATO forces in South Asia das disturbed precarious balance of power between regional players including India, Russia, China and Pakistan.

A look at India's foreign policy since independence shows that she has aligned itself with a dominant power to gain influence in the region. After independence from British rule in 1947, ruling Congress party with its socialist leader Jawahar Lal Nehru aligned her with communist USSR. The break-up of USSR in early 1990s forced India to rethink its strategy to either become a power in its own right or align itself with America or neighboring China. China was a difficult option considering their competing interest to gain access to energy sources, regional dominance and economic competition. America on the other hand was a better option because it had a large Indian immigrant community that could influence the policy makers; it was market for outsourcing of Indian skilled labor and it was located far off so would always rely on the local partner for safeguarding its interest.

The key question to ask in this equation is to understand the convergence of interests of these two countries in broader regional context. The answer probably is that India feels insecure from presence of a nuclear Pakistan at its borders. Research reports of their intellectuals suggest they would prefer Pakistan divided into smaller pieces that would rely on India for economic viability and security needs.

America on the other hand is nervous about a Muslim nuclear power that could be a threat to its strategic interests as well as possibility of Islamic extremist laying their hands on these nuclear weapons. America also needs a foothold in the region to keep an eye on growing powers Russia and China.

If this theory of Indo-American interest in the division of Pakistan is real then how would the region look like? One scenario was published by New York Times in which Federally Administered Tribal Area (FATA) region of Pakistan was merged with Afghanistan, Baluchistan was converted into an independent state including some parts of Iran as well. Truncated Pakistan in this scenario is comprised of provinces of Punjab & Sindh.

India seems to forget thousand years history of the region. Enlargement of Afghanistan would mean that there will be a nation of 65 million on its borders that has been source of attacks on its land throughout history. Establishment of Mughal Empire that ruled India for 500 years emerged from lands of Afghanistan. Before that Mahmood Ghaznavi, Ahmed Shah Abdali and Taimur Lane invaded India by creating bases in Afghanistan. Afghanistan with no agricultural and industrial resources of its own would be a nation of starving, battle hardened and ambitious people. These Aghfans will resume their attacks on rich lands of India for wealth and pursuing ambition of reinstatement of Muslim rule there. Recreation of this force would be much more dangerous for India to contain than multiethnic country of present day Pakistan. India should appreciate sacrifices made by Pakistan to contain these forces of extremism from reaching India. In absence of this buffer India would have been a frontline state in the war on terror. This would have created an unsustainable pressure for a country that is home to over 200 different ethnicities including some that are seeking succession from federation.

The other unknown in this emerging scenario is apparent complacency of China and Russia who have substantial strategic interest in South Asian region.

It is surprising to note that Russia makes a big diplomatic noise whenever America signs any kind of security deal with a nation in Europe but it remains mute when announcement is made about a large force deployment in South Asia. Presence of a foreign army is a direct threat to interest of China but they have not made any diplomatic efforts to object to it.

There could be many explanations for Russia and China's complacent behavior. One could be that the lesson learned by Russia in Afghanistan was that it is a place where an army dies from thousand small wounds inflicted by people who have a long history of gorilla fights. It is possible that another reason for their neutrality is that in their calculation American involvement in Afghanistan strains its capability to respond to aggression anywhere else. This scenario was played out during Russo-Georgian conflict when America could not provide any support to its ally Georgia despite past promises. Third explanation could be that both Russia and China understands that real source of American influence is their economic might and consumer markets. A major military operation would require substantial financial commitment which could further undermine an already ailing economy.

This will create an opportunity for these two powers to promote a new multi polar world order. The terrorist incidents in India could be in retaliation to its alignment with America. It is easy to point finger at Pakistan for terrorist incidents but real master minds could be located else where in the region. It will be naïve to believe that India's close association with America through nuclear, security and economic deals is unnoticed in Moscow and Beijing.

Balance between nations can not be achieved until all members of global community decide that only diplomatic channels will be used to resolved conflicts. Presence of foreign forces in South Asia will continue to result in insurgencies, terrorist attacks and extremism. Russia and China should come forward to play their role in international platforms to solve regional issues. America should focus more on improving lives of their people by creating new job opportunities and improving their economy.

South Asian Region: tug of war in South Asia
(November 9, 2010 & January 11, 2011)

"America does not have permanent friends, only permanent interests" is a famous phrase elaborating American approach towards foreign policy. President Obama's visit to India has proved this point once again. While he refrained from mentioning Pakistan in his speeches but he did boosted morale of his guests by endorsing Indian permanent membership in United Nations Security Council. Although this announcement may not actually help gaining a seat but it does indicate that America considers India its strategic partner in South Asia. This marks formal departure of India, from being a socialist country, to joining capitalist block lead by United States of America. In historic perspective this is untangling of the final knot of cold war era as one of the strongest allies of former communist superpower in South Asia aligns itself with West.

In early 1970s America, with help from Pakistan, broke diplomatic ice with China which consequently provided abundance of cheap manufacturing labor for American companies. This resulted in boom times for both countries as product prices remained stable in America while China got inducted into global economy. In last two decades China, growing at an annual rate of over 8% has emerged as second largest economy in the world with over 2.6 trillion dollars of foreign reserves. To maintain its economic growth China has gained access to steady supply of rare metals, commodities and fossil fuels by forging alliances in Africa and Middle East. China has started building a network of sea ports in Pakistan, Bangladesh, Myanmar as well as a land port in Nepal to create logistic route for its shipments in and out of the country. China is helping economies of its partners through soft loans, bridge finance and grants without any direct interference in their domestic affairs. This rising influence worries policy planners in Delhi and Washington.

China throughout its history has played a dominant role in South and South East Asia.

Although China has competed with Japan for regional influence for over thousand years, its one key distinguishing characteristic has been never to go beyond their seas. This has changed, as first time in its history China may be extending its reach beyond South China Seas. They have carefully chosen their expansion plans to include countries that are rich in mineral resources to satisfy the hunger of their vast manufacturing appetite. They have executed plans to have direct influence in Africa & Asia while they have formed a strategic alliance with Brazil and Turkey for an indirect influence in South America and Europe respectively. First phase of their strategy was to use their vast cash resources to build a network of sea ports in Asia and Africa. These ports are fully financed, built and operated by Chinese companies. The next phase in their development is just starting which is to have trade and security pacts with these nations to ensure smooth sailing of Chinese merchant ships from these ports. Recent naval influence exerted by Chinese navy in South China seas is a message to the world to be aware of challenging them in their backyard.

American strategy to contain Chinese influence is based on two principles which are to promote regional competition and pressure Chinese economy to adopt open market policies. Japan, Singapore and South Korea have been traditional US partners to protect its interests in South East Asia. Taiwan and Philippines are allies in South China seas. Israel and Saudi Arabia provide strategic influence in Middle East. Egypt and South Africa provide partnership on the African continent. In South Asia, India is a new partner and will be included in major negotiations with Afghanistan, Iran and Pakistan. In the last few months America and Europe has been steadily increasing pressure on China to appreciate its currency. If this happens it will increase the unit cost of production, if all other inputs are held constant, which will make Chinese products less competitive. In this scenario India can benefit as American companies shift their factory floor there. With an English speaking population, American businesses already have experience in utilizing it as an off shore center for back office services.

During eight years of President George Bush America embarked on strategy of expanding NATO to approach former Soviet state of Ukraine & Gerogia to become members along with plans for missile defense system in Poland. This produced angry response from Russia so much so that it had to create a military crisis in South Ossetia to express its intent to use force if needed. When President Obama took oath of office, he immediately embarked on mending relations with Russia through a public display of pressing a reset button. From media polls it is quite clear that Prime Minister Putin, a passionate Russian nationalist, might emerge as a leading contender to resume his second tenure as President of Russia in 2012. If that happens no one should be in any doubt that Russia would accelerate creation of a regional organization of former Soviet states to create a cartel of commodity rich countries. Recent signing of a currency deal between Russia and China is a step in creating an economic collaboration between this emerging block.

India is a large country with second largest population after China. Despite practicing a caste system in its social structure, it promotes its image as the largest democracy in the world. Inclusion of India in United Nations Security Council as a permanent member coupled with change in veto rules could provide a counter balance to Chinese influence in South and South-East Asia. Any body that is surprised by President Obama's endorsement of Indian candidacy for UNSC has not been following the gradual built-up of this relationship. It started with President Clinton who openly supported deeper relationship with India over Pakistan. Later it was President Bush who offered India civil nuclear deal. With Adoption of capitalism, large numbers of non-resident Indians (NRI) in western countries and a democratic government, it is likely that India will form of a trade and security alliance with West. There is a possibility that NATO will remake itself to be a global alliance with India as its ally in South Asia.

Analysts should not be surprised if in the next stage of development America sign a security pact with India with a caveat to shift Afghan responsibility on Indian shoulders. This step will kill many birds with one arrow. First, it will encircle nuclear Pakistan on both eastern & western borders. Second, it will create a regional power struggle between India and China thereby distracting it from other parts of the world. Third, it will allow India to engage with Iran on American behalf. Fourth, it will install a friendly gatekeeper to Central Asian natural resources to contain Chinese interests.

Pakistani policy planners make a wrong judgment when they assume that Republican's are more Pakistan friendly than Democrats. They must understand that American foreign policy is jointly developed by these two parties in close coordination with career diplomats. For Pakistan, it is an opportunity to rethink their foreign policy approach. They have to first decide if they want to be a security or an economic state but while doing that they must remember that a weak economy can not be strong militarily. From American perspective Pakistan has always been a tactically important country whether to contain communism through a bloody war as a font line state with Russia in Afghanistan or fight stateless terrorists in its FATA regions. On the other hand from Pakistan's perspective America has been a strategically important country. First it is a large market for Pakistani exports; second America is one of the largest suppliers of military equipment; and third it is home to over 750,000 Pakistani immigrants sending billions in foreign remittances. But Pakistan must remember that, to make its American friends happy, it can not adopt a hostile stance with any of its neighbor. Unfriendly comments from Indian ministers and military brass is an intentional attempt to keep Pakistan guessing its next move. India can not afford to put breaks on its economic growth by engaging in any form of war in the region. This is an opportunity for Pakistan to convince India that a neutral position on major disagreements is in best interest of both countries. Pak-China relationship on the other hand can grow stronger to contain tide of Indian influence in South Asia and neutralize their intended hold on Afghanistan.

Geo-political power is usually a by-product of economic success. Three of the five permanent members of UN Security Council, Britain, US and France, are dealing with economic recessions while fourth Russia is struggling with dwindling regional influence and internal social issues. With economic success of Brazil, Turkey and India it is unlikely that these nations would relegate their geo-political interest to the UN Security Council run by nations that rely on their investments to finance budget deficits.

Internal stability in Pakistan is important to pursue a successful foreign policy. Pakistan has to focus on economic growth; strengthen political institutions and reduce provincial disagreements. The first step could be to organize an all party's conference to formulate a foreign policy position on which everyone agrees.

South Asia: moving pieces of foreign policy
(September 25, 2011)

Many foreign policy experts compare their craft to the game of chess. The difference is that in foreign policy chess board half the pieces are invisible. Combine this with paranoia that results from fear of unknown and the situation becomes quite intricate. No one can predict exact course of events but that should not prevent planners to prepare a combination of likely scenarios.

Events of last few months will have significant impact on future shape of the world. First, it was Arab spring that is now moving into its final phase seeking the departure of Bashar al Assad of Syria. Second, attack on US embassy in Kabul which was followed by assassination of Burhanuddin Rabbani, President of Afghan High Peace Council. Third, President of Palestinian Authority Mahmoud Abbas submitted formal application to United Nations to seek admission as a full member. These events may seem separate but they are all connected as our basic premise is that US focus is now shifting from Middle East to South Asia.

After World War II, Israel became one of the center pieces of American foreign policy to maintain its influence on oil rich Middle Eastern countries. Fear of Israel's military might enabled America to sell billions of dollars of weapons as well as provide security umbrella for steady flow of oil. But after 9/11 this importance has gone down for many reasons. First, America now enjoys direct presence of its military in key Middle Eastern countries including Saudi Arabia, Bahrain, Oman, Kuwait and Iraq which gives it a direct control of over 55% of proven oil reserves. Second, American economy has taken a downward spiral requiring careful planning to allocate resources. This change in strategic position might have prompted America to force a solution to Palestinian question through other means since stalled negotiations between the parties could not be restarted. Before submission of formal application for a UN membership an environment was created that would force Israel to get serious in peace negotiations.

Turkey, a major American ally, changed its position from a friend of Israel to an apparent hostility after death of 9 Turkish citizens during an attack on a Gaza aid flotilla. What surprised people was lack of American interest to bridge differences between its two strategic allies. As Turkey increased diplomatic pressure on Israel, US signed a major radar shield agreement with Turkey which showed their continued strategic alliance. During same time military establishment of Egypt, which is strongest American ally among Arabs, expressed doubts that they will be able to hold public pressure to honor their peace agreement with Israel. Similarly another ally Saudi Arabia openly supported Palestinian bid for UN membership. These coordinated events seem unlikely to be chance happenings without American consent.

Second move in this strategic shift was the announcement by Palestinian authority to submit their application for statehood to UN. One would imagine that America, a major contributor of aid, would put all its weight to dissuade Palestine by asking their mutual friend Turkey to use their influence. But instead it allowed momentum to build for this historic event.

Anyone who has ever been involved in policy formulation knows that long standing positions are not publically changed overnight even though it might be in the plans. Position of Israel is morally weak as it was the same UN that granted it statehood almost fifty years ago. For public consumption America will veto Palestinian bid but it is widely expected that it will face world condemnation for this act especially from its African, South American and Muslim allies. That backlash could provide impetus for America to depart from its extensive support to Israel and focus fully on South Asia where the action will be for rest of this century. Israel's overtures to China and Russia indicate that they are aware of this shift in policy and are seeking to hedge their position.

Why is America so much interested in South Asia? A close look at the map provides ample evidence in support of it. South Asia is home to two ambitious powers i.e. India and China.

Asia is home to three of the six declared nuclear powers i.e. India, China and Pakistan. It is home to fastest growing economies of the world i.e. India, China, as well as in close proximity to established ones like Japan and South Korea. It is home to half the population of the world. It is a gateway between Asia and Europe commonly known as Eurasia. In order to maintain its influence in the region America needed strong military presence to guard this gateway of Euroasia. One of the key factors to convince sovereign states to allow military bases is fear. Fear of an existence of a large disruptive force that can dislodge intricate balance of power between countries and result in widespread chaos. In South Korea it was expansion of communism that allowed stationing of American forces. In Japan it is growing power of China. In Middle East it is shia resurgence of Iran. In Germany it was the twice catastrophic rise of Aryan nationalism. In South Asia forces of terrorism and extremism will provide justification to acquire bases.

American decision to form bases in Afghanistan is justified because of its historic geopolitical position as a gateway to resource rich Central Asia, its small population, and insignificant military strength. But this approach had three inherent challenges i.e. Afghanistan does not have a favorable disposition to foreign military presence on its soil; the opposition of China and Russia to US bases and paranoia of Pakistan that America seeks to control its nuclear weapons.

China is still few decades away from projecting its military power internationally during which time it has to resolve some of its internal weaknesses. Unrest in Xinjiang province by terrorists was an alarm that worked in American favor. Position of China was softened by giving them assurances of access to the mineral and energy resources of Central Asia.

Russian position was neutralized when Obama administration pressed the reset button as soon as he came into office by assuring to contain the expansion plans of NATO and allowing Russia to maintain its influence on resource rich Central Asian countries. America also softened their support for Chechen separatist movement as a compromise.

The remaining hurdle in this equation is deterioration of relations between America and Pakistan. Pakistan must realize that its internal divisions, weak economy and its reliance on foreign weapons do not provide it the necessary strength to take an aggressive position against a major power. At the same time America must not ignore that as second largest Muslim country with a large organized military equipped with nuclear weapons, it will be mutually beneficial to align interest rather than embark on a divergent path. Pakistan has a long history of aligning its interest with America at critical junctures. Pakistan will have no major objection to American presence in Afghanistan but its growing strategic ties with arch rival India raises red flags in Islamabad. American insistence of dealing directly with Taliban without consultation also raises concern. These are issues that can be resolved if both countries step back from undiplomatic language and engage in negotiations.

Pakistan must engage in an intense diplomacy to clearly define its strategic interest to its friends and gain their support. China, Saudi Arabia and Turkey can play a key role in providing assurances to Pakistan and Afghanistan that their interests will be safeguarded.

The diplomatic chess board is in an active mode and all powers are actively engaged in the game. Wars will not be ended until there is a check mate that creates a stalemate.

Reorganizing UN: a new vision
(May 2, 2005)

First item in UN charter states that nations of the world are determined to save succeeding generations from scourge of war, which twice in our lifetime has brought untold sorrow to mankind. But this first promise has been broken at least five times in last 65 years; Korean war in 1950s, American invasion of Vietnam in 1960s, Russian occupation of Afghanistan in 1970s, conflict in Bosnia in 1990s, Iraq's invasion of Kuwait and most recently, American occupation of Iraq and Afghanistan. Legal premise may suggest that these were not wars but the fact is that countless innocent lives were lost in these armed conflicts regardless of the legitimacy of these actions. These events raise questions about effectiveness of UN in resolving conflict among its member countries. It is a vast subject but we will briefly touch upon organization of UN and its role in solving conflicts.

Office of Secretary General and Secretary General Kofi Annan has been the topic of many debates after disclosure of irregularities in UN oil- for- food program. This program was designed to help Iraq gain access to food and medicine during 10 years of economic sanctions for pursuing acquisition of weapons of mass destruction. These scandals have drawn attention to the administration of UN. The organization is broken down into the General Assembly (GA), Security Council, Secretariat, Economic Social Council, and International Court of Justice and Trusteeship. GA is comprised of all member states mandated with a charter to discuss any item that facilitates social, political and economic cooperation between nations. Security Council, comprised of 5 permanent members and 10 elected members, is more focused in resolving disputes between members and advice corrective actions against nations that can endanger international peace and stability. The secretariat headed by Secretary General works as an administrative wing as well as a diplomatic anchor between member countries.

Article II of the charter gives equal sovereign rights to all member nations but it is undermined by creating a privileged class of Permanent members of UNSC with a veto power.

These permanent members can stop any resolution that is brought to the Security Council by vetoing it. On many occasions this veto power came into play in resolving international conflicts seriously damaging the effectiveness of UN in discharging its charter responsibilities. Many world leaders have stressed reforming United Nations. Secretary General Kofi Annan has called on world leaders to reach a new global deal to tackle challenges of development, security and human rights and to overhaul the UN.

Eventually, UN has to become a body where all countries are equal in their membership rights or else it will lose its legitimacy. It is a good sign that it is considering to expand this exclusive club by increasing the number of its permanent members from 5 to 7. Japan, Brazil and India are all striving to gain access to these two additional seats. If members cannot agree to abolish permanent membership of the Security Council it can at least try to balance it by giving it representation from all cultures of the world.

Muslim countries that represent almost 33 percent of global population do not even have one permanent seat on Security Council. There are many countries that can be considered for this seat including Pakistan, Egypt, Turkey and Indonesia. Pakistan is the most qualified choice to represent the Muslim world. Pakistan makes substantial contribution to peace keeping efforts as well as enjoys close diplomatic relations with Middle Eastern countries. Africa is probably the poorest and most neglected continent in the world. UN should give Africa its due share on world stage by allocating a permanent Security Council seat to an African nation.

UN Secretariat operates as an international bureaucracy with a lot of waste and inefficiency built into the system. It has recently reorganized its country teams by creating 58 "UN Houses" to provide common office space to various agencies operating in those countries. But even this approach cannot produce substantial savings for it. Instead of managing its social program itself, UN should rely on host governments to lend staff for execution of various programs.

Key role of UN is to ensure peace and harmony among its member states. Unfortunately, it is in this role that it has proved to be most ineffective. UN resolutions have only become pieces of paper with no recourse available in cases of its breach. India has repeatedly ignored UN resolutions regarding Kashmir issue but Pakistan has no recourse available to get those resolutions honored. Like other multilateral organizations, especially EU, UN should have minimum requirements for its member states. These requirements should cover social, political and economic parameters to ensure compliance of human rights by member countries. Instead of America imposing its doctrine of democracy, UN should assume that role and make it a condition for its members to follow.

Other challenge UN faces is containment of world powers in initiating unilateral actions against other countries. America totally ignored UN Security Council by unilaterally deciding to initiate Iraq war in 2003. This independent action has opened doors for other nations to use it as precedence in taking preemptive actions against their neighboring countries. Strengthening diplomatic arm of UN and forming a permanent military establishment to take necessary corrective actions against nations that are committing crimes against humanity can avoid such situations. Crisis in Darfur is an excellent example where UN military intervention might be required to prevent genocide of innocent people. Composition of this military unit can be based on demographics of its member countries.

UN must not be seen as a talk shop and a club for the privileged few. It must become a final arbiter on decisions that shape future of the world. Economic, social and political deprivation gives rise to frustration and anger that ultimately result in conflict. UN will have to tackle many serious issues in years to come: Climate change, terrorism, nuclear proliferation, poverty and child labor are among them. Concerted efforts by all countries will be needed to tackles these issues.

Reorganizing UN: Nationalism vs. Globalization
(February 1, 2006)

For almost 50 years of last century globalization was an international response to save the world from a disaster like World War II. Philosophers, economists and politicians all believed that we live in a global village and that interests of mankind are intertwined. Globalization, as an economic philosophy meant that flow of capital, both human and intellectual, should move freely between political boundaries of countries. Transcontinental corporations were encouraged to promote their own unique culture instead of adjusting to local traditions and cultures. But all this changed after 9/11 when a group of terrorists struck a blow in the heart of American dream.

American leaders spearheaded globalization efforts with capitalism used as a weapon against communism. After the fall of Union of Soviet Socialist Republic (USSR), American leadership got a boost of confidence in their beliefs and values. They considered it a universal message of equality, peace and prosperity. Throughout 1990s American economy single handedly lifted the whole world with unprecedented growth in jobs, introduction of consumer communication technology, and unprecedented rise in stock market valuations creating young millionaires. Clinton administration focused more inward than outward during eight years of his term in office. Many American intellectuals with global ambitions did not agree with this restraint in exerting American influence in world affairs. After 9/11 these intellectuals found a motive to promote their global agenda and found a leader willing to implement it.

American rallying cry to either be with us or against us brought forward nationalism as a strong force against globalization. This is evident from a fatal blow to European constitution turned down by most of its member countries. It has prompted old powers France and Germany to break away from American influence and become independent in their foreign policy with support from popular public opinion.

It has encouraged Iran to defy world pressure and pursue its nuclear program by igniting nationalist sentiment among its people.

In this hostile environment, proponents of globalization have to come up with a new approach to curb this emerging nationalistic tide. The first step in this direction is freeing global economy from regional influences by creating international organizations. In the aftermath of American quagmire in Iraq it should be obvious that United Nations is much more relevant in world affairs than it ever was. It is about time that charter of UN is expanded to include global economic cooperation. A UN securities & Exchange commission (UNSEC) should be formed, and a UN electronic stock exchange (UNSE) should be initiated and regulated by this body.

Companies with transcontinental business interests should be allowed to list on this stock exchange and given an ability to raise capital worldwide. UNSEC can formulate listing requirements for this stock exchange. Listing on UNSE will make financial sense for these corporations who spent millions of dollars to conform to domestic accounting standards of each country they are operating in. It will help mutual funds to save expenses in maintaining local trading desks in different countries that can be replaced by a central investment team. It will assist individual investors to participate in global economy by investing in these UNSE listed securities.

The Bank for International Settlement (BIS), based in Basel, Switzerland, has been operating since 1930 to provide coordination between 55 central banks of the world. Role of BIS should be extended further to eliminate any single country currency used as a trading unit. Currently US dollar is considered a default trading currency. Recently Euro, Japanese Yen and Chinese Yuan have tried to extend their international influence but have not succeeded in replacing dollar as a trading unit. This economic influence of a national currency sometimes becomes a hurdle to the spread of globalization. BIS should come up with an international currency unit and set the conversion rates for each member currency.

Third most important element of spreading globalization is curbing recent tide of immigration controls in developed countries. For centuries mankind has migrated to greener pastures in search of opportunity and survival. It was only in 20th century that countries, to safeguard their political and economic interests, introduced passport and visa regime. These controls have created population imbalances which translate into environmental damage in some cases. Proponent of immigration controls is using nationalistic security reasons to further their agenda. With advent of computer technologies and convenient data storage, it is not difficult for countries to prevent criminals from entering their borders. UN should work with International Labor Organization (ILO) to coordinate immigration of people between countries. Each country needing immigrants can put forward their need to the international organization along with qualification requirements for applicants. Those interested to migrate can submit their applications to this international body using Internet and other communication technologies. Similarly, companies listed on UNSE should be given special permission to hire globally with no travel restriction on their employees. ILO or UN citizen commission can issue special travel documents to these employees. EU sanguine visa can provide valuable insight to prepare this program. Member countries can be allowed access to this data to prevent any unwanted people entering their borders. A country can submit an objection to travel with reasonable proof to prevent entry of any of these people in their borders.

All these ideas may seem utopian or unrealistic but without global economic institutions the forces of nationalism will continue gaining strength and dividing world in different civilizations constantly in war with each other. The creation of a truly global village, providing equal opportunity for all citizens, will eliminate appeal of terrorist organizations and make the world a safer place.

Reorganizing UN: emergence of regional platforms
(September 6, 2008)

Since its inception in 1945 UN has proved to be ineffective in preventing major world conflicts. Permanent members have vetoed on UN resolutions whenever it suited their national interest and rejected UN altogether when it was not possible to get a resolution in their favor. America brought its case against Iraq before UN to seek cooperation and authorize war to replace autocratic ruler Saddam Hussain. To make its case for war evidence of existence of weapons of mass destruction (WMD) was prepared. America made it clear that they will engage in a war with or without approval of the world body which was actually mandated to prevent such wars. The members of general assembly and Security Council expressed serious doubts about existence of WMD and refrained from extending any cooperation. Former General Secretary Kofi Annan tried to prevent Iraq war by emphasizing importance of diplomatic isolation for Saddam and by providing support to opposition in Iraq. He was ridiculed and embroiled in corruption charges which later proved baseless. He has been redeemed when America accepted their failure to locate any WMD in Iraq and accepting failure in nation building in the aftermath of fall of Baghdad. After 5 years of war it is now clear that if America had listened to world we might still have to deal with an Iraqi dictator but destruction of one of the oldest civilization might have been prevented with tremendous loss of human lives as collateral damage.

American invasion of Iraq have provided diplomatic precedence for other nations to ignore UN in persuasion of their national interest without brining them to the floor of Security Council. Russian actions in Georgia are a clear indication that in the new world order UN is increasingly irrelevant. We have two options available to reinstate lost credibility of this organization.

First option is to change structure of UN Security Council to democratize special powers of permanent members.

Second option is more radical which is to disband the organization into smaller regional entities with cooperation agreements in place between them.

Changing dynamics of the world has made it clear that we are moving clearly towards a multi-polar world in which US, Russia, China, Brazil, India and Iran will play a significant role. These competing world powers will need a client organization to exercise their powers on satellites. America already has NATO in place to use their influence on Western European countries. In the aftermath of Georgian situation and American security agreement with Poland, Russia can reinstate its long forgotten WARSAW pact with a new name allowing membership to former USSR states. Shanghai Cooperation Organization (SCO) can serve this purpose. China will use ASEAN and other regional arrangements to create its sphere of influence while India will rely on SAARC members as their client. Middle Eastern and Muslim countries can restructure Organization of Islamic Cooperation (OIC) to create a platform for negotiating with other blocks. Brazil, with strong backing from Argentina, can change the scope of regional trade agreement Mercosur among South American nations to include foreign policy and mutual security. African Union with strong leadership from South Africa and support from Ethiopia can form their own block.

Emergence of these regional organizations can make it possible for the world to negotiate peace. Globalization of politics has proved to be wrong as regional interests based on culture, language, religion and shared borders are stronger. It is not possible for a North American leader to fully understand and appreciate concerns of South Americans as Brazil can do. Each organization with a strong economic and military sponsor can make it possible to negotiate fair agreements backed by a genuine interest to implement it. It is always better to have a cold war with fine balance rather than an actual war with tremendous loss of innocent lives as collateral damage. It is very important to achieve a new balance which might be possible when the whole world is engaged through organizations promoting their regional interests.

United Nations is costing global humanity close to US$5 billion every year without much progress to show. UN has not been able to prevent famine in Ethiopia or genocide in Rwanda & Darfur by acting too slowly because of competing interest of permanent members. All of us need to come together and form a new world order that incorporates regional interest rather than making the world hostage to veto powers of five countries.

Reorganizing UN: state vs non-state actors
(January 22, 2009)

The diplomatic language of an era is influenced by the dominant power and their proxy states. In current era many terms have evolved to assume new meanings and become part of diplomatic lexicon. Reference to non-state actors that plan and execute terrorist acts has become a common occurrence. Non-state actors have been present throughout human history so this is not a new phenomenon. In 8th century ruler of Sindh Raja Dahir was given an ultimatum by Hajjaj ibn Yusuf for his inability to prevent pirate attacks on Muslim trading vessels. After one of those piracy incidents Dahir was given warning to return confiscated merchandize and kidnapped people or face wrath of the Muslim empire. His failure to comply with the envoy's demand resulted in invasion of Sindh. In 18th century East India Company became a non-state actor to exert military power to protect its trading interest in India. East India Company laid foundation for eventual colonization of India by British Empire.

Throughout history major powers have used non-state actors to pressure other states to succumb to their wishes. Afghan resistance movement, a non-state actor, against occupation of Russia, was supported by United States openly and termed it legitimate in all international forums. While same resistance movement to throw an American sponsored proxy rule in Kabul is called a terrorist organization. A significant point from these examples is that any government aspiring to eliminate non-state actors is fooling itself and trying to achieve an unattainable task. After terror incidents in Mumbai, President Zardari issued a statement that a non-state actor within Pakistan's sovereign borders might be responsible for these acts. By issuing this statement in haste he virtually issued a license to other states to intervene in Pakistan's to prevent future attacks.

Perception emerging from redefinition of non-state actors is the assumption that actions of non-state actors are almost always illegal and counter to state interests while state has legitimate right to engage in a military expedition without reprisal.

Israeli attack on Gaza killing large number of innocent citizens including employees of United Nations were not condemned as a terrorist act anywhere in the world only because these actions were initiated by a state in the name of its security. Israel broke all rules of engagement by deliberately throwing bombs, some filled with white phosphorous, on civilian population using pretext that those were hideouts of terrorist without showing proper evidence in support of the claim. They even attacked UN food warehouses claiming that bullets were fired from there. On the other hand Hamas which won a popular election were not allowed to acquire legitimacy of a state actor and hence deprived of its democratic right to rule and become a party to peace negotiation. When Israel blocked access to Gaza from land, sea and air, Hamas' armed actions to for its national security concerns were termed acts of terrorism.

Most influential non-state actor on the world stage is United Nations as a multilateral platform to broker negotiations between states. Structure of UN is such that five permanent members enjoy extraordinary powers in the Security Council while all other nations have to comply with the whims of those powers. The power struggle between these powers largely defines the outcome of a conflict. Sanctions against a nation are totally ineffective if that nation is supported by a major power. On the other hand a nation is put in a corner when no major power is willing to support its cause. There have been many resolutions against Israel and India to resolve the Palestine and Kashmir conflict but these nations blatantly refused to comply without any serious sanctions imposed against them. On the other hand sanctions against Iraq for their aspirations to become a regional power resulted in deaths of over 500,000 children while no one came forward to plead their case. US Secretary of State Madeline Albright famously quoted that those deaths were an inevitable collateral damage.

Administration of President Barack Obama emphasized time and again that they believe in using soft or diplomatic power to resolve conflicts and protect their interest. If they are serious in achieving their stated objectives then they have to remove the anomalies in their definition of terrorism and non-state actors. It is ironic that introduction of democracy in Iraq at the cost of innocent civilian lives is justifiable while results of an election under US watch in Gaza are not acceptable.

Discrepancies in American diplomatic lingo will further tarnish their image and push world towards a new order with many poles of influence. American values are very close to Islamic faith and there is no reason a conciliatory discourse can not be established. We hope Obama administration will bring the two civilizations closer by resolving injustices around the world and restructuring the UN to reflect new realities.

Middle East: Iraq and its future
(September 14, 2005)

Many writers including myself have predicted that Iraq might be divided into three autonomous states i.e. Shiite majority south, Kurd majority north and Sunni majority north east. Many people expressed their reservation about that prediction and considered it a simplistic view. But it seems that this will soon become a reality as is evident from draft constitution of Iraq. Though the interim government has still not reached an agreement on the draft and has requested second extension in deadline to approve it. Dynamics on ground indicate that it will be promulgated even if Sunnis do not fully consent to it. Majority of constituent body, around 80%, is comprised of Shiite and Kurd leaders who are in favor of a federalist system. Many observers feel this is a precursor to the break up of Iraq into three states.

Before we comment on the prevailing condition in Iraq, it is important to analyze history which provides a very important benchmark to understand behavior and attitude of a nation. Iraq, or Mesopotamia as it was called before present era, was at cross roads between expanding Islamic empire from Arabia and Christian dominated west sharing its border with Turkey. For almost its entire history Iraqis were progressive people adopting advancement in technology and science as well as contributing towards intellectual evolution of mankind. First known pictographic writings were found in Iraq. During its 5000 years of recorded history, Mesopotamia was considered cradle of civilization but its importance to modern world was revealed after large oil reserves were found there.

In modern history Iraq can be compared to Afghanistan in terms of psychology of its people and its geo-political position in their respective regions. Afghanistan for thousands of years, served as a gateway for ambitious Central Asian kings to invade rich lands of India.

The people of Afghanistan were accustomed to armies marching through their land and so maintaining weapons became a way of life for them. In last century Mujahedeen, as they were referred to by Americans, raised arms against invasion of Russia and ultimately forced their withdrawal in haste. Similarly Iraq was a gateway between Arab Middle East to Europe. It has experienced armies marching through its lands to either reach Mediterranean region or European invaders subjugating oil rich Middle East.

Iraq was carved out of larger Arabia after the defeat of Ottoman Empire in First World War and in 1920 became part of British Empire. It was never a totally Arab country in its ethnic make-up. It shared borders with Shiite majority Iran on one side and on the other had a substantial Kurdish population who never totally felt being part of the Iraqi identity. Declining economic condition of Britain forced it to install King Faisal 1 and converted it into a kingdom. British maintained their proxy control of Iraq until 1941 when an anti-British leader Rashid Ali al-Gaylani overthrew the King and established his republican rule. British could never again gain control of the territory from succession of Iraq's military and political leaders. After many bloody coups, Baath party took control in 1963 under the leadership of Col. Abd al-Salam Aref that culminated in the elevation of Saddam Hussein to power in 1979.

For large part of 20th century, Iraq had been a battleground between various Western and Asian powers to gain access to its large oil reserves. Throughout these turbulent times, Iraqi people have maintained their unity but ambitious leaders supported by foreign powers never allowed peace to prevail in the region. Saddam's expansionist ambitions prompted America to make him its chief enemy. This enmity first resulted in the Gulf War of 1991 after forced annexation of Kuwait by Iraq and then led to complete American occupation after second Iraq war in 2003.

In modern times it is difficult for any power to maintain absolute control of a country as is evident from the failure of America in Vietnam, Germany in Poland and Russia in Afghanistan.

The most successful strategy is the one pursued by British Empire for most part of 19th and 20th century, which is to encourage ethnic and sectarian divisions among people to weaken their resolve for liberty. It seems that Britain is not only contributing armed forces but also sharing its hundreds of years of colonial experience with Americans.

Strongman Saddam Hussain under his iron fist was able to maintain a unified Iraqi identity until he was removed by American invasion. His removal from power eliminated the lid that held the society together and created a vacuum that is largely responsible for the civil war. American policy of allowing dismantling of Iraqi army and removal of Baathist from government institutions has created a void that is also playing its part in the current chaos. The first piece of American strategy in Iraq is to promote ethnic and sectarian division by emphasizing differences in the Sunni and Shiite communities. Although Kurds are Sunnis in their religious following but combining them with Arab Sunnis will remove the demographic advantage of Shiite. So the ethnic card is played to divide the society into three competing groups.

Breakup of Iraq during occupation will squarely put blame on American shoulders. So over a decade or two a buffer period has to be ensued during which a wider gulf will be created among communities using intelligence assets created on the ground. New constitution was drafted under supervision of transitional government in 2005 which contains a provision that allows a group of regional governors to decide to succeed from center and become autonomous. Break up of Iraq into oil rich Shiite and Kurd region will result in their continued military dependence on America and award of oil concessions to protect themselves from any aggression from Iran or predominantly Sunni Arab states. It will provide a much-needed stronghold for America to keep its influence on other oil rich countries i.e. Kuwait and Saudi Arabia.

Actions taken to satisfy thirst for energy and economic gains might make sense in short term but in long term break up of Iraq could destabilize the region so severely that it could put world peace in serious jeopardy.

Let us try to predict probable outcome of break up of the region. To begin with, there would be an economic reliance of Sunni-Iraq on Shiite controlled oil riches. Economic turmoil could produce millions of youth with no jobs leading them to fall into the hands of terrorist organizations to inflict injury on the world. The continued presence of America to protect the Shiite-Iraq could induce Iran to pursue its quest for nuclear weapons, seriously endangering regional peace as well as creating an arms race. China's anxiety over interruptions in its oil supplies could induce them to support Iranian ambitions as a counter to American interest. It will further divide the world into two poles. Economically empowered Iraqi-Kurds could finance separatist movements in Kurdish region of Turkey. Turkish proximity to Europe will create a ripple effect of these incidents in EU thereby further complicating matters.

Best scenario for long-term peace in the region is introduction of a parliamentary democracy in Iraq with President as head of state rotated between Kurds, Shiite and Sunnis according to a predetermined formula. Iraq could be divided into 5 or 6 administrative provinces with their own local assemblies under regional governors operating as representatives of the President. This provincial government could be financed through a national pool of oil revenues as well as local taxes. This system of government is successfully run in India with over 200 sects and ethnicities. India, which has a long history of friendship with Iraq, can share her experience with the interim Iraqi government to prepare a draft constitution that ensures a united Iraq with equal rights given to all segments of the society. The Organization of Islamic Cooperation (OIC) and Gulf Cooperation Council (GCC) can play an important role in formulation of a draft constitution to ensure successful transfer of power to an elected parliament.

Break up of Iraq would damage American credibility and its intention to bring peace to the region. Any decrease in its influence will provide further opportunity to China to strengthen its defense and economic ties with Middle Eastern countries as it has done in Africa. America should only aid Iraq to safeguard its own future; not become its architect.

Middle East: no peace on the horizon
(July 28, 2006)

It seems that the precarious balance between Israel and its neighbors is once again broken. Western media blame Hezbollah for breaking peace by ambushing the Israeli soldiers; killing some and kidnapping two. Israel retaliated with full force by bombarding Beirut for last 16 days and entering Lebanese territory with an objective to strike at the strongholds of Hezbollah. First of all, the skirmishes between Israeli militia and Palestinian organizations have been going on forever without any real break. Israel has repeatedly bombarded Palestinian and Hezbollah positions during last 10-15 years killing many activists as well as civilians. Secondly, since Muslim resistance organizations are no match for military strength of Israel, they had to resolve to gorilla tactics to retaliate against occupation of their territory and to get the release of their prisoners held in jails.

US diplomatic response to this conflict has been controversial. It is first time that America has refused to push Israel for a quick ceasefire. American officials have, in fact, encouraged Israeli advancement into Lebanese territory. It serves two purposes. First, it takes attention away from Iraq and provides a source to uplift public support for the administration. Secondly, it helps America use Israel as a front line state to fight Muslim activist organizations in Middle East. America has been quick to blame Syria and Iran for supporting Hezbollah thereby making them part of the conflict. This conflict helps Republican Party gain support for their candidates during upcoming congressional elections by making their case for war against terrorism.

International response has been mixed. Russia, France and Germany have condemned Israel's aggression causing heavy civilian casualties to fight a political organization with militaristic bent. United Nations Secretary, General Kofi Annan, has criticized bombing of Beirut and destruction of UN observation post.

Muslim countries in their official response are divided as always. Countries with significant American influence like Saudi Arabia, Jordan and Egypt have made Hezbollah responsible for this conflict. But most surprisingly, Muslim institutions like Organization of Islamic Cooperation (OIC) and Arab League have not been able to bring parties to the negotiations to attain cease-fire. So far there has been no emergency meeting of heads of Muslim states to form a united front to address this crisis. OIC has only conducted an ambassadorial level meeting which issued a weakly worded communiqué to ask Israel to cease hostilities and allow initiation of humanitarian aid for affected civilians. Western countries have called a meeting in Rome without adequate Muslim representation to address situation. OIC and Arab League were not made part of Rome meeting. The result of that conference, naturally, was a failure.

Another dynamic in play here is that Muslim masses have lost trust in their governments to represent their interest in domestic and international affairs. They consider their governments to be non-representative, exploitative and agents of the West. Western media has continually questioned the validity, ethics and moral values of Muslim faith labeling almost all terrorists as Islamic terrorists. This has further alienated masses that consider radical organizations as guardians of their faith against unprovoked aggression. Militant organizations Al Qaeda and Hezbollah understand this dynamic very well and use it to their advantage to gain finances, recruits and local community protection. Since there is no Muslim country strong enough to stand up to military might of America and Israel, Muslims largely feel that gorilla fight is their only option to respond to armed aggression in their lands. They have seen this scenario in play in Afghanistan, Iraq and now in Lebanon where Hezbollah has stood up to sophisticated armory of Israel.

Peace cannot be attained unless all of us agree that we have a serious crisis at hand, which can quickly convert to a global war. It is unrealistic to negotiate peace without involving Muslim institutions OIC, GCC and Arab League.

The strategy by West to try to divide the Muslim world into Shiite and Sunni sects can turn dangerous. This attempt might work at government level but masses understand this play and are united as one Ummah. Each passing day in Israel-Lebanese war is creating deeper support for Lebanese. This could ultimately result in upheavals in countries with authoritarian rulers considered proxies of West and introduction of more radical governments which could produce more conflicts throughout the region.

Wars do not solve any conflicts. They are only used to vent anger and frustrations building up for decades. In the end, peace is always attainted sitting around a table reaching a compromise that is equitable and fair. Israel's efforts to build walls and buffer zones are unrealistic unless its neighbors see her as a reliable friend and a trusted partner.

Appendix I: Objectives Resolution

Note: The Objectives Resolution was passed by the Constituent Assembly of Pakistan in March, 1949, and was made a substantive part of the Constitution of Pakistan by the Revival of Constitution of 1973 Order, 1985 (P.O.No.14 of 1985), Art.2 and Sch.item 2 (with effect from March 2, 1985).

Text of the Objectives Resolution

Whereas sovereignty over the entire universe belongs to Allah Almighty alone and the authority which He has delegated to the State of Pakistan, through its people for being exercised within the limits prescribed by Him is a sacred trust;

This Constituent Assembly representing the people of Pakistan resolves to frame a Constitution for the sovereign independent State of Pakistan;

Wherein the State shall exercise its powers and authority through the chosen representatives of the people;
Wherein the principles of democracy, freedom, equality, tolerance and social justice as enunciated by Islam shall be fully observed;
Wherein the Muslims shall be enabled to order their lives in the individual and collective spheres in accordance with the teachings and requirements of Islam as set out in the Holy Quran and the Sunnah;
Wherein adequate provision shall be made for the minorities to freely profess and practice their religions and develop their cultures;
Wherein the territories now included in or in accession with Pakistan and such other territories as may hereafter be included in or accede to Pakistan shall form a Federation wherein the units will be autonomous with such boundaries and limitations on their powers and authority as may be prescribed;
Wherein shall be guaranteed fundamental rights including equality of status, of opportunity and before law, social, economic and political justice, and freedom of thought, expression, belief, faith, worship and association, subject to law and public morality;
Wherein adequate provisions shall be made to safeguard the legitimate interests of minorities and backward and depressed

classes;

Wherein the independence of the Judiciary shall be fully secured;
Wherein the integrity of the territories of the Federation, its independence and all its rights including its sovereign rights on land, sea and air shall be safeguarded;

So that the people of Pakistan may prosper and attain their rightful and honored place amongst the nations of the World and make their full contribution towards international peace and progress and happiness of humanity.

Appendix II: CHARTER OF DEMOCRACY

We the elected leaders of Pakistan have deliberated on the political crisis in our beloved homeland, the threats to its survival, the erosion of the federation's unity, the military's subordination of all state institutions, the marginalisation of civil society, the mockery of the Constitution and representative institutions, growing poverty, unemployment and inequality, brutalisation of society, breakdown of rule of law and, the unprecedented hardships facing our people under a military dictatorship, which has pushed our beloved country to the brink of a total disaster;

Noting the most devastating and traumatic experiences that our nation experienced under military dictatorships that played havoc with the nation's destiny and created conditions disallowing the progress of our people and the flowering of democracy. Even after removal from office they undermined the people's mandate and the sovereign will of the people;

Drawing history's lesson that the military dictatorship and the nation cannot co-exist – as military involvement adversely affect the economy and the democratic institutions as well as the defence capabilities, and the integrity of the country – the nation needs a new direction different from a militaristic and regimental approach of the Bonapartist regimes, as the current one;

Taking serious exception to the vilification campaign against the representatives of the people, in particular, and the civilians, in general, the victimisation of political leaders/workers and their media trials under a Draconian law in the name of accountability, in order to divide and eliminate the representative political parties, to Gerrymander a king's party and concoct legitimacy to prolong the military rule;

Noting our responsibility to our people to set an alternative direction for the country saving it from its present predicaments on an economically sustainable, socially progressive, politically democratic and pluralist, federally cooperative, ideologically tolerant, internationally respectable and regionally peaceful basis in the larger interests of the peoples of Pakistan to decide once for all that only the people and no one else has the sovereign right to govern through their elected representatives, as conceived by the democrat par excellence, Father of the Nation Quaid-i-Azam Mohammed Ali Jinnah;

Reaffirming our commitment to undiluted democracy and universally recognised fundamental rights, the rights of a vibrant opposition, internal party democracy, ideological/political tolerance, bipartisan working of the parliament through powerful committee system, a cooperative federation with no discrimination against federating units, the decentralisation and devolution of power, maximum provincial autonomy, the empowerment of the people at the grassroots level, the emancipation of our people from poverty, ignorance, want and disease, the uplift of women and minorities, the elimination of klashnikov culture, a free and independent media, an independent judiciary, a neutral civil service, rule of law and merit, the settlement of disputes with the neighbours through peaceful means, honouring international contracts, laws/covenants and sovereign guarantees, so as to achieve a responsible and civilised status in the comity of nations through a foreign policy that suits our national interests;

Calling upon the people of Pakistan to join hands to save our motherland from the clutches of military dictatorship and to defend their fundamental, social, political and economic rights and for a democratic, federal, modern and progressive Pakistan as dreamt by the Founder of the nation; have adopted the following, "Charter of Democracy";

A. CONSTITUTIONAL AMENDMENTS

1. The 1973 Constitution as on 12th October 1999 before the military coup shall be restored with the provisions of joint electorates, minorities, and women reserved seats on closed party list in the Parliament, the lowering of the voting age, and the increase in seats in parliament and the Legal Framework Order, 2000 and the Seventeenth Constitutional Amendment shall be repealed accordingly.

2. The appointment of the governors, three services chiefs and the CJCSC shall be made by the chief executive who is the prime minister, as per the 1973 Constitution.

3. (a) The recommendations for appointment of judges to superior judiciary shall be formulated through a commission, which shall comprise of the following: i. The chairman shall be a chief justice, who has never previously taken oath under the PCO.

ii. The members of the commission shall be the chief justices of the provincial high courts who have not taken oath under the PCO, failing which the senior most judge of that high court who has not taken oath shall be the member

iii. Vice-Chairmen of Pakistan and Vice-Chairmen of Provincial Bar Association with respect to the appointment of judges to their concerned province

iv. President of Supreme Court Bar Association

v. Presidents of High Court Bar Associations of Karachi, Lahore, Peshawar, and Quetta with respect to the appointment of judges to their concerned province

vi. Federal Minister for Law and Justice

vii. Attorney General of Pakistan

(a-i) The commission shall forward a panel of three names for each vacancy to the prime minister, who shall forward one name for confirmation to joint parliamentary committee for confirmation of the nomination through a transparent public hearing process.

(a-ii) The joint parliamentary committee shall comprise of 50 per cent members from the treasury benches and the remaining 50 per cent from opposition parties based on their strength in the parliament nominated by respective parliamentary leaders.

(b) No judge shall take oath under any Provisional Constitutional Order or any other oath that is contradictory to the exact language of the original oath prescribed in the Constitution of 1973.

(c) Administrative mechanism will be instituted for the prevention of misconduct, implementation of code of ethics, and removal of judges on such charges brought to its attention by any citizen through the proposed commission for appointment of Judges. (d) All special courts including anti-terrorism and accountability courts shall be abolished and such cases be tried in ordinary courts. Further to create a set of rules and procedures whereby, the arbitrary powers of the chief justices over the assignment of cases to various judges and the transfer of judges to various benches such powers shall be exercised by the Chief Justice and two senior most judges sitting together.

4. A Federal Constitutional Court will be set up to resolve constitutional issues, giving equal representation to each of the federating units, whose members may be judges or persons qualified to be judges of the Supreme Court, constituted for a six-year period. The Supreme and High Courts will hear regular civil and criminal cases. The appointment of judges shall be made in the same manner as for judges of higher judiciary.

5. The Concurrent List in the Constitution will be abolished. A new NFC award will be announced.

6. The reserved seats for women in the national and provincial assemblies will be allocated to the parties on the basis of the number of votes polled in the general elections by each party.

7. The strength of the Senate of Pakistan shall be increased to give representation to minorities in the Senate.

8. FATA shall be included in the NWFP province in consultation with them.

9. Northern Areas shall be developed by giving it a special status and further empowering the Northern Areas Legislative Council to provide people of Northern Areas access to justice and human rights.

10. Local bodies election will be held on party basis through provincial election commissions in respective provinces and constitutional protection will be given to the local bodies to make them autonomous and answerable to their respective assemblies as well as to the people through regular courts of law.

B. CODE OF CONDUCT

11. National Security Council will be abolished. Defence Cabinet Committee will be headed by prime minister and will have a permanent secretariat. The prime minister may appoint a federal security adviser to process intelligence reports for the prime minister. The efficacy of the higher defence and security structure, created two decades ago, will be reviewed. The Joint Services Command structure will be strengthened and made more effective and headed in rotation among the three services by law. 12. The ban on a 'prime minister not being eligible for a third term of office' will be abolished.

13. (a) Truth and Reconciliation Commission be established to acknowledge victims of torture, imprisonment, state-sponsored persecution, targeted legislation, and politically motivated accountability. The commission will also examine and report its findings on military coups and civil removals of governments from 1996.

(b) A commission shall also examine and identify the causes of and fix responsibility and make recommendations in the light thereof for incidences such as Kargil.

(c) Accountability of NAB and other Ehtesab operators to identify and hold accountable abuse of office by NAB operators through purgery and perversion of justice and violation of human rights since its establishment.

(d) To replace politically motivated NAB with an independent accountability commission, whose chairman shall be nominated by the prime minister in consultation with the leader of opposition and confirmed by a joint parliamentary committee with 50 per cent members from treasury benches and remaining 50 per cent from opposition parties in same manner as appointment of judges through transparent public hearing. The confirmed nominee shall meet the standard of political impartiality, judicial propriety, moderate views expressed through his judgements and would have not dealt.

14. The press and electronic media will be allowed its independence. Access to information will become law after parliamentary debate and public scrutiny.

15. The chairmen of public accounts committee in the national and provincial assemblies will be appointed by the leaders of opposition in the concerned assemblies.

16. An effective Nuclear Command and Control system under the Defence Cabinet Committee will be put in place to avoid any possibility of leakage or proliferation.

17. Peaceful relations with India and Afghanistan will be pursued without prejudice to outstanding disputes.

18. Kashmir dispute should be settled in accordance with the UN Resolutions and the aspirations of the people of Jammu and Kashmir.

19. Governance will be improved to help the common citizen, by giving access to quality social services like education, health, job generation, curbing price hike, combating illegal redundancies, and curbing lavish spendings in civil and military establishments as ostentious causes great resentment amongst the teeming millions. We pledge to promote and practice simplicity, at all levels.

20. Women, minorities, and the under privileged will be provided equal opportunities in all walks of life.

21. We will respect the electoral mandate of representative governments that accepts the due role of the opposition and declare neither shall undermine each other through extra constitutional ways.

22. We shall not join a military regime or any military sponsored government. No party shall solicit the support of military to come into power or to dislodge a democratic government.

23. To prevent corruption and floor crossing all votes for the Senate and indirect seats will be by open identifiable ballot. Those violating the party discipline in the poll shall stand disqualified by a letter from the parliamentary party leader to the concerned Speaker or the Chairman Senate with a copy to the Election Commission for notification purposes within 14 days of receipt of letter failing which it will be deemed to have been notified on the expiry of that period.

24. All military and judicial officers will be required to file annual assets and income declarations like Parliamentarians to make them accountable to the public.

25. National Democracy Commission shall be established to promote and develop a democratic culture in the country and provide assistance to political parties for capacity building on the basis of their seats in parliament in a transparent manner.

26. Terrorism and militancy are by-products of military dictatorship, negation of democracy, are strongly condemned, and will be vigorously confronted.

C. FREE AND FAIR ELECTIONS

27. There shall be an independent, autonomous, and impartial election commission. The prime minister shall in consultation with leader of opposition forward up to three names for each position of chief election commissioner, members of election commission, and secretary to joint parliamentary committee, constituted on the same pattern as for appointment of judges in superior judiciary, through transparent public hearing process. In case of no consensus, both prime minister and leader of opposition shall forward separate lists to the joint parliamentary committee for consideration. Provincial election commissioner shall be appointed on the same pattern by committees of respective provincial assemblies.

28. All contesting political parties will be ensured a level playing field in the elections by the release of all political prisoners and the

unconditional return of all political exiles. Elections shall be open to all political parties and political personalities. The graduation requirement of eligibility which has led to corruption and fake degrees will be repealed.

29. Local bodies elections will be held within three months of the holding of general elections.

30. The concerned election authority shall suspend and appoint neutral administrators for all local bodies from the date of formation of a caretaker government for holding of general elections till the elections are held.

31. There shall be a neutral caretaker government to hold free, fair, and transparent elections. The members of the said government and their immediate relatives shall not contest elections.

D. CIVIL – MILITARY RELATIONS

32. The ISI, MI and other security agencies shall be accountable to the elected government through Prime Minister Sectt, Ministry of Defence, and Cabinet Division respectively. Their budgets will be approved by DCC after recommendations are prepared by the respective ministry. The political wings of all intelligence agencies will be disbanded. A committee will be formed to cut waste and bloat in the armed forces and security agencies in the interest of the defence and security of the country. All senior postings in these agencies shall be made with the approval of the government through respective ministry.

33. All indemnities and savings introduced by military regimes in the constitution shall be reviewed.

34. Defence budget shall be placed before the parliament for debate and approval.

35. Military land allotment and cantonment jurisdictions will come under the purview of defence ministry. A commission shall be set up to review, scrutinise, and examine the legitimacy of all such land allotment rules, regulations, and policies, along with all cases of state land allotment including those of military urban and agricultural land allotments since 12th October, 1999 to hold those accountable who have indulged in malpractices, profiteering, and favouritism.

36. Rules of business of the federal and provincial governments shall be reviewed to bring them in conformity with parliamentary form of government.

Appendix III: Full text of Kerry-Lugar-Bergman bill

AT THE FIRST SESSION

Begun and held at the City of Washington on Tuesday,
the sixth day of January, two thousand and nine

An Act

To authorize appropriations for fiscal years 2010 through 2014 to promote an enhanced strategic partnership with Pakistan and its people, and for other purposes.

BE IT ENACTED BY THE SENATE AND HOUSE OF REPRESENTATIVES OF THE UNITED STATES OF AMERICA IN CONGRESS ASSEMBLED,

SECTION 1. Short title; table of contents.

(a) Short title. — This Act may be cited as the "Enhanced Partnership with Pakistan Act of 2009".

(b) Table of contents. — The table of contents for this Act is as follows:

SEC. 2. Definitions.

In this Act:

(1) APPROPRIATE CONGRESSIONAL COMMITTEES.—Except as otherwise provided in this Act, the term "appropriate congressional committees" means the Committees on Appropriations and Foreign Relations of the Senate and the Committees on Appropriations and Foreign Affairs of the House of Representatives.

(2) COUNTERINSURGENCY.—The term "counterinsurgency" means efforts to defeat organized movements that seek to overthrow the duly constituted Governments of Pakistan and Afghanistan through violent means.

(3) COUNTERTERRORISM.—The term "counterterrorism" means efforts to combat al Qaeda and other foreign terrorist organizations that are designated by the Secretary of State in accordance with section 219 of the Immigration and Nationality Act (8 U.S.C. 1189), or other individuals and entities engaged in terrorist activity or support for such activity.

(4) FATA.—The term "FATA" means the Federally Administered Tribal Areas of Pakistan.

(5) FRONTIER CRIMES REGULATION.—The term "Frontier Crimes Regulation" means the Frontier Crimes Regulation, codified under British law in 1901, and applicable to the FATA.

(6) IMPACT EVALUATION RESEARCH.—The term "impact evaluation research" means the application of research methods and statistical analysis to measure the extent to which change in a

population-based outcome can be attributed to program intervention instead of other environmental factors.

(7) MAJOR DEFENSE EQUIPMENT. — The term "major defense equipment" has the meaning given the term in section 47(6) of the Arms Export Control Act (22 U.S.C. 2794(6)).

(8) NWFP. — The term "NWFP" means the North West Frontier Province of Pakistan, which has Peshawar as its provincial capital.

(9) OPERATIONS RESEARCH. — The term "operations research" means the application of social science research methods, statistical analysis, and other appropriate scientific methods to judge, compare, and improve policies and program outcomes, from the earliest stages of defining and designing programs through their development and implementation, with the objective of the rapid dissemination of conclusions and concrete impact on programming.

(10) SECURITY FORCES OF PAKISTAN. — The term "security forces of Pakistan" means the military and intelligence services of the Government of Pakistan, including the Armed Forces, Inter-Services Intelligence Directorate, Intelligence Bureau, police forces, levies, Frontier Corps, and Frontier Constabulary.

(11) SECURITY-RELATED ASSISTANCE. — The term "security-related assistance" —

(A) means —

(i) grant assistance to carry out section 23 of the Arms Export Control Act (22 U.S.C. 2763); and

(ii) assistance under chapter 2 of part II of the Foreign Assistance Act of 1961 (22 U.S.C. 2311 et. seq); but

(B) does not include —

(i) assistance authorized to be appropriated or otherwise made available under any provision of law that is funded from accounts within budget function 050 (National Defense); and

(ii) amounts appropriated or otherwise available to the Pakistan Counterinsurgency Capability Fund established under the Supplemental Appropriations Act, 2009 (Public Law 111–32).

SEC. 3. Findings.

Congress finds the following:

(1) The people of the Islamic Republic of Pakistan and the United States share a long history of friendship and comity, and the interests of both nations are well-served by strengthening and deepening this friendship.

(2) Since 2001, the United States has contributed more than $15,000,000,000 to Pakistan, of which more than $10,000,000,000 has been security-related assistance and direct payments.

(3) With the free and fair election of February 18, 2008, Pakistan returned to civilian rule, reversing years of political tension and mounting popular concern over military rule and Pakistan's own democratic reform and political development.

(4) Pakistan is a major non-NATO ally of the United States and has been a valuable partner in the battle against al Qaeda and the Taliban, but much more remains to be accomplished by both nations.

(5) The struggle against al Qaeda, the Taliban, and affiliated terrorist groups has led to the deaths of several thousand Pakistani civilians and members of the security forces of Pakistan over the past seven years.

(6) Despite killing or capturing hundreds of al Qaeda operatives and other terrorists — including major al Qaeda leaders, such as Khalid Sheikh Muhammad, Ramzi bin al-Shibh, and Abu Faraj al-Libi — the FATA, parts of the NWFP, Quetta in Balochistan, and Muridke in Punjab remain a sanctuary for al Qaeda, the Afghan Taliban, the Terikh-e Taliban and affiliated groups from which these groups organize terrorist actions against Pakistan and other countries.

(7) The security forces of Pakistan have struggled to contain a Taliban-backed insurgency, recently taking direct action against those who threaten Pakistan's security and stability, including military operations in the FATA and the NWFP.

(8) On March 27, 2009, President Obama noted, "Multiple intelligence estimates have warned that al Qaeda is actively planning attacks on the United States homeland from its safe-haven in Pakistan.".

(9) According to a Government Accountability Office report (GAO-08-622), "since 2003, the [A]dministration's national security strategies and Congress have recognized that a comprehensive plan that includes all elements of national power — diplomatic, military, intelligence, development assistance, economic, and law enforcement support — was needed to address the terrorist threat emanating from the FATA" and that such a strategy was also mandated by section 7102(b)(3) of the Intelligence Reform and Terrorism Prevention Act of 2004 (Public Law 108–458; 22 U.S.C. 2656f note) and section 2042(b)(2) of the Implementing the Recommendations of the 9/11 Commission Act of 2007 (Public Law 110–53; 22 U.S.C. 2375 note).

(10) During 2008 and 2009, the people of Pakistan have been especially hard hit by rising food and commodity prices and severe energy shortages, with 2/3 of the population living on less than $2 a day and 1/5 of the population living below the poverty line according to the United Nations Development Program.

(11) Economic growth is a fundamental foundation for human security and national stability in Pakistan, a country with more than 175,000,000 people, an annual population growth rate of two percent, and a ranking of 136 out of 177 countries [141 out of 182 countries in 2009] in the United Nations Human Development Index.

(12) The 2009 Pakistani military offensive in the NWFP and the FATA displaced millions of residents in one of the gravest humanitarian crises Pakistan has faced, and despite the heroic efforts of Pakistanis to respond to the needs of the displaced

millions and facilitate the return of many, it has highlighted the need for Pakistan to develop an effective national counterinsurgency strategy.

SEC. 4. Statement of principles.

Congress declares that the relationship between the United States and Pakistan should be based on the following principles:

(1) Pakistan is a critical friend and ally to the United States, both in times of strife and in times of peace, and the two countries share many common goals, including combating terrorism and violent radicalism, solidifying democracy and rule of law in Pakistan, and promoting the social and economic development of Pakistan.

(2) United States assistance to Pakistan is intended to supplement, not supplant, Pakistan's own efforts in building a stable, secure, and prosperous Pakistan.

(3) The United States requires a balanced, integrated, countrywide strategy for Pakistan that provides assistance throughout the country and does not disproportionately focus on security-related assistance or one particular area or province.

(4) The United States supports Pakistan's struggle against extremist elements and recognizes the profound sacrifice made by Pakistan in the fight against terrorism, including the loss of more than 1,900 soldiers and police since 2001 in combat with al Qaeda, the Taliban, and other extremist and terrorist groups.

(5) The United States intends to work with the Government of Pakistan—

(A) to build mutual trust and confidence by actively and consistently pursuing a sustained, long-term, multifaceted relationship between the two countries, devoted to strengthening the mutual security, stability, and prosperity of both countries;

(B) to support the people of Pakistan and their democratic government in their efforts to consolidate democracy, including strengthening Pakistan's parliament, helping Pakistan reestablish an independent and transparent judicial system, and working to extend the rule of law in all areas in Pakistan;

(C) to promote sustainable long-term development and infrastructure projects, including in healthcare, education, water management, and energy programs, in all areas of Pakistan, that are sustained and supported by each successive democratic government in Pakistan;

(D) to ensure that all the people of Pakistan, including those living in areas governed by the Frontier Crimes Regulation, have access to public, modernized education and vocational training to enable them to provide for themselves, for their families, and for a more prosperous future for their children;

(E) to support the strengthening of core curricula and the quality of schools across Pakistan, including madrassas, in order to improve the prospects for Pakistani children's futures and eliminate incitements to violence and intolerance;

(F) to encourage and promote public-private partnerships in Pakistan in order to bolster ongoing development efforts and strengthen economic prospects, especially with respect to opportunities to build civic responsibility and professional skills of the people of Pakistan, including support for institutions of higher learning with international accreditation;

(G) to expand people-to-people engagement between the two countries, through increased educational, technical, and cultural exchanges and other methods;

(H) to encourage the development of local analytical capacity to measure program effectiveness and progress on an integrated basis, especially across the areas of United States assistance and payments to Pakistan, and increase accountability for how such assistance and payments are being spent;

(I) to assist Pakistan's efforts to improve counterterrorism financing and anti-money laundering regulatory structure in order to achieve international standards and encourage Pakistan to apply for "Financial Action Task Force" observer status and adhere to the United Nations International Convention for the Suppression of the Financing of Terrorism;

(J) to strengthen Pakistan's counterinsurgency and counterterrorism strategy to help prevent any territory of Pakistan from being used as a base or conduit for terrorist attacks in Pakistan or elsewhere;

(K) to strengthen Pakistan's efforts to develop strong and effective law enforcement and national defense forces under civilian leadership;

(L) to achieve full cooperation in matters of counter-proliferation of nuclear materials and related networks;

(M) to strengthen Pakistan's efforts to gain control of its under-governed areas and address the threat posed by any person or group that conducts violence, sabotage, or other terrorist activities in Pakistan or its neighboring countries; and

(N) to explore means to consult with and utilize the relevant expertise and skills of the Pakistani-American community.

TITLE I — Democratic, Economic, and Development Assistance for Pakistan

SEC. 101. Authorization of assistance.

(a) In general. — The President is authorized to provide assistance to Pakistan —

(1) to support the consolidation of democratic institutions;

(2) to support the expansion of rule of law, build the capacity of government institutions, and promote respect for internationally-recognized human rights;

(3) to promote economic freedoms and sustainable economic development;

(4) to support investment in people, including those displaced in on-going counterinsurgency operations; and

(5) to strengthen public diplomacy.

(b) Activities supported. — Activities that may be supported by assistance under subsection (a) include the following:

(1) To support democratic institutions in Pakistan in order to strengthen civilian rule and long-term stability, including assistance such as —

(A) support for efforts to strengthen Pakistan's institutions, including the capacity of the National Parliament of Pakistan, such as enhancing the capacity of committees to oversee government activities, including national security issues, enhancing the ability of members of parliament to respond to constituents, and supporting of parliamentary leadership;

(B) support for voter education and civil society training as well as appropriate support for political party capacity building and responsiveness to the needs of all the people of Pakistan; and

(C) support for strengthening the capacity of the civilian Government of Pakistan to carry out its responsibilities at the national, provincial, and local levels.

(2) To support Pakistan's efforts to expand rule of law, build the capacity, transparency, and trust in government institutions, and promote internationally recognized human rights, including assistance such as —

(A) supporting the establishment of frameworks that promote government transparency and criminalize corruption in both the government and private sector;

(B) support for police professionalization, including training regarding use of force, human rights, and community policing;

(C) support for independent, efficient, and effective judicial and criminal justice systems, such as case management, training, and efforts to enhance the rule of law to all areas in Pakistan;

(D) support for the implementation of legal and political reforms in the FATA;

(E) support to counter the narcotics trade;

(F) support for internationally recognized human rights, including strengthening civil society and nongovernmental organizations working in the area of internationally recognized human rights, as well as organizations that focus on protection of women and girls, promotion of freedom of religion and religious tolerance, and protection of ethnic or religious minorities; and

(G) support for promotion of a responsible, capable, and independent media.

(3) To support economic freedom and economic development in Pakistan, including—

(A) programs that support sustainable economic growth, including in rural areas, and the sustainable management of natural resources through investments in water resource management systems;

(B) expansion of agricultural and rural development, such as farm-to-market roads, systems to prevent spoilage and waste, and other small-scale infrastructure improvements;

(C) investments in energy, including energy generation and cross-border infrastructure projects with Afghanistan;

(D) employment generation, including increasing investment in infrastructure projects, including construction of roads and the continued development of a national aviation industry and aviation infrastructure, as well as support for small and medium enterprises;

(E) worker rights, including the right to form labor unions and legally enforce provisions safeguarding the rights of workers and local community stakeholders;

(F) access to microfinance for small business establishment and income generation, particularly for women; and

(G) countering radicalization by providing economic, social, educational, and vocational opportunities and life-skills training to at-risk youth.

(4) To support investments in people, particularly women and children, including—

(A) promoting modern, public primary and secondary education and vocational and technical training, including programs to assist in the development of modern, nationwide school curriculums [sic.] for public, private, and religious schools; support for the proper oversight of all educational institutions, including religious schools, as required by Pakistani law; initiatives to enhance access to education and vocational and technical training for women and girls and to increase women's literacy, with a special emphasis on helping girls stay in school; and construction and maintenance of libraries and public schools;

(B) programs relating to higher education to ensure a breadth and consistency of Pakistani graduates, including through public-private partnerships;

(C) improving quality public health to eliminate diseases such as hepatitis and to reduce maternal and under-five mortality rates;

(D) building capacity for nongovernmental and civil society organizations, particularly organizations with demonstrated experience in delivering services to the people of Pakistan, particularly to women, children, and other vulnerable populations; and

(E) support for refugees and internally displaced persons and long-term development in regions of Pakistan where internal conflict has caused large-scale displacement.

(5) To strengthen public diplomacy to combat militant extremism and promote a better understanding of the United States, including—

(A) encouraging civil society, respected scholars, and other leaders to speak out against militancy and violence; and

(B) expanded exchange activities under the Fulbright Program, the International Visitor Leadership Program, the Youth Exchange and Study Program, and related programs administered by the Department of State designed to promote mutual understanding and interfaith dialogue and expand sister institution programs between United States and Pakistani schools and universities.

(c) Additional and Related Activities. —

(1) AVAILABILITY OF AMOUNTS FOR PAKISTANI POLICE PROFESSIONALIZATION, EQUIPPING, AND TRAINING. — Not less than $150,000,000 of the amounts appropriated for fiscal year 2010 pursuant to the authorization of appropriations under section 102 should be made available for assistance to Pakistan under this section for police professionalization, equipping, and training.

(2) AVAILABILITY OF AMOUNTS FOR ADMINISTRATIVE EXPENSES. — Up to $10,000,000 of the amounts appropriated for each fiscal year pursuant to the authorization of appropriations under section 102 may be made available for administrative expenses of civilian departments and agencies of the United States Government in connection with the provision of assistance under this section. Such amounts shall be in addition to amounts otherwise available for such purposes.

(3) UTILIZING PAKISTANI ORGANIZATIONS. — The President is encouraged, as appropriate, to utilize Pakistani firms and community and local nongovernmental organizations in Pakistan, including through host country contracts, and to work with local leaders to provide assistance under this section.

(4) USE OF DIRECT EXPENDITURES. — Amounts appropriated for each fiscal year pursuant to the authorization of appropriations under section 102 or otherwise made available to carry out this section shall be utilized to the maximum extent possible as direct expenditures for projects and programs, subject to existing reporting and notification requirements.

(5) CHIEF OF MISSION FUND. — Of the amounts appropriated for each fiscal year pursuant to the authorization of

appropriations under section 102, up to $5,000,000 may be used by the Secretary of State to establish a fund for use by the Chief of Mission in Pakistan to provide assistance to Pakistan under this title or the Foreign Assistance Act of 1961 (22 U.S.C. 2151 et seq.) to address urgent needs or opportunities, consistent with the purposes of this section, or for purposes of humanitarian relief. The fund established pursuant to this paragraph may be referred to as the "Chief of Mission Fund".

(6) SENSE OF CONGRESS. — It is the sense of Congress that —

(A) the United States should provide robust assistance to the people of Pakistan who have been displaced as a result of ongoing conflict and violence in Pakistan and support international efforts to coordinate assistance to refugees and internally displaced persons in Pakistan, including by providing support to international and nongovernmental organizations for this purpose;

(B) the Administrator of the United States Agency for International Development should support the development objectives of the Refugee Affected and Host Areas (RAHA) Initiative in Pakistan to address livelihoods, health, education, infrastructure development, and environmental restoration in identified parts of the country where Afghan refugees have lived; and

(C) the United States should have a coordinated, strategic communications strategy to engage the people of Pakistan and to help ensure the success of the measures authorized by this title.

(d) Notification. — For fiscal years 2010 through 2014, the President shall notify the appropriate congressional committees not later than 15 days before obligating any assistance under this section as budgetary support to the Government of Pakistan or any element of the Government of Pakistan and shall include in such notification a description of the purpose and conditions attached to any such budgetary support.

SEC. 102. Authorization of appropriations.

(a) In general. — There are authorized to be appropriated to the President, for the purposes of providing assistance to Pakistan under this title and to provide assistance to Pakistan under the Foreign Assistance Act of 1961 (22 U.S.C. 2151 et seq.), up to $1,500,000,000 for each of the fiscal years 2010 through 2014.

(b) Availability of Funds. —

(1) IN GENERAL. — Of the amounts appropriated in each fiscal year pursuant to the authorization of appropriations in subsection (a) —

(A) none of the amounts appropriated for assistance to Pakistan may be made available after the date that is 60 days after the date of the enactment of this Act unless the Pakistan Assistance Strategy Report has been submitted to the appropriate congressional committees pursuant to section 301(a); and

(B) not more than $750,000,000 may be made available for assistance to Pakistan unless the President's Special Representative to Afghanistan and Pakistan submits to the appropriate congressional committees during such fiscal year —

(i) a certification that assistance provided to Pakistan under this title or the Foreign Assistance Act of 1961 to date has made or is making reasonable progress toward achieving the principal objectives of United States assistance to Pakistan contained in the Pakistan Assistance Strategy Report; and

(ii) a memorandum explaining the reasons justifying the certification described in clause (i).

(2) MAKER OF CERTIFICATION. — In the event of a vacancy in, or the termination of, the position of the President's Special Representative to Afghanistan and Pakistan, the certification and memorandum described under paragraph (1)(B) may be made by the Secretary of State.

(c) Waiver. — The Secretary of State may waive the limitations in subsection (b) if the Secretary determines, and certifies to the appropriate congressional committees, that it is in the national security interests of the United States to do so.

(d) Sense of Congress on foreign assistance funds. — It is the sense of Congress that, subject to an improving political and economic climate in Pakistan, there should be authorized to be appropriated up to $1,500,000,000 for each of the fiscal years 2015 through 2019 for the purpose of providing assistance to Pakistan under the Foreign Assistance Act of 1961.

SEC. 103. Auditing.

(a) Assistance Authorized. — The Inspector General of the Department of State, the Inspector General of the United States Agency for International Development, and the inspectors general of other Federal departments and agencies (other than the Inspector General of the Department of Defense) carrying out programs, projects, and activities using amounts appropriated to carry out this title shall audit, investigate, and oversee the obligation and expenditure of such amounts.

(b) Authorization for In-Country Presence. — The Inspector General of the Department of State and the Inspector General of the United States Agency for International Development, after consultation with the Secretary of State and the Administrator of the United States Agency for International Development, are authorized to establish field offices in Pakistan with sufficient staff from each of the Offices of the Inspector General, respectively, to carry out subsection (a).

(c) Authorization of appropriations. —

(1) IN GENERAL. — Of the amounts authorized to be appropriated under section 102 for each of the fiscal years 2010 through 2014, up to $30,000,000 for each fiscal year is authorized to be made available to carry out this section.

(2) RELATION TO OTHER AVAILABLE FUNDS. — Amounts made available under paragraph (1) are in addition to amounts otherwise available for such purposes.

TITLE II—Security assistance for Pakistan

SEC. 201. Purposes of assistance.

The purposes of assistance under this title are—

(1) to support Pakistan's paramount national security need to fight and win the ongoing counterinsurgency within its borders in accordance with its national security interests;

(2) to work with the Government of Pakistan to improve Pakistan's border security and control and help prevent any Pakistani territory from being used as a base or conduit for terrorist attacks in Pakistan, or elsewhere;

(3) to work in close cooperation with the Government of Pakistan to coordinate action against extremist and terrorist targets; and

(4) to help strengthen the institutions of democratic governance and promote control of military institutions by a democratically elected civilian government.

SEC. 202. Authorization of assistance.

(a) International Military Education and Training.—

(1) IN GENERAL.—There are authorized to be appropriated such sums as may be necessary for each of the fiscal years 2010 through 2014 for assistance under chapter 5 of part II of the Foreign Assistance Act of 1961 (22 U.S.C. 2347 et seq.; relating to international military education and training) for Pakistan, including expanded international military education and training (commonly known as "E–IMET").

(2) USE OF FUNDS.—It is the sense of Congress that a substantial amount of funds made available to carry out this subsection for a fiscal year should be used to pay for courses of study and training in counterinsurgency and civil-military relations.

(b) Foreign Military Financing Program.—

(1) IN GENERAL. — There are authorized to be appropriated such sums as may be necessary for each of the fiscal years 2010 through 2014 for grant assistance under section 23 of the Arms Export Control Act (22 U.S.C. 2763; relating to the Foreign Military Financing program) for the purchase of defense articles, defense services, and military education and training for Pakistan.

(2) USE OF FUNDS. —

(A) IN GENERAL. — A significant portion of the amount made available to carry out this subsection for a fiscal year shall be for the purchase of defense articles, defense services, and military education and training for activities relating to counterinsurgency and counterterrorism operations in Pakistan.

(B) SENSE OF CONGRESS. — It is the sense of Congress that a significant majority of funds made available to carry out this subsection for a fiscal year should be used for the purpose described in subparagraph (A).

(3) ADDITIONAL AUTHORITY. — Except as provided in sections 3 and 102 of the Arms Export Control Act, the second section 620J of the Foreign Assistance Act of 1961 (as added by Public Law 110–161), and any provision of an Act making appropriations for the Department of State, foreign operations, and related programs that restricts assistance to the government of any country whose duly elected head of government is deposed by military coup or decree, and except as otherwise provided in this title, amounts authorized to be made available to carry out paragraph (2) for fiscal years 2010 and 2011 are authorized to be made available notwithstanding any other provision of law.

(4) DEFINITIONS. — In this section, the terms "defense articles", "defense services", and "military education and training" have the meaning given such terms in section 644 of the Foreign Assistance Act of 1961 (22 U.S.C. 2403).

(c) Sense of Congress. — It is the sense of Congress that the United States should facilitate Pakistan's establishment of a program to provide reconstruction assistance, including through Pakistan's military as appropriate, in areas damaged by combat operations.

(d) Exchange Program between military and civilian personnel of Pakistan and certain other countries. —

(1) IN GENERAL. — The Secretary of State is authorized to establish an exchange program between —

(A) military and civilian personnel of Pakistan; and

(B)(i) military and civilian personnel of countries determined by the Secretary of State to be in the process of consolidating and strengthening a democratic form of government; or

(ii) military and civilian personnel of North Atlantic Treaty Organization member countries, in order to foster greater mutual respect for and understanding of the principle of civilian rule of the military.

(2) ELEMENTS OF PROGRAM. — The program authorized under paragraph (1) may include conferences, seminars, exchanges, and other events, distribution of publications and reimbursements of expenses of foreign military personnel participating in the program, including transportation, translation and administrative expenses.

(3) ROLE OF NONGOVERNMENTAL ORGANIZATIONS. — Amounts authorized to be appropriated to carry out this section for a fiscal year are authorized to be made available for nongovernmental organizations to facilitate the implementation of the program authorized under paragraph (1).

(4) AUTHORIZATION OF APPROPRIATIONS. — There are authorized to be appropriated such sums as may be necessary for each of the fiscal years 2010 through 2014 to carry out the program established by this subsection.

SEC. 203. Limitations on certain assistance.

(a) Limitation on security-related assistance. — For fiscal years 2011 through 2014, no security-related assistance may be provided to Pakistan in a fiscal year until the Secretary of State, under the direction of the President, makes the certification required under subsection (c) for such fiscal year.

(b) Limitation on Arms Transfers. — For fiscal years 2012 through 2014, no letter of offer to sell major defense equipment to Pakistan may be issued pursuant to the Arms Export Control Act (22 U.S.C. 2751 et seq.) and no license to export major defense equipment to Pakistan may be issued pursuant to such Act in a fiscal year until the Secretary of State, under the direction of the President, makes the certification required under subsection (c) for such fiscal year.

(c) Certification. — The certification required by this subsection is a certification by the Secretary of State, under the direction of the President, to the appropriate congressional committees that—

(1) the Government of Pakistan is continuing to cooperate with the United States in efforts to dismantle supplier networks relating to the acquisition of nuclear weapons-related materials, such as providing relevant information from or direct access to Pakistani nationals associated with such networks;

(2) the Government of Pakistan during the preceding fiscal year has demonstrated a sustained commitment to and is making significant efforts towards combating terrorist groups, consistent with the purposes of assistance described in section 201, including taking into account the extent to which the Government of Pakistan has made progress on matters such as —

(A) ceasing support, including by any elements within the Pakistan military or its intelligence agency, to extremist and terrorist groups, particularly to any group that has conducted attacks against United States or coalition forces in Afghanistan, or against the territory or people of neighboring countries;

(B) preventing al Qaeda, the Taliban and associated terrorist groups, such as Lashkar-e-Taiba and Jaish-e-Mohammed, from operating in the territory of Pakistan, including carrying out cross-border attacks into neighboring countries, closing terrorist camps in the FATA, dismantling terrorist bases of operations in other parts of the country, including Quetta and Muridke, and taking action when provided with intelligence about high-level terrorist targets; and

(C) strengthening counterterrorism and anti-money laundering laws; and

(3) the security forces of Pakistan are not materially and substantially subverting the political or judicial processes of Pakistan.

(d) Certain payments. —

(1) IN GENERAL. — Subject to paragraph (2), none of the funds appropriated for security-related assistance for fiscal years 2010 through 2014, or any amounts appropriated to the Pakistan Counterinsurgency Capability Fund established under the Supplemental Appropriations Act, 2009 (Public Law 111–32), may be obligated or expended to make payments relating to —

(A) the Letter of Offer and Acceptance PK–D–YAD signed between the Governments of the United States of America and Pakistan on September 30, 2006;

(B) the Letter of Offer and Acceptance PK–D–NAP signed between the Governments of the United States of America and Pakistan on September 30, 2006; and

(C) the Letter of Offer and Acceptance PK–D–SAF signed between the Governments of the United States of America and Pakistan on September 30, 2006.

(2) EXCEPTION. — Funds appropriated for security-related assistance for fiscal years 2010 through 2014 may be used for construction and related activities carried out pursuant to the Letters of Offer and Acceptance described in paragraph (1).

(e) Waiver. —

(1) IN GENERAL. — The Secretary of State, under the direction of the President, may waive the limitations contained in subsections (a), (b), and (d) for a fiscal year if the Secretary of State determines

that is important to the national security interests of the United States to do so.

(2) PRIOR NOTICE OF WAIVER. — The Secretary of State, under the direction of the President, may not exercise the authority of paragraph (1) until 7 days after the Secretary of State provides to the appropriate congressional committees a written notice of the intent to issue to waiver and the reasons therefor. The notice may be submitted in classified or unclassified form, as necessary.

(f) Appropriate Congressional Committees Defined. — In this section, the term "appropriate congressional committees" means —

(1) the Committee on Foreign Affairs, the Committee on Armed Services, the Committee on Oversight and Government Reform, and the Permanent Select Committee on Intelligence of the House of Representatives; and

(2) the Committee on Foreign Relations, the Committee on Armed Services, and the Select Committee on Intelligence of the Senate.

SEC. 204. Pakistan Counterinsurgency Capability Fund.

(a) For Fiscal Year 2010. —

(1) IN GENERAL. — For fiscal year 2010, the Department of State's Pakistan Counterinsurgency Capability Fund established under the Supplemental Appropriations Act, 2009 (Public Law 111–32), hereinafter in this section referred to as the "Fund", shall consist of the following:

(A) Amounts appropriated to carry out this subsection (which may not include any amounts appropriated to carry out title I of this Act).

(B) Amounts otherwise available to the Secretary of State to carry out this subsection.

(2) PURPOSES OF FUND. — Amounts in the Fund made available to carry out this subsection for any fiscal year are authorized to be used by the Secretary of State, with the concurrence of the

Secretary of Defense, to build and maintain the counterinsurgency capability of Pakistan under the same terms and conditions (except as otherwise provided in this subsection) that are applicable to amounts made available under the Fund for fiscal year 2009.

(3) TRANSFER AUTHORITY. —

(A) IN GENERAL. — The Secretary of State is authorized to transfer amounts in the Fund made available to carry out this subsection for any fiscal year to the Department of Defense's Pakistan Counterinsurgency Fund established under the Supplemental Appropriations Act, 2009 (Public Law 111–32) and such amounts may be transferred back to the Fund if the Secretary of Defense, with the concurrence of the Secretary of State, determines that such amounts are not needed for the purposes for which initially transferred.

(B) TREATMENT OF TRANSFERRED FUNDS. — Subject to subsections (d) and (e) of section 203, transfers from the Fund under the authority of subparagraph (A) shall be merged with and be available for the same purposes and for the same time period as amounts in the Department of Defense's Pakistan Counterinsurgency Fund.

(C) RELATION TO OTHER AUTHORITIES. — The authority to provide assistance under this subsection is in addition to any other authority to provide assistance to foreign countries.

(D) NOTIFICATION. — The Secretary of State shall, not less than 15 days prior to making transfers from the Fund under subparagraph (A), notify the appropriate congressional committees in writing of the details of any such transfer.

(b) Submission of Notifications. — Any notification required by this section may be submitted in classified or unclassified form, as necessary.

(c) Appropriate Congressional Committees Defined. — In this section, the term "appropriate congressional committees" means —

(1) the Committee on Appropriations, the Committee on Armed Services, and the Committee on Foreign Affairs of the House of Representatives; and

(2) the Committee on Appropriations, the Committee on Armed Services, and the Committee on Foreign Relations of the Senate.

SEC. 205. Requirements for civilian control of certain assistance.

(a) Requirements. —

(1) IN GENERAL. — For fiscal years 2010 through 2014, any direct cash security-related assistance or non-assistance payments by the United States to the Government of Pakistan may only be provided or made to civilian authorities of a civilian government of Pakistan.

(2) DOCUMENTATION. — For fiscal years 2010 through 2014, the Secretary of State, in coordination with the Secretary of Defense, shall ensure that civilian authorities of a civilian government of Pakistan have received a copy of final documentation provided to the United States related to non-assistance payments provided or made to the Government of Pakistan.

(b) Waiver. —

(1) SECURITY-RELATED ASSISTANCE. — The Secretary of State, in consultation with the Secretary of Defense, may waive the requirements of subsection (a) with respect to security-related assistance described in subsection (a) funded from accounts within budget function 150 (International Affairs) if the Secretary of State certifies to the appropriate congressional committees that the waiver is important to the national security interest of the United States.

(2) NON-ASSISTANCE PAYMENTS. — The Secretary of Defense, in consultation with the Secretary of State, may waive the requirements of subsection (a) with respect to non-assistance payments described in subsection (a) funded from accounts within budget function 050 (National Defense) if the Secretary of Defense certifies to the appropriate congressional committees that

the waiver is important to the national security interest of the United States.

(c) Application to certain activities. — Nothing in this section shall apply with respect to —

(1) any activities subject to reporting requirements under title V of the National Security Act of 1947 (50 U.S.C. 413 et seq.);

(2) any assistance to promote democratic elections or public participation in democratic processes;

(3) any assistance or payments if the Secretary of State determines and certifies to the appropriate congressional committees that subsequent to the termination of assistance or payments a democratically elected government has taken office;

(4) any assistance or payments made pursuant to section 1208 of the Ronald W. Reagan National Defense Authorization Act for Fiscal Year 2005 (Public Law 108–375; 118 Stat. 2086), as amended;

(5) any payments made pursuant to the Acquisition and Cross-Servicing Agreement between the Department of Defense of the United States of America and the Ministry of Defense of the Islamic Republic of Pakistan; and

(6) any assistance or payments made pursuant to section 943 of the Duncan Hunter National Defense Authorization Act for Fiscal Year 2009 (Public Law 110–417; 122 Stat. 4578).

(d) Definitions. — In this section —

(1) the term "appropriate congressional committees" means the Committees on Appropriations, Armed Services, and Foreign Affairs of the House of Representatives and the Committees on Appropriations, Armed Services, and Foreign Relations of the Senate; and

(2) the term "civilian government of Pakistan" does not include any government of Pakistan whose duly elected head of government is deposed by military coup or decree.

TITLE III—Strategy, accountability, monitoring, and other provisions

SEC. 301. Strategy Reports.

(a) Pakistan Assistance Strategy Report.—Not later than 45 days after the date of enactment of this Act, the Secretary of State shall submit to the appropriate congressional committees a report describing United States policy and strategy with respect to assistance to Pakistan under this Act. The report shall include the following:

(1) A description of the principal objectives of United States assistance to Pakistan to be provided under title I of this Act.

(2) A general description of the specific programs, projects, and activities designed to achieve the purposes of section 101 and the respective funding levels for such programs, projects, and activities for fiscal years 2010 through 2014.

(3) A plan for program monitoring, operations research, and impact evaluation research for assistance authorized under title I of this Act.

(4) A description of the role to be played by Pakistani national, regional, and local officials and members of Pakistani civil society and local private sector, civic, religious, and tribal leaders in helping to identify and implement programs and projects for which assistance is to be provided under this Act, and of consultations with such representatives in developing the strategy.

(5) A description of the steps taken, or to be taken, to ensure assistance provided under this Act is not awarded to individuals or entities affiliated with terrorist organizations.

(6) A projection of the levels of assistance to be provided to Pakistan under this Act, broken down into the following categories as described in the annual "Report on the Criteria and Methodology for Determining the Eligibility of Candidate Countries for Millennium Challenge Account Assistance":

(A) Civil liberties.

(B) Political rights.

(C) Voice and accountability.

(D) Government effectiveness.

(E) Rule of law.

(F) Control of corruption.

(G) Immunization rates.

(H) Public expenditure on health.

(I) Girls' primary education completion rate.

(J) Public expenditure on primary education.

(K) Natural resource management.

(L) Business start-up.

(M) Land rights and access.

(N) Trade policy.

(O) Regulatory quality.

(P) Inflation control.

(Q) Fiscal policy.

(7) An analysis for the suitable replacement for existing Pakistani helicopters, including recommendations for sustainment and training.

(b) Comprehensive regional strategy report.—

(1) SENSE OF CONGRESS.—It is the sense of Congress that the achievement of United States national security goals to eliminate terrorist threats and close safe havens in Pakistan requires the development of a comprehensive plan that utilizes all elements of

national power, including in coordination and cooperation with other concerned governments, and that it is critical to Pakistan's long-term prosperity and security to strengthen regional relationships among India, Pakistan, and Afghanistan.

(2) COMPREHENSIVE REGIONAL SECURITY STRATEGY. – The President shall develop a comprehensive interagency regional security strategy to eliminate terrorist threats and close safe havens in Pakistan, including by working with the Government of Pakistan and other relevant governments and organizations in the region and elsewhere, as appropriate, to best implement effective counterinsurgency and counterterrorism efforts in and near the border areas of Pakistan and Afghanistan, including the FATA, the NWFP, parts of Balochistan, and parts of Punjab.

(3) REPORT. –

(A) IN GENERAL. – Not later than 180 days after the date of the enactment of this Act, the President shall submit to the appropriate congressional committees a report on the comprehensive regional security strategy required under paragraph (2).

(B) CONTENTS. – The report shall include a copy of the comprehensive regional security strategy, including specifications of goals, and proposed timelines and budgets for implementation of the strategy.

(C) APPROPRIATE CONGRESSIONAL COMMITTEES DEFINED. – In this paragraph, the term "appropriate congressional committees" means –

(i) the Committee on Appropriations, the Committee on Armed Services, the Committee on Foreign Affairs, and the Permanent Select Committee on Intelligence of the House of Representatives; and

(ii) the Committee on Appropriations, the Committee on Armed Services, the Committee on Foreign Relations, and the Select Committee on Intelligence of the Senate.

(c) Security-related assistance plan. — Not later than 180 days after the date of the enactment of this Act, the Secretary of State shall submit to the appropriate congressional committees a plan for the proposed use of amounts authorized for security-related assistance for each of the fiscal years 2010 through 2014. Such plan shall include an assessment of how the use of such amounts complements or otherwise is related to amounts described in section 204.

SEC. 302. Monitoring Reports.

(a) Semi-Annual Monitoring Report. — Not later than 180 days after the submission of the Pakistan Assistance Strategy Report pursuant to section 301(a), and every 180 days thereafter through September 30, 2014, the Secretary of State, in consultation with the Secretary of Defense, shall submit to the appropriate congressional committees a report that describes the assistance provided under this Act during the preceding 180-day period. The report shall include —

(1) a description of all assistance by program, project, and activity, as well as by geographic area, provided pursuant to title I of this Act during the period covered by the report, including the amount of assistance provided for each program or project, and with respect to the first report a description of all amounts made available for assistance to Pakistan during fiscal year 2009, including a description of each program, project, and activity for which funds were made available;

(2) a list of persons or entities from the United States or other countries that have received funds in excess of $100,000 to conduct projects under title I of this Act during the period covered by the report, which may be included in a classified annex, if necessary to avoid a security risk, and a justification for the classification;

(3) with respect to the plan described in section 301(a)(3), updates to such plan and a description of best practices to improve the impact of the assistance authorized under title I of this Act;

(4) an assessment of the effectiveness of assistance provided under title I of this Act during the period covered by the report in

achieving desired objectives and outcomes as guided by the plan described in section 301(a)(3), and as updated pursuant to paragraph (3) of this subsection, including a systematic, qualitative, and where possible, quantitative basis for assessing whether desired outcomes are achieved and a timeline for completion of each project and program;

(5) a description of any shortfall in United States financial, physical, technical, or human resources that hinder the effective use and monitoring of such funds;

(6) a description of any negative impact, including the absorptive capacity of the region for which the resources are intended, of United States bilateral or multilateral assistance and recommendations for modification of funding, if any;

(7) any incidents or reports of waste, fraud, and abuse of expenditures under title I of this Act;

(8) the amount of funds authorized to be appropriated pursuant to section 102 that were used during the reporting period for administrative expenses or for audits and program reviews pursuant to the authority under sections 101(c)(2) and 103;

(9) a description of the expenditures made from any Chief of Mission Fund established pursuant to section 101(c)(5) during the period covered by the report, the purposes for which such expenditures were made, and a list of the recipients of any expenditures from the Chief of Mission Fund in excess of $100,000;

(10) an accounting of assistance provided to Pakistan under title I of this Act, broken down into the categories set forth in section 301(a)(6);

(11) an evaluation of efforts undertaken by the Government of Pakistan to —

(A) disrupt, dismantle, and defeat al Qaeda, the Taliban, and other extremist and terrorist groups in the FATA and settled areas;

(B) eliminate the safe havens of such forces in Pakistan;

(C) close terrorist camps, including those of Lashkar-e-Taiba and Jaish-e-Mohammed;

(D) cease all support for extremist and terrorist groups;

(E) prevent attacks into neighboring countries;

(F) increase oversight over curriculum in madrassas, including closing madrassas with direct links to the Taliban or other extremist and terrorist groups; and

(G) improve counterterrorism financing and anti-money laundering laws, apply for observer status for the Financial Action Task Force, and take steps to adhere to the United Nations International Convention for the Suppression of Financing of Terrorism;

(12) a detailed description of Pakistan's efforts to prevent proliferation of nuclear-related material and expertise;

(13) an assessment of whether assistance provided to Pakistan has directly or indirectly aided the expansion of Pakistan's nuclear weapons program, whether by the diversion of United States assistance or the reallocation of Pakistan's financial resources that would otherwise be spent for programs and activities unrelated to its nuclear weapons program;

(14) a detailed description of the extent to which funds obligated and expended pursuant to section 202(b) meet the requirements of such section; and

(15) an assessment of the extent to which the Government of Pakistan exercises effective civilian control of the military, including a description of the extent to which civilian executive leaders and parliament exercise oversight and approval of military budgets, the chain of command, the process of promotion for senior military leaders, civilian involvement in strategic guidance and planning, and military involvement in civil administration.

(b) Government Accountability Office Reports. —

(1) PAKISTAN ASSISTANCE STRATEGY REPORT. — Not later than one year after the submission of the Pakistan Assistance Strategy Report pursuant to section 301(a), the Comptroller General of the United States shall submit to the appropriate congressional committees a report that contains —

(A) a review of, and comments addressing, the Pakistan Assistance Strategy Report;

(B) recommendations relating to any additional actions the Comptroller General believes could help improve the efficiency and effectiveness of United States efforts to meet the objectives of this Act;

(C) a detailed description of the expenditures made by Pakistan pursuant to grant assistance under section 23 of the Arms Export Control Act (22 U.S.C. 2763; relating to the Foreign Military Financing program); and

(D) an assessment of the impact of the assistance on the security and stability of Pakistan.

(2) CERTIFICATION REPORT. — Not later than 120 days after the date on which the President makes the certification described in section 203(c) for a fiscal year, the Comptroller General of the United States shall conduct an independent analysis of the certification described in such section and shall submit to the appropriate congressional committees a report containing the results of the independent analysis.

(c) Submission. — The Secretary of State may submit the reports required by this section in conjunction with other reports relating to Pakistan required under other provisions of law, including sections 1116 and 1117 of the Supplemental Appropriations Act, 2009 (Public Law 111–32; 123 Stat. 1906 and 1907).

(d) Appropriate congressional committees defined. — In this section, the term "appropriate congressional committees" means —

(1) the Committee on Appropriations, the Committee on Armed Services, and the Committee on Foreign Affairs of the House of Representatives; and

(2) the Committee on Appropriations, the Committee on Armed Services, and the Committee on Foreign Relations of the Senate.

SPEAKER OF THE HOUSE OF REPRESENTATIVES

VICE PRESIDENT OF THE UNITED STATES AND PRESIDENT OF THE SENATE

Appendix IV: National Reconciliation Ordinance
"AN ORDINANCE to promote national reconciliation

WHEREAS it is expedient to promote national reconciliation, foster mutual trust and confidence amongst holders of public office and remove the vestiges of political vendetta and victimisation, to make the election process more transparent and to amend certain laws for that purpose and for matters connected therewith and ancillary thereto:

AND WHEREAS the National Assembly is not in session and the president is satisfied that circumstances exist, which render it necessary to take immediate action;

NOW, THEREFORE, in exercise of the powers conferred by clause (1) of Article (89) of the Constitution of the Islamic Republic of Pakistan, the president is pleased to make and promulgate the following Ordinance:

1. Short title and commencement.

(1) This ordinance may be called the National Reconciliation Ordinance, 2007

(2) It shall come into force at once.

2. Amendment of section 494, Act V of 1898.

In the Code of Criminal Procedure, 1898 (Act V of 1898), section 494 shall be renumbered as sub-section (1) thereof and after sub-section (1) renumbered as aforesaid, the following sub-section (2) and (3) shall be added, namely:

"(2) Notwithstanding anything to the contrary in sub-section(1), the federal government or a provincial government may, before the judgment is pronounced by a trial court, withdraw from the prosecution of any person including an absconding accused who is found to be falsely involved for political reasons or through political victimization in any case initiated between 1st day of

January, 1986 to 12th day of October, 1999 and upon such withdrawal clause (a) and clause (b) of sub-section (1) shall apply.

(3) For the purposes of exercise of powers under sub-section (2) the federal government and the provincial government may each constitute a review board to review the entire record of the case and furnish recommendations as to their withdrawal or otherwise.

(4) The review board in case of Federal Government shall be headed by a retired judge of the Supreme Court with Attorney-General and Federal Law Secretary as its members and in case of Provincial Government it shall be headed by a retired judge of the high court with Advocate-General and/or Prosecutor-General and Provincial Law Secretary as its members.

(5) A review board undertaking review of a case may direct the public prosecutor or any other authority concerned to furnish to it the record of the case."

3. Amendment of section 39, Act LXXXV of 1976.- (1) In the Representation of the People Act, 1976 (LXXXV of 1976), in section 39, after sub-section (6), the following new sub-section (7) shall be added, namely:

"(7) After consolidation of results the Returning Officer shall give to such contesting candidates and their election agents as are present during the consolidation proceedings, a copy of the result of the count notified to the commission immediately against proper receipt and shall also post a copy thereof to the other candidates and election agents".

4. Amendment of section 18, Ordinance XVIII of 1999.

In the National Accountability Ordinance, 1999 (XVIII of 1999), hereinafter referred to as the said Ordinance, in section 18, in clause (e), for the full stop at the end a colon shall be substituted and thereafter the following proviso shall be added, namely:

"Provided that no sitting member of Parliament or a Provincial

Assembly shall be arrested without taking into consideration the recommendations of the Special Parliamentary Committee on Ethics referred to in clause (aa) or Special Committee of the Provincial Assembly on Ethics referred to in clause (aaa) of section 24, respectively."

5. Amendment of section 24, Ordinance XVIII of 1999.

In the said ordinance, in section 24, (i) in clause (a) for the full stop at the end a colon shall be substituted and thereafter the following proviso shall be inserted, namely.

"Provided that no sitting member of Parliament or a Provincial Assembly shall be arrested without taking into consideration the recommendations of Special Parliamentary Committee on Ethics or Special Committee of the Provincial Assembly on Ethics referred to in clause (aa) and (aaa), respectively, before which the entire material and evidence shall be placed by the chairman, NAB."; and (ii) after clause (a), amended as aforesaid, the following new clauses (aa) and (aaa) shall be inserted, namely;

(aa) The Special Parliamentary Committee on Ethics referred to in the proviso to clause (a) above shall consist of a chairman who shall be a member of either House of Parliament and eight members each from the National Assembly and Senate to be selected by the Speaker, National Assembly and Chairman Senate, respectively, on the recommendations of Leader of the House and Leader of the Opposition of their respective houses, with equal representation from both sides.

(aaa) The Special Committee of the Provincial Assembly on Ethics shall consist of a chairman and eight members to be selected by the Speaker of the Provincial Assembly on the recommendation of Leader of the House and Leader of the Opposition, with equal representation from both sides."

6. Amendment of section 31A, Ordinance XVIII of 1999.

In the said Ordinance, in section 31A, in clause (a), for the full stop at the end a colon shall be substituted and thereafter the following new clause (aa) shall be inserted, namely:

"(aa) An order or judgment passed by the Court in absentia against an accused is void ab initio and shall not be acted upon."

7. Insertion of new section, Ordinance, XVIII of 1999.

In the said Ordinance, after section 33, the following new section shall be inserted, namely:

"33A. Withdrawal and termination of prolonged pending proceedings initiated prior to 12th October, 1999.

(1) Notwithstanding anything contained in this Ordinance or any other law for the time being in force, proceedings under investigation or pending in any court including a high court and the Supreme Court of Pakistan initiated by or on a reference by the National Accountability Bureau inside or outside Pakistan, including proceedings continued under section 33, requests for mutual assistance and civil party to proceedings initiated by the Federal Government before the 12th day of October, 1999 against holders of public office stand withdrawn and terminated with immediate effect and such holders of public office shall also not be liable to any action in

future as well under this Ordinance for acts having been

done in good faith before the said date;

Provided that those proceedings shall not be withdrawn and terminated which relate to cases registered in connection with the cooperative societies and other financial and investment companies or in which no appeal, revision or constitutional petition has been filed against final judgment and order of the Court or in which an appellate or
revisional order or an order in constitutional petition has become final or in which voluntary return or plea bargain has been accepted by the Chairman, National Accountability Bureau under section 25 or recommendations of the Conciliation Committee have been accepted by the Governor, State bank of Pakistan under

section 25A.

(2) No action or claim by way of suit, prosecution, complaint or other civil or criminal proceeding shall lie against the Federal, Provincial or Local Gover ment, the National Accountability Bureau or any of their officers and functionaries for any act or thing done or intended to be done in good faith pursuant to the withdrawal and termination of cases under sub-section (1) unless they have deliberately misused authority in violation of law."

2093288R00171

Printed in Great Britain
by Amazon.co.uk, Ltd.,
Marston Gate.